# FR JOHN FAHY

John Minogue.

8 WOODVIEW.

Jim Madden

# Fr John Fahy (1893-1969)

*Radical Republican
and Agrarian Activist*

the columba press

First published in 2012 by
the columba press
55A Spruce Avenue, Stillorgan Industrial Park,
Blackrock, Co Dublin

Cover by Bill Bolger
Origination by The Columba Press
Printed by Gemini International Limited

ISBN 978 1 85607 763 7

# Contents

# Acknowledgements

I wish to thank many people who helped me while preparing and writing this book.

Gearóid Ó Tuathaigh, Professor Emeritus in History, National University of Ireland, Galway, kindly agreed to read the manuscript and wrote the Foreword.

Fr Declan Kelly, Clonfert Diocesan Archivist, was most generous with his time and advice. His encyclopaedic knowledge of Clonfert diocesan history was greatly valued. I found myself regularly returning to his own publications for information and clarification.

The assistance of Ronan Hegarty, a postgraduate student in the Dept of Information Systems and Library Studies UCD, in sourcing archival material was invaluable.

Margaret Kelly, Ben Killeen and Tom Moran, who were actively involved in Lia Fáil in Lusmagh, shared with me their memories of Fr Fahy and those stirring times.

Members of Fr Fahy's extended family, particularly his niece Mrs Nora Cooney, his nephews Br Máirtín Fahy (RIP) and Tom Fahy and his wife Maureen and grandnephew Jimmy Cooney were most hospitable on my visits to them. They provided interesting photographs and my conversations with them helped to determine the final shape of the book.

Ruairí Ó Brádaigh, former Chief of Staff of the IRA and President of Republican Sinn Féin, put his extensive files relating to Fr Fahy at my disposal and his personal reminiscences broadened the scope of this work.

In Maynooth University Susan Durack, Librarian, gave an early boost to my research by pointing me in the right direction and Cora Hennelly, President's Office, St Patrick's College, went to great lengths to unearth an ordination photo of Fr Fahy.

The librarians in Galway City Library, the staff at the Galway City and County Library headquarters at Cathedral Square, the librarians in Athlone, Banagher and Birr public libraries and the staff in the James Hardiman Library, National University of

Ireland Galway, were all extremely helpful in responding to my many requests.

In the National University of Ireland Galway I wish to thank Dr Tony Varley, School of Political Science and Sociology, An tOllamh Dáibhí Ó Cróinín, Roinn na Staire and my brother John A. Madden, Professor Emeritus in Classics, for providing valuable references and suggestions.

Fr Tom Murray, archivist for the diocese of Ardagh and Clonmacnoise, provided valuable information which he sourced in All Hallows College, Dublin and in Longford.

Author and journalist Rosita Sweetman readily agreed to have an abridged version of the chapter on Dan McCarthy and The National Land League from her book *On Our Knees* included here.

Jim Fahy, RTÉ Western Editor, was similarly accommodating regarding his chapter on 'The Fahys – Clanricarde's Opponents' which first appeared in *Clanricarde Country*.

Many people made press cuttings, photographs, family correspondence and other material relevant to the Fr Fahy narrative available to me. Others shared recollections and stories about him that helped to give a broader picture of a complex man. Among those, I wish to thank especially the following: Margaret Barton, Brendan Bennett, Liam and Leonie Byrne, Paddy Byrne, John Callanan, P. J. Callanan, Nancy Cannon, Fr Dermot Carthy, Fr Joe Clarke, Gerry Cloonan, John Joe Conwell, Michael Coonan, Marie Corcoran, Kieran Donegan (RIP), Donal Donnelly, Linda Dowling, Ray Downes, Paddy Doyle, Michael Flynn, Nuala Flynn, Pat Gallagher, Fr Gerard Geraghty, John Gilligan, Fr Cronan Glynn, Mary Hanrahan, John Holohan, Fr Phil Hearty, Brigid Horan, Pat Hynes, Joachim Kelly, Martin Kelly, Patrick Kelly, Lily Kelly, Seamus Kelly, Tim Kelly, John Kelly, Peter Kenny, Sarah Lantry, Mary Larkin, Thomas and Toni Larkin, John Mahon, Joe Mannion, Rory Masterson, Joe Moran, Pat Moylan, Mary Mulvey, Patsy McGuinness, Fr John Naughton, An tAth Pádraig Ó Fiannachta, John Rigney, Tom Ruane, Bishop Michael Smith (Meath), Pauline and Jim Sullivan, Peter Sullivan, Fr Cathal Stanley, Michael Stephens, Seán Treacy and Mary Whelan.

Mary Flynn typed what was at times a difficult manuscript in a most professional manner, for which I particularly thank her.

Finally, I am indebted to my wife Aideen and son John, who provided support, encouragement, constructive criticism and much practical help at all stages of this undertaking.

# Foreword

The life and public career of Fr John Fahy (1893-1969) conjoins two recurring themes in modern Irish history: waves of agrarian agitation on behalf of the rural underclass (a feature since the later eighteenth century) and the figure of the turbulent or 'rebel' priest. By the time the Irish Free State came into existence in 1922, both of these themes were entering their final phase, as dramatic, dynamic forces in Irish political and social life. The land war and successive land acts of the period 1879-1922 had brought about one kind of 'social revolution', namely, the creation of a large farmer-owner class in rural Ireland, with the virtual buy-out of the old landlord class. Within the Catholic church in Ireland, tighter episcopal control and stricter discipline had all but closed the political space long-occupied by agitating 'rebel' priests. In one sense, therefore, Fr John Fahy may well be considered something of a colourful anachronism. However, even the final phase of a long-active historical force in Irish life is deserving of attention, and the story of Fr John Fahy is a story well worth the telling.

The decimation of the rural underclass (labourers, cottiers and smallholders) during the famine, and through the continuing drain of emigration in the half-century following the famine, transformed the class structure of rural Ireland. With industrialisation confined to the north-east region, agriculture was the mainstay of the Irish economy. Outside of Belfast, urban growth largely rested on commercial and administrative functions and a degree of modest manufacturing for local markets (the few export-orientated products manufactured outside of Ulster are well-known and were mainly related to agriculture – brewing, distilling, dairy and animal products). Dublin was principally a commercial, administrative and 'services' capital, rather than an industrial city. Together with the leadership of a commercial and political middle-class in the towns and cities, the comfortable farmer of the countryside had come to dominate rural culture (including political and social movements) in the area that became the Free State in 1922. In Connacht, this leadership was

overwhelmingly Catholic in religion, and the Catholic church itself was a central institution of the prevailing social order.

Of course, the dominance of the comfortable middle-class
did not go uncontested, during the several key episodes of the
land struggle in the decades preceding 1922, or for a long time
after. The trade unions sought to organise workers in town and
countryside; smallholders (and landless labourers), despite
their diminishing numbers, sporadically agitated for improved
wages or more land. This latter demand, of course, was the crux
of the issue: as the implementation of the land acts clearly
demonstrated, neither rent reductions, secure tenancy nor attractive purchasing terms for one's holding could solve the
problem of smallholders who simply did not have enough land
to support themselves and their families, even in the much-
vaunted 'frugal comfort'. Land redistribution was the cry of the
economically non-viable smallholders (and of many landless
labourers). The Irish Land Commission, though it continued to
acquire and to redistribute land in the decades after 1922, could
never meet all of the demands of the desperate claimants for
'extra land', not least in the congested areas of the west. The result was a continuing, sporadically intense, agitation among
smallholders for a more aggressive state policy and programme
of land redistribution, and in particular for the break-up of the
larger 'ranches' and the outlawing of further land acquisition
(land 'grabbing' as it was emotively denounced) by commercial
farmers or, worst of all, by 'outsiders'.

The plight of these land-hungry smallholders, in despair at
their own straitened circumstances and the dismal prospects of
their children, unless they should choose to emigrate, prompted
various political initiatives to seek a remedy to their difficulties.
The anti-annuities campaign of the late twenties and early thirt-
ies was one such campaign, and the sorry plight of the smallholders also provided the initial impetus for the founding of
Clann na Talmhan in the late 1930s. But it seemed that the tide of
history (and the workings of the market) would not be turned.
As the haemorrhage of emigration during the 1950s (more than
400,000 net emigration in one decade) emptied out the rural
west in particular, Fr John Fahy, a priest of the Clonfert diocese
and a militant republican (he was prominent in the IRB while in
his early ministry in Scotland), launched an initiative of his own.

Fr Fahy's aggressive rhetoric and methods of agitation owed more to the tradition of direct action agrarian secret societies than to the electoral politics and parliamentary lobbying of Clann na Talmhan or other farmers' organisations. The story of Fr Fahy, his background, political activism, rhetoric and action (not least through his sulphuric newspaper and organisation of the late 1950s, *Lia Fáil*) is here told in this engaging and well documented book by Jim Madden. The reader will, no doubt, form his own judgement on Fr Fahy's championing of the smallholders of the west in the decades when, as Peadar O'Donnell (an ally of Fr Fahy's in several campaigns) remarked, they were 'disappearing into history'. Few will deny that he had strong convictions and a genuine concern (and sense of indignation) for the plight of the rural smallholders, or that he had personal courage, lived simply and was personally generous to the poor and marginalised of his parishes in his time. But it is also incontestable (as the illustrative documentation – pamphlets, newspaper writings, personal and public letters – included in this book clearly demonstrates) that he was habitually intemperate in public controversy, prone to xenophobic statements (the all too common references to the menace of Jews and Freemasons and 'aliens' acquiring land and oppressing the poor), and frequently deployed a strong vein of venom in his denunciation of his foes and in the general flow of his polemics.

Given the notoriety that he achieved through his public statements, speeches and activities, it may seem to many that Fr Fahy was permitted a remarkable latitude by successive bishops of Clonfert (notwithstanding frequent rebukes and warnings by bishops and, on Fr Fahy's part, equally frequent undertakings, never adhered to, to correct his behaviour and come into line with canon law and episcopal instructions). It is true that his behaviour ultimately caused his demotion from parish priest to curate. But the latitude allowed him for many years, and through many turbulent episodes, may have been due, in some measure, to his unshakable loyalty to Catholic doctrine and devotional practice, and to the general militancy of his stand against heretics and sundry other backsliders, at home and abroad. His own simple life, and the fact that his rhetoric (and general sympathy) for the 'underdog' in rural Ireland, tapped into a strong historical sense of victimhood among Irish Catholics, probably contributed further to the indulgence granted him as a public (and highly divisive) controversialist.

For all his energy, passion and sense of righteousness, however, Fr John Fahy laboured in a cause that ultimately failed. The workings of the market, and the Irish social 'safety-valve' of emigration down through the decades, relentlessly thinned out the ranks of the rural smallholders. In time, the logic of the 'Common Market' would accelerate this process. One can only imagine what Fr Fahy, were he alive, might have said of the 'alien' controls from Brussels that have shaped Irish agriculture in recent decades!

Fr John Fahy died peacefully in 1969. The list of mourners reported as attending his funeral, and the warm tributes of many of the obituaries published in a variety of newspapers and magazines after his death, may serve to remind us of some of the ambiguities and contradictions that pervade Irish attitudes to the 'land question' and to the role of the 'agitator' in movements of social protest on behalf of the underdog.

*Gearóid Ó Tuathaigh,*
*Professor Emeritus in History,*
*National University of Ireland, Galway.*

## *Author's Preface*

I often met Fr John Fahy when he came from Lusmagh to shop in Banagher. As a priest of the Clonfert diocese, he was interested that I was attending St Joseph's College, Garbally Park, Ballinasloe, which was the Clonfert diocesan college. Later when he became aware that I was going to Dublin to continue my studies, he suggested that I might undertake some research for him in the National Library.

At that time I was unaware that Fr Fahy had a national reputation as far back as the 1920s. In adult life I gradually got to know more about him and my interest in his political ideas, activities and legacy intensified. I became aware subsequently that there were references to Fr Fahy in several important historical publications.

In the *Dictionary of Irish Biography* (2009), Laurence White describes his career – based on information supplied by Fr Declan Kelly – as

a stormy duality of radical politics and orthodox Catholic belief and practice, accentuated by an eccentric personality.

Professor Gearóid Ó Tuathaigh, in *The Land Question, Politics and Irish Society 1922-1960* (1982), suggested that

The career and work of Fr John Fahy with his short-lived paper *Lia Fáil* is worthy of serious attention.

His friend and mentor Peadar O'Donnell in *There will be Another Day* (1963) wrote of Fr Fahy that

he had a great gift for leadership; even his occasional incoherence seemed to emphasise his leadership as in the case of Big Jim (a reference to Jim Larkin, the Irish Labour leader and founder of The Irish Transport and General Workers Union).

Tom Fahy from Roo, Craughwell, in an essay about his uncle in *Killeenadeema – History and Heritage* (2008) felt that a book could and should be written about his political activities.

Michael McInerney in his biography of Peadar O'Donnell (1974) said that Fr Fahy while waging his campaign for the abolition of the land annuities in the 1920s was

as radical a man as ever had been seen in Ireland.

My early encounters with Fr John sparked my curiosity about his life. Later on, my reading of 19th and 20th century Irish history gave me the impetus to undertake this biography. The highly-respected former Republican and later Fianna Fáil minister Seán Moylan once wrote that

History is best understood if one has a conception of the personalities of those who make it.

In this book, therefore, I have tried to place Fr Fahy among his contemporaries. People like Bishop Dignan, Bishop Philbin, Peadar O'Donnell, Mary MacSwiney, Éamon de Valera and many others, whose lives intersected with Fr Fahy at crucial times, feature in the following pages.

It is clear then, that there are compelling reasons for writing the lifestory of a priest who at one time led what he called a Land Army with up to 10,000 members in eleven counties, who almost single-handedly wrote and produced a newspaper, who spent time in jail where he considered himself to be a prisoner of conscience and who at different stages of his life caused many a headache for the rulers of church and state.

I have endeavoured to follow Seán Moylan's further advice to any biographer

not to make the mistake of making the subject a whale among minnows.

Finally I would like to say that I alone am responsible for any errors of fact or interpretation which occur in the text.

*Jim Madden*
*Harbour Road*
*Banagher*
*Co. Offaly*
*Lá Fhéile Bríde, 2012*

CHAPTER ONE

# Historical Background

In the century following the defeat of the Irish at Kinsale in 1601, the English colonists took possession of nearly ninety per cent of the land of Ireland, a development that would have enormous consequences for the course of Irish history over the next three centuries. Rebellions, uprisings, famine and agrarian unrest would mark the struggles of the native Catholic Irish to regain their lost inheritance.

The Irish scholar Daniel Corkery (1878-1964) – poet, playwright, novelist, critic and nationalist – was of the view that land, as well as religion and nationalism, was a central theme of Irish literature. From novelists like Canon Sheehan, Charles J. Kickham, Peadar O'Donnell and John McGahern to the poet Patrick Kavanagh and the playwright John B. Keane, it is clear that land in Ireland has been responsible for what Terence Dooley in *The Land for the People* (2004) calls

> the hot flashes of anger and dispute that throw into relief
> deep-lying hatreds and fierce loyalties.

It didn't need to be a large fertile tract of land for those hatreds and loyalties to be aroused.

In his poem *Epic*, Kavanagh describes a violent row in 1938 between his neighbours over

> … who owned
> That half a rood of rock, a no-man's land
> Surrounded by our pitchfork-armed claims.
> I heard the Duffys shouting 'Damn your soul!'
> And old McCabe stripped to the waist, seen
> Step the plot defying blue cast-steel –
> 'Here is the march along these iron stones.'
> That was the year of the Munich bother.

John B. Keane's 1960's powerful character The Bull McCabe rages against the speculator, Dee, who threatens to outbid him for a small field long coveted by The Bull. In language almost identical to what Fr Fahy had used over thirty years earlier in his famous *Catechism*, McCabe bellows with all the force his mighty frame can muster that 'I won't be wronged in my own village, in my own country by an imported land-grabber.'

The Irish obsession with land is beautifully caught in McCabe's words as he anticipates the moment he can finally call this field his own:

> I watched this field for 40 years and my father before me watched it for 40 more. I know every rib of grass and every thistle and every whitethorn bush that bounds it … This is a sweet little field, this is an independent little field that wants eatin'.

It could be argued too that land, religion and nationalism dominated much of Fr Fahy's life. They were woven seamlessly into almost every facet of his daily existence. He considered them so inextricably linked as to be indivisible.

John Fahy grew up in a part of south-east Galway which had been at the forefront of the Land War in the decades prior to his birth. That area from Loughrea and the Sliabh Aughty mountains to the river Shannon (Lough Derg) included the parishes of Kilnadeema, Abbey-Duniry, Woodford, Tynagh, Ballinakill and Portumna. Events in some of these parishes made international headlines through the bravery and heroism displayed by the local tenant farmers and their supporters during evictions on the Clanricarde and other estates. The evictions carried out in a merciless manner by armed soldiers and police on helpless tenants only helped to strengthen the resolve of the dispossessed.

In 1870 less than 3 per cent of the people owned the land they farmed. These were in the words of Canon Joseph Guinan in the first lines of his novel *Annamore*:

> … the bad old days previous to the Land Acts, when most Irish farmers were tenants-at-will – that is occupying owners without a shred of security of tenure beyond the landlord's own sweet will, not infrequently a capricious and tyrannical one.

The agitation to confront this tyranny of unjust rents often imposed by an absentee landlord class led to the launching in

Woodford in October 1886 of The Plan of Campaign at a meeting attended by up to 4000 people. It was resolved to operate the plan along the following lines.

The tenants would approach the landlord or his agent and seek an immediate substantial reduction in their rent. Refusal to meet this demand would result in the withholding of the rents which would then be lodged in an estate account to be used in cases where extreme hardship was being experienced by evicted tenants. Land thus unoccupied would not be rented by any other tenants. Those who failed to uphold this agreement would face the prospect of immediate boycott.

The spirit of resistance among the tenants and an abiding belief in their cause were nowhere more in evidence than in their heroic defence of the homes of Thomas Saunders (1886) and 'Doc' Tully (1888). Even if their efforts against the battering ram brigade were ultimately unsuccessful in preventing the evictions, their courage and bravery galvanised the vast majority of the tenants to lend their support to a struggle that would, in a few decades, transform the social structures of rural Ireland.

Saunders' home became immortalised as Saunders' Fort while Tully, who had a smallholding of about seventeen acres and was a boat-builder by trade, got his nickname 'Doctor' because of his very influential contribution to the planning and execution of the Plan of Campaign. On one occasion he urged the tenants to dispense 'leaden pills' to the local landlord and his agents.

In their efforts to secure the 3 Fs – Fair Rent, Fixity of Tenure and Free Sale – the tenants of South-East Galway were greatly supported and ably led by the Bishop of Clonfert Patrick Duggan and by priests such as Rev Patrick Coen, Rev Patrick Costelloe, Rev Patrick Egan and Rev William Roche.

It was surely significant too, that it was Bishop Duggan who in August 1884 was singled out by Michael Cusack to be patron of the Gaelic Athletic Association, which the Clareman was about to launch. However because of his advancing years and decreasing energy, Bishop Duggan, while fully supportive of Cusack's initiative, declined the invitation. Instead, the bishop suggested that his younger, more energetic and equally supportive Episcopal colleague Dr Croke, Archbishop of Cashel, be asked to act as patron of the new organisation.

Through much agitation, great communal turmoil and suffering, and a succession of Land Acts reluctantly extracted from the British government, the power of the landlords in Galway and across the country was gradually broken.

It was into this highly-charged politically volatile landscape that the young John Fahy emerged in 1893.

CHAPTER TWO

## *The Early Years*

John Fahy was born on 14 June 1893 in Burroge, Killeenadeema, Loughrea, Co. Galway. His parents John and Honora (née Davock) had twelve children. The family were hard working farming people. John was baptised in the local church on 17 June and his parents had invited Matthew and Brigid Bowes to act as godparents.

John's father had been active in The Land League and on one celebrated occasion he is reputed to have bested, single-handedly, a party of mounted Royal Irish Constabulary who attempted to break up a Land League meeting in the vicinity of Loughrea.

After National School John Fahy enrolled in 1907 as a boarder in the Clonfert diocesan college St Joseph's, The Pines, Creagh, Ballinasloe which moved in 1923 to Garbally Park, formerly the seat of the Earls of Clancarthy. He matriculated on 12 September 1911 and entered the national seminary St Patrick's College Maynooth to study for the priesthood. According to historian Dr Brian Murphy he spent two years in 3rd year, passing into Theology in 1914-15 and becoming a sub-deacon in his final year. Throughout his years in the seminary, John, like most of the students there, was acutely aware of the political events unfolding outside the walls of the college.

The outbreak of the Great War in 1914 aroused strong pro-German sentiments among some of the staff and students. Fr P. J. Corish in his history of Maynooth (1995) suggests that among a section of the college community England's difficulty might be seen as Ireland's opportunity. He went on to relate how the Administrative Council of Maynooth early in 1916

> had to deal with a request from the recruiting officer, who claimed the right to come into the college and interview students and employees. He was told that on no condition would he be allowed to speak to students, and he might speak to the workmen only if he could produce specific authorisation. He appealed to higher authority, which inclined

to support the college. In the end he had to be content with what for him must have been an unsatisfactory compromise, that he might stand at the gate at the time the workmen were going out and speak to them if they were willing to listen.

Easter Week 1916 was a particularly tense time in Maynooth. On Easter Monday, shortly after midday, Dr Thomas O'Doherty Dean of St Joseph's and later to become Bishop of Clonfert, arrived back in the college from the city with the news that 'Dublin was up.'

The preparations for the annual sports, which were normally held in Easter week during the holiday period, were complete but on this occasion as news gradually filtered through about the Rising, all interest in sporting matters faded as recalled in *Vexilla Regis* (1966) by Fr Michael Casey (Elphin), then a junior student in Maynooth. 'A spirit of patriotic enthusiasm roused all our emotions' was how he remembered those stirring times.

Later in the afternoon of that fateful Easter Monday, the sound of marching men armed with rifles rang out from the main college entrance. Fr Casey's narrative continues:

We were brought very quickly and very closely to a realisation of the real meaning of what was happening when we saw Donal Ó Buachalla and his men of Maynooth marching determinedly across the peaceful, flower-bordered avenue of St Joseph's Square in the direction of the President's quarters, and as we gazed in wonder we witnessed a lovely scene. Those loyal men of Ireland humbly knelt on the gravelled terrace to receive the blessing of the President and then, as they proudly marched off again to join their comrades in Dublin, we could not restrain our feelings, and from the crowded windows we cheered them as they set out on their way to danger and to death for us and for the land we loved so much.

In dealing with that episode, Fr Corish adds some significant details to Fr Casey's recollections. When those Volunteers from Maynooth town knelt before the President's Arch and begged the blessing of the President, Fr John Hogan, he told Ó Buachalla – later appointed Governor-General by de Valera in 1932 – and his comrades that he could not bless their 'foolish and most ill-advised expedition' and urged them to go home. Fr. Corish contends that the Volunteers told the President that they would not go home, repeated the request for his blessing and said that if he didn't give it, they would go without it. Fr Hogan then told them that he would bless them as far as their spiritual needs were concerned but that he was totally opposed to what they were doing.

Having obtained the blessing, Ó Buachalla and his men left the college and marched along the banks of the Royal Canal and headed for Dublin to play their part in the Rising.

Extensive drilling by the students took place all that week, sometimes in secluded corners, at other times in prominent locations in the college grounds. John Fahy, by now fast emerging as a leader, urged the student body to get actively involved in the insurrection in the capital as their predecessors had done over a century before during the rebellion of 1798. As was noted in an appreciation of Fr John in the Garbally College annual *The Fountain* in 1970 after his death:

> Wiser counsel prevailed. They were all aware that survival in the battle would be no guarantee for survival in Maynooth and nobody wanted to part with a devoted comrade.

After their release from prison in June 1917, the surviving leaders of 1916 drafted an address to Woodrow Wilson, the American president, and invited the public to sign it. Almost all the students of Maynooth put their names to that document.

When the British Government passed a law in April 1918 introducing military conscription to Ireland, all the Irish political parties opposed the move and at the Mansion House Conference resolved to send a delegation to the bishops who were meeting at that time in Maynooth.

One of the delegates, Éamon de Valera, by now President of Sinn Féin and who some years earlier had taught mathematics in the college, got a rousing welcome from the students as soon as he appeared. Almost certainly this was the first time for John Fahy to set eyes on a man to whom he would initially give unquestioning loyalty. In later years he deemed de Valera to be the author of many of Ireland's ills.

CHAPTER THREE

## In Scotland

John Fahy was ordained a priest in St Brendan's Cathedral, Loughrea, by Bishop Thomas O'Doherty of Clonfert on 28 September 1919.

Many Irish dioceses at that time had an adequate number of priests and Clonfert was no exception. Fr John was sent on loan to the diocese of Dunkeld, Scotland where he served at St Joseph's, Dundee 1919-20 and at St Andrew's Pro-Cathedral, Dundee 1920-21.

From the outset Fr John immersed himself in activities aimed at improving the miserable conditions under which many Irish emigrants lived. The working environment for Irish priests constantly presented a range of challenges in those early decades of the 20th century. Often parishioners had to contend with living in squalid overcrowded slums, lack of employment opportunities, poor working conditions and little or nothing by way of social security or unemployment assistance. Anti-Catholic and anti-Irish bigotry were encountered on a daily basis. Migratory workers from Donegal were regularly attacked as they disembarked in Glasgow from the cattle-boats which had ferried them from Derry. Commenting on a labour procession aimed at improving workers' conditions the *Christian Scotsman* noted that

> At the tail end of the procession was a contingent of Irish priests, shaven and shorn and shovel-hatted, fat as pigs that are bound for Liptons.

Fr Fahy quickly established close links with Robert Stewart a leading communist in Dundee at the time and a tireless advocate on behalf of the slum-dwellers and workers striving to improve their lot.

The War of Independence was raging fiercely in Ireland and Fr Fahy was intent on contributing in every way possible to the struggle at home to break the link with England. From the start of his spell in Dundee he was active at leadership level both as Chaplain and Captain of the 3rd Battalion of the 1st Scottish Brigade of the Irish Republican Army (IRA).

Lena McDonald made an application to the Pensions Office on 21 October 1938. She had been active in getting munitions from Dundee and Glasgow to Ireland during The Troubles as a member of the 1st Scottish Brigade, 3rd Batt., Dundee Co., IRA. She describes the scale of the operation and concludes her application by stating that

> Fr John Fahy of Ballinkill, Co Galway, can cover my statement for the 1919 period as at that time he was a curate in Dundee and I took orders from him as Captain of the Brigade.

He regularly spoke on behalf of the Dundee Sinn Féin Club and availed of every opportunity to attack British policy in Ireland and the atrocities perpetrated, particularly by the Black and Tans. Fr Fahy fully supported the decision of the Lord Mayor of Cork, Terence MacSwiney, to embark on a hunger-strike and he challenged priests who suggested that MacSwiney should be refused the sacraments to a public debate on the morality of hunger strikes.

On Sunday night 14 November 1920, a young priest, Fr Michael Griffin, who had been ordained in 1916 and who was on loan from Clonfert to Galway diocese where he worked in the city parish of Rahoon, was lured on some pretext from his presbytery. His body was found in a shallow bog grave a week later with a bullet wound to his head and the finger of suspicion pointed to the Auxiliaries. Fr Declan Kelly in his Clonfert diocesan history *Meadow of the Miracles* states that Fr Griffin was not on a sick call 'as he did not bring his holy oils or the Blessed Eucharist'.

Fr Fahy made the journey home for the funeral but was late in arriving for the removal. He maintained an all-night vigil beside the remains of Fr Griffin in Loughrea Cathedral. Fr Griffin's grave is located to the left of the entrance to St Brendan's Cathedral.

Already Fr Fahy's concerns for the temporal as well as the spiritual needs of the people he served were fully formed and sharply defined. It is a measure of his commitment to the Republican cause, his organisational skills and force of personality that in less than two years serving in Dundee he was elected president of the Scottish Division of the Irish Republican Movement.

The esteem in which Fr Fahy was held by the Catholics of Dundee and the factors which motivated him at that time as a priest and as a republican may be gauged from the following report in the *Connacht Tribune* (1 July 1922) which describes a function held to mark his departure from Scotland.

*The Priest in Politics*
*Closetoken clergyman's interesting references at Dundee*
*God and Religion Must Come First*
On Wednesday, 14 June, the Rev John Fahy, of Clostoken, Loughrea, Co Galway, late curate of St Andrew's Pro-Cathedral, Dundee, addressed a crowded meeting in the Foresters' Hall in that city. The occasion was the presentation of a five-seater touring motor car, an illuminated address, and a handsomely inscribed pocketbook from the Irish and Catholics of the city, with whom he had worked for only eighteen months, as a token of their filial love and admiration. The Rev Monsignor Turner VG, was in the chair. During his opening address the Monsignor said:

The last great Irish demonstration that we took part in was more in the open, under the green canopy of heaven. On that occasion we welcomed to Dundee a great churchman and patriot, Archbishop Mannix. On this occasion we welcome back to our midst a great churchman and a great patriot also.

The Monsignor went on to say that Father Fahy was a holy and saintly priest, and was revered by all on account of his hard-working and zealous nature. Some of his curates had risen to fame as Canons of Cathedral Chapters, and others to the presidency of colleges in Ireland, and Father Fahy would be no exception to the rule. The chairman told some amusing anecdotes of Ireland, and coupled them with the adventures of Father with his 'Old Tin Lizzie,' which he had borrowed from a friend to assist him with his scattered congregation in Co Galway. He wound up his discourse by wishing Father Fahy the best of luck in his career, and said that he would feel hurt if he (Father Fahy) did not feel as much at home now as he did before he left the city for the green hills of Erin.

An Irish concert followed, in which the songs and dances were ably performed by the artistes.

Mr Hugh Traynor, President of Saint Andrew's sports' committee, in handing over the illuminated address, which is a great work of art, and bears a photograph of Father Fahy (the whole of which was the work of Father Dominic, of Lawside Convent), remarked that Father Fahy was one of the hardest-working priests who had come to Dundee, and that he was always to be found teaching the young men of the parish Irish games, etc.

Mr A. McLean, of St Joseph's parish, in handing over the wallet, asked Father Fahy to accept it as a token of respect from the people of Dundee. He added that they could say many fine things, but after listening to the reading of the address, any words from him would be superfluous.

In replying to the presentation, Father Fahy thanked the people for the unique presentation which they had given him to take back with him to Ireland, and said that he had put his work as a priest among them in an incomparably higher position than his work as an Irishman. But Ireland's war came on and he did all in his power to help the forces fighting for Ireland's right. And so he went into the war, and went in wholeheartedly, and he was glad to say that, later, he had confirmation of his action from the Moses of the Irish race, Dr Mannix, the great Archbishop of Melbourne, who blessed the banner of that section of the Irish Republican army to which he (Father Fahy) was attached. He went on to say that some in their mistaken fervour put Ireland first and God second, but he was with those who put God first, and in the irony of providence the position in Ireland today is, that we who have put God first have Ireland first also, because we have not compromised or swerved or wobbled, but are true to the principles we stood for under the Irish Republican government, and will remain true to them until the Irish nation freely and deliberately destroys them.

After some amusing stories, Father Fahy thanked all who were concerned in the presentation – for the fine new motor car, for the artistic and beautifully-wrought illuminated address, and for the wallet. He especially thanked the committee, one of whom, by the way, was Miss Lena MacDonald, who served a long term of imprisonment for gun-running in 1921.

On his arrival in Dundee on Tuesday evening, Father Fahy was met at the station by a few of his Irish brother priests, and they proceeded in taxis to St Andrew's Pro-Cathedral, where he was the guest of Monsignor Turner. On Wednesday a reception was held in the Queen's Hotel in his honour. This was attended by all the priests of the diocese, and many prominent local people.

## CHAPTER FOUR

## *Bishop John Dignan*

In the course of a long and sometimes turbulent life, Fr Fahy's words and actions occasionally propelled him, as will be seen, to national prominence.

Dr Patrick Murray in his fascinating study *Oracles of God – The Roman Catholic Church and Irish Politics 1922-1937* (pp 27-28) – states that during the 1920s and 1930s Fr Fahy was

> able to break the criminal law, serve a term in prison, deliver speeches denying the legitimacy of the State and openly involve himself in IRA activity, without incurring any penalty more severe than a transfer to an inhospitable curacy where he persisted in his defiance of the Free State regime. The relative leniency with which Fahy was treated may be attributed to the fact that John Dignan, Bishop of Clonfert since 1924, was an avowed Republican.

Dr John Dignan was Bishop of Clonfert for almost thirty years, 1924-1953. It was inevitable therefore that his life and the life of Fr Fahy would be inextricably linked at regular intervals, ecclesiastically and politically during that long episcopacy. A brief look at aspects of Bishop Dignan's life, concentrating particularly on his political outlook, may help to shed some light on what was at times a difficult, strained and even tempestuous relationship, though not without a great deal of mutual respect between two men of strong convictions and impeccable republican credentials.

John Dignan was born in 1880 in Ballygar, Co. Galway. He was ordained in 1903 and taught in St Joseph's College, The Pines, Ballinasloe where he was president from 1904 to 1919. He then worked in the parish of Abbey-Duniry until his appointment as Bishop of Clonfert in 1924.

From the time of his ordination he was active in Sinn Féin and was elected president of the East Galway branch in 1917. He played a major role in setting up Sinn Féin Courts in Co.

Galway. His outspoken republican comments and speeches meant that he was closely monitored by the RIC and British forces operating in Galway. The Black and Tans raided his house in April 1921 but he had received a tip-off from the RIC and evaded what in all probability would have been for him a fatal encounter had he been at home when they called.

Fr Dignan nominated an anti-Treaty candidate in the Pact Election held in 1922 while his bishop Dr O'Doherty nominated pro-Treaty candidates. Bishop O'Doherty transferred to Galway in 1923 and Fr. Dignan was appointed Bishop of Clonfert in July 1924. In his consecration homily he commented unfavourably on the state of the country under Cumann na nGaedheal. The country he contended was 'morally, economically even nationally slipping slowly into the abysmal pit of confusion and disorder.' But he urged his Sinn Féin listeners to obey, as he did, the rule of the majority in the firm hope and belief that in a short time the Republican Party was certain to be returned to power. The very strong pro-republican tone of Bishop Dignan's comments was enough for Archbishop Gilmartin of Tuam to confide to an episcopal colleague that 'after that I'm finished consecrating bishops.'

Bishop Dignan was presented with an illuminated address by the Galway Sinn Féin Clubs on which he wrote 'colourless, brainless, Cumann na nGaedheal.'

Some months after his consecration as bishop he said in an address to the Gaelic League quoted in the *Connacht Tribune* (14 June 1924) that he

> believed not only in a free Ireland but in a Gaelic Ireland and it was almost a duty on all Irish people who loved their country and revered their religion to stem the wave of paganism and materialism and sin that now swept the world by erecting around their coasts the barrier of the language.

Bishop Dignan's consecration was deemed to be of great importance politically as he was the most senior Irish churchman to take such a pro-republican stance since the Treaty.

When Éamon de Valera was released from prison in July 1924 one of the first people he sought out was Bishop Dignan.

One of Dev's supporters in a letter to Frank Aiken felt sufficiently upbeat by the turn of events that he commented that 'our stock is rising, we're getting respectable again.' Patrick Murray in dealing with this period states that

> Dignan dealt another blow to the Free State in November 1925 when, as chairman of the County Homes Committee he renounced the practice of obliging public officials to sign the declaration of allegiance, supporting an engineer who refused to do so.

A contributor to *An Phoblacht* in November 1925 praised the public pronouncements of Bishop Dignan and other republican clerics who

> by their actions in refusing to use the sacraments as pro-Treaty weapons saved the church from appearing to be a mere wing of Mr Cosgrave's party.

By 1929 the activities of Fr Fahy provoked what developed into a serious church-state controversy. However, the subtle negotiating skills and steely determination displayed by the bishop ensured on the one hand that the legal apparatus of the Free State government did not encroach unduly on his ecclesiastical patch and at the same time he was seen to have dealt decisively if not somewhat leniently with an openly defiant curate. A peace of sorts was eventually restored, not without Dr Dignan's patience being stretched almost to breaking point. But his episcopal authority remained undiluted and his republican principles retained their pristine purity.

On 20 June 1933 Bishop Dignan, still the most republican-minded member of the Irish hierarchy, was selected by his colleagues to deliver an address to the Maynooth Union in which he

> warned parents and others of the grave disloyalty and disobedience they committed in sending students to Trinity College, which came under the ban of the Holy See.

He went on to state that

> Trinity College's atmosphere, traditions and *genius loci* were as hostile to the Catholic Faith as ever.

Bishop Dignan wrote frequently and eloquently in attempting to foster community harmony and national well-being. In 1936 he was invited by the Minister for Local Government and Public Health, Seán MacEntee, to become Chairman of the Committee of Management of the National Health Insurance Society.

In October 1944 he published a pamphlet titled *Social security: outlines of a scheme of a national health insurance* which was 'an attempt to work out in detail the application of Catholic social teaching to a particular sector of Irish life.'

It was, according to F. S. L. Lyons in *Ireland since the Famine* (1970), the most striking contribution to the debate and his thoroughly comprehensive scheme proved

> much too comprehensive, it was soon made plain, for the official mind to digest or the official purse to afford.

Dr Dignan denounced as un-Christian the existing social services. The minister, on the other hand, saw a certain merit in a system 'incorporating the Christian ideal of frugal sufficiency'. The bishop declared, according to Whyte in *Church and State* (1971), that

> the whole Poor Law legislation, the Medical Charities Act and similar legislation should be blotted out from our Statute Book and from our memory. The system is tainted at its root and it reeks now as it did when introduced, of destitution, pauperism and degradation.

This criticism of the state's almost non-existent social services, reminiscent as they were at least in part of the Poor Law, did not endear him to the minister who eventually requested Dr Dignan to resign as Chairman.

According to Patrick Murray (p. 165 fn.) the resignation was offered and accepted but not before the bishop conveyed in forceful terms to the minister 'that his behaviour imperilled the democratic character of the State.'

Another factor which very likely caused friction between MacEntee and the bishop was the appointment by Bishop Dignan of Seán MacBride, an eminent Senior Counsel, as Chairman of the Portiuncula Hospital Consultative Committee which oversaw the construction and opening of the new hospital on 9 April 1945. MacBride had organised the first Saor Éire Convention in 1931 and was Chief of Staff of the IRA 1936-38. He was a noted defender of republican prisoners at the time he received the invitation from Bishop Dignan and was clearly a staunch opponent of MacEntee's Fianna Fáil government. He was the son of Major John MacBride, executed in 1916 and of Maud Gonne who so intoxicated the poet Yeats.

Bishop Dignan always expressed himself in an uncompromising and original manner. His independence of thought and sense of justice were nowhere more in evidence according to Murray than during

> the term of the first Costello government (1948-1951) he showed sympathy for Noel Browne's point of view when the latter was the object of major episcopal disapproval.

Among the bishop's notes on Department of Health proposals for a Mother and Child service is the following: 'personally hold very strongly that there is nothing in the scheme opposed to Catholic teaching.'

These are glimpses of the man to whom Fr Fahy was answerable from shortly after his return from Scotland and for the following twenty-nine years up to 1953.

CHAPTER FIVE

# The Influence of Peadar O'Donnell

Fr Fahy's first appointment on his return in 1921 to Ireland was at Eyrecourt where, according to Fr Kevin Egan, he had a strained and difficult working relationship with his parish priest, Fr Martin Leahy who was a strong supporter of the Treaty.

Clostoken was to be Fr John's next appointment from 1923 to 1925. He was constantly supporting and promoting opposition to the government through his active involvement in the IRA whether as chaplain, organiser or recruiting officer for East Galway. Dr Brian Murphy in his extensively researched chapter in *Radical Irish Priests 1660-1970* recounts (p. 188) that Fr Fahy heckled the Free State Minister for Agriculture, Patrick Hogan from Kilrickle, at a pro-Treaty election meeting in August 1923 at Loughrea. Fr Fahy on that occasion shouted out, in response to critical comments made by government supporters about the republican candidate Frank Fahy, 'that he didn't sell his country, neither did Terence MacSwiney nor Mary MacSwiney'. This provoked Michael Tierney from Ballymacward, Professor of Greek in University College Dublin and the man mainly credited with that university's move in the 1960s from Earlsfort Terrace to the extensive Belfield campus, to ask Fr Fahy if he was 'prepared to accept responsibility for all the banks and post offices that had been plundered during the last twelve months and for the deeds committed during that period by the party he came there to represent'.

As a student Michael Tierney (1894-1975) had been a contemporary of John Fahy in The Pines, Ballinasloe. He was a brilliant student and after graduation studied in Athens, Berlin and at the Sorbonne. At twenty-nine he was appointed Professor of Greek in University College Dublin in 1923 and served as president from 1947 to 1964.

Professor Tierney won a by-election in Mayo-North for Cumann na nGaedheal in 1925 and represented the National University of Ireland constituency 1927-1932. He served in Seanad Éireann 1938-1944. He married Eibhlín, daughter of Eoin MacNéil whose biography he wrote.

Despite their common Galway heritage Fr Fahy and Professor Tierney were at opposite ends of the political spectrum. Tierney and Professor James Hogan UCC, brother of Paddy Hogan Agriculture Minister, were regular contributors to *United Ireland*, the influential journal which reflected concerns and policies of the Cosgrave party.

Both Hogan and Tierney were gravely concerned about the dangers of communism. In their writings they praised the corporate state as developed in Italy. Professor Tierney considered that

the corporate state had evolved a scheme of social and political organisation so suited to modern conditions that every civilised country would adapt it to its own needs …
The corporate state must come to Ireland as elsewhere.

Professor Lyons argued that the

doctrines formulated in United Ireland … owed as much to another Italian as they did to Mussolini. The teachings of Pope Pius XI in the encyclical *Quadragesimo Anno* laid heavy emphasis upon vocational organisation and representation within the state and it was this stream of thought that was likely to be more influential in Catholic Ireland.

Those years during the 1920s were very tumultuous ones in Ireland. The War of Independence, The Treaty and its aftermath, the disastrous Civil War, the failed Army Mutiny, the suppression of the report from the Boundary Commission, the murder of Kevin O'Higgins, vice-president of the Executive Council, in turn followed by extremely divisive election campaigns, left the country almost ungovernable.

And yet despite the mayhem so often in evidence, the achievements of the Cumann na nGaedheal government led by W. T. Cosgrave were extraordinary. In general its members were, in the words of Kevin O'Higgins, 'probably the most conservative-minded revolutionaries that ever put through a successful revolution.' That so many of its leaders had no previous ministerial experience made their accomplishments all the more remarkable. All the institutions of state and the structures of local government as we know them today were set up with little resources and the Irish Free State was internationally recognised.

Divisions on the republican side with Éamon de Valera and his newly formed Fianna Fáil party opting to enter Dáil Éireann in 1927 left a strong physical force rump operating outside the confines of parliamentary democratic activities. This group in turn gradually divided into two main factions. One group was opposed to all that the Treaty represented and felt further betrayed by de Valera's embrace of constitutional politics. Its leaders were very socially conservative when seeking solutions to the problems daily facing the country and the members remained for the most part loyal to their Catholic religious roots despite regularly being denounced by churchmen across the land.

The other strand in the republican family, with Peadar O'Donnell to the fore, increasingly advanced more far-reaching solutions to the country's economic and social ills. They voiced their frustration at the government's lack of progress in these crucial areas. While the Tricolour had replaced the Union Jack over Dublin Castle, widespread poverty still stalked the land. The ill-treatment of republican prisoners continued and a resolution to the running sore of the land annuity payments to the British government was nowhere in sight. These annuities were the repayment of loans which the British government had made to Irish farmers to buy out their landlords before the Irish Free State had come into existence. The Cumann na nGaedheal government collected and passed on these payments. It was to this socially conscious latter group, largely through the influence of O'Donnell, that Fr Fahy was inexorably drawn.

These radical republicans, often branded as socialists and even communists and instigators of civil unrest, hoped through their political action to breathe new life into the ongoing struggle for what they argued would be real independence.

A brief look at the life of Peadar O'Donnell, regarded as the ultimate socialist radical revolutionary, might help to explain why a man like Fr Fahy found himself attracted to the political and social message promoted so convincingly and selflessly by this man from Dungloe, Co Donegal.

O'Donnell (1893-1986) qualified as a teacher but after a short time took up a position as an organiser for the Irish Transport and General Workers' Union. He joined the IRA in 1919 and took the republican side in the Civil War. He was captured with Liam Mellows after the fall of the Four Courts and was in jail until 1924.

O'Donnell was editor of *An Phoblacht*, the official organ of the IRA (1926-1930), and used that journal to expound what for the Ireland of the 1920s was his radical political manifesto. Writing on 29 October 1927, he said that

> the bankers, ranchers, brokers, lawyers will never join in a revolutionary effort to save the country … we must seek to organise the have-nothings and have-littles.

On 24 December, also in *An Phoblacht*, he wrote that

> until Ireland drops all this wordy cant about sovereignty, and gets to work to make that sovereignty active against the forces of conquest that are now exacting tribute from our working folk, all we can say is that Ireland is jabbering in her sleep.

O'Donnell's wife Lile (nee O'Donel), a native of Swinford, Co. Mayo, was financially independent which allowed him to give up his union job and concentrate on his political and literary activities. O'Donnell was a founder member of Saor Éire in 1931 and established the Republican Congress in 1935. He organised and fought with the Connolly Column on the Republican side in the Spanish Civil War in 1936.

He was a gifted journalist and novelist and found time between 1946 and 1954 to edit the famous magazine *The Bell* which was a great platform for young writers like James Plunkett, Patrick Kavanagh, Anthony Cronin and Brendan Behan. One volume of his autobiography *There will be Another Day* (Dolmen Press, 1963) outlines in detail his fierce struggle against the continued payment of the land annuities to England.

Historian Roy Foster in his *Modern Ireland 1600-1972* wrote (1989, p 548) that

> An Phoblacht, particularly under Peadar O'Donnell's editorship, remains the record of an alternative politics in the 1930s and 1940s much as *The Bell* … stands as a record of an alternative culture.

Fr Fahy was transferred in 1926 to Bullaun, outside Loughrea, around the time that O'Donnell was conducting a campaign of non-payment of land annuities in his native Donegal.

Their paths would cross in the following years and Fr Fahy's actions ensured that Bullaun and his own name would reverberate with significant political, legal and ecclesiastical fallout across the land.

## CHAPTER SIX

## *Biddy Nevin's cattle 'rescued'*

Peadar O'Donnell's campaign against the payment of land annuities in The Rosses area of Co. Donegal, begun in the 1925-26
period, had by 1928 virtually collapsed. Fr Fahy had been organising resistance from his base in Bullaun surrounded by a
tightly-knit group of like-minded supporters including the OC
of the local IRA unit. The most prominent among the younger
members of this group were Martin Fahy, Mick Silver, John Joe
Kennedy and Michael Seery. He was also supported by what
O'Donnell called 'veterans of the land war', outstanding among
them Tom Kenny, Pat Gannon and Eamonn Corbett a close
friend of Liam Mellows.

Fr Fahy wrote a play based on the 1880s Plan of Campaign
during the land war and it was performed in Loughrea. His
group was working closely with a small number of Fianna Fáil
supporters and in collaboration with the IRA created a movement called The Anti-Tribute League whose main aim was to
thwart, by whatever means, the payment of annuities to
England. An Anti-Tribute campaign catechism bearing the unmistakable fingerprints of Fr John was produced and widely circulated. It was published by O'Donnell in *An Phoblacht*. The following are extracts from it:

A T C
(Anti Tribute Campaign)

Q. How did England establish a claim to the land of
   Ireland?
A. By robbery.
Q. What is rent?
A. Rent is a tribute of slavery enforced by the arms of
   the robber-landlord.
Q. What is a landlord?
A. A landlord is a descendant of a land robber.
Q. Who pays rents to landlords?

A.   Only slaves.

Q.   What is a bailiff?

A.   A bailiff is a land robber's assistant.

Q.   What should be done with a bailiff … a landlord?

A T C 3

(Anti Tribute Campaign)

Q.   Who passed the Land Acts?

A.   The British Government.

Q.   Why?

A.   To make Ireland pay her garrison, the landlords.

Q.   To pay them for what?

A.   For the land of Ireland.

Q.   Had the landlords any title to the land of Ireland?

A.   None whatsoever.

Q.   Why?

A.   Because they got it by robbery, and murder.

Q.   What else did the landlords do?

A.   They enslaved Ireland for England.

Q.   Were there never a Land Act how would the land be today?

A.   It would be free.

Q.   What did the Land Acts effect?

A.   They compelled the Irish people to buy Ireland from the landlords.

Q.   How?

A.   By making them pay annuities.

Q.   Are the Irish people bound by the Land Acts?

A.   Not at all!

Q.   Should they pay the annuities?

A.   NOT AT ALL!

Q.   Why?

A.   A land robber should not be paid for robbed land.

Around this time Fr John also wrote a document called *The Oath and the Annuities*. His lifelong disregard for those elected to political office on however strong a mandate is clearly evident in the following extract taken from that publication:

We allow awful monstrosities to thrive in this land of ours. It is past time to start slashing them down. Public representatives are often despicable humbugs. May we hope that even at this late hour they will face this question of the Oath as it ought to be faced – a most treasonable crime against Ireland. May Ireland vomit out of her mouth every traitorous monster who dares befoul her with the beastly stain of treason. Personally, I would not execute those who stand for the Oath by either hanging or shooting. I would disembowel them slowly and then saw their heads off with a cross-cut.

Fr Fahy invited Peadar O'Donnell, whose Donegal campaign was now at an end, to come to Galway and use his considerable talents in combination with the Bullaun group. O'Donnell had no hesitation in accepting the invitation for a number of reasons. He was well aware of the unity of purpose and single-minded determination of Fr John and his group in pursuing their objectives. An additional attraction for him was that he

> was eager to light a fire on Paddy Hogan's doorstep and here certainly were the makings.

Paddy Hogan has been widely acclaimed as an innovative and progressive Minister for Agriculture. For example, he successfully guided the 1923 Land Act through Dáil Éireann and was responsible for setting up the Agricultural Credit Corporation and The Irish Sugar Company, two institutions which were to have very positive influences on the long-term development of Irish agriculture. But, in the words of Professor Joe Lee of UCC,

> as the lawyer son of a senior Land Commission official he instinctively equated the ordinary farmer with the 200-acre man, when only 8000 out of 382,000 holdings belonged to this category in 1930.

Hogan didn't seem to take fully into account that as well as a small group of very large farmers, there was also a majority of small and medium sized farmers and a large cohort of farm labourers. The interests of all these groups were often in direct conflict with each other. His best known campaign slogan was

One more sow
One more cow
One more acre under the plough.

O'Donnell recalls in *Another Day* the opening sentence of Fr Fahy's first letter to him:

> To be sure you are the one man in Ireland making a stand for the old Gael.

Not long after O'Donnell's arrival in January 1929 in Bullaun the parish priest asked Fr John one Sunday to appeal to the parishioners for funds to build a curate's house. Fr John began his sermon in a low-key manner and after declaring to the congregation his reluctance to be requesting money from them, he skilfully availed of the opportunity presented to him to drive home his anti-annuities message. He put it to them that if they had money to give away, would it not be wiser to help him build a new residence with it rather than send their hard-earned money to Britain in the form of land annuities. O'Donnell takes up the story thus:

> The startled Parish Priest popped out of the sacristy door, but Father John had no eyes for him. He was too busy advising his people to make two halves of the land annuity, take one half of it with them into the village and buy the makings of a celebration, and give the other half to him. The congregation, watching the Parish Priest in a dither, was in a mood to cheer by the time Father John finished his sermon.

A memo to members of the Executive Council reveals that on the following Sunday Fr Fahy read Mary MacSwiney's outline of a proposed new republican constitution called the Declaration of Independence from the altar and then urged the congregation to join the IRA.

On 18 February cattle were seized from Corcorans of Benmore, New Inn and impounded in Loughrea. According to Supt Doyle in his note to the Justice Department (26 March 1929):

> Fr Fahy came into Loughrea with some others with no apparent reason except to make a rescue of the cattle from the pound. The guards in Loughrea, on their suspicions being aroused, took suitable precautions and nothing happened.

Later that night the authorities moved the cattle to Galway City pound from where they were rescued during the night. Supt Doyle's final comment on that rescue was that

It is not unreasonable to assume that Fr Fahy who has strong Irregular leanings was the ... instigator.

A week later a bailiff seized two cattle from Biddy Nevin, Ballymurray, Bullaun for failure to pay annuities. Fr Fahy, according to O'Donnell in *Another Day* (p 97), was working with a group of men erecting a graveyard wall when the bailiff passed driving the cattle towards Loughrea. On a command from Fr John the men rushed on to the road to take the cattle from the bailiff who drew his revolver and fired into the air. All the men except Fr John retreated. He now physically attacked the bailiff and sent him 'staggering into the ditch with a thrust of his shoulder'. He further threatened the bailiff not to follow the cattle as 'something might happen to him'. The bailiff having recovered sufficiently got on his bicycle and went looking for help. O'Donnell concludes his description of that episode by stating that

Young Cooney, one of the road workers, sprinted back to give Father John a helping hand, and he took over the cattle. At Father John's bidding, Cooney turned the cattle in on the land of a man named Kane, an ex-soldier of the 1914-18 war in which he lost a leg. Kane rose to it, and when the guards came swarming down on the scene the cows were safely tucked away in his byre.

Dr Brian Murphy's account of the incident differs in some respects from O'Donnell's recollections. He states that having seized two cattle from Miss Bridget Nevin of Ballymurray, Loughrea the bailiff's path was blocked at Bullaun by a crowd of fifteen to twenty men:

Fr Fahy urged the crowd to act but when no one made a move he seized a whip or stick from one of them and drove the cattle back. Only after he called them 'a crowd of cowards' did the men join in rescuing the cattle.

Jimmy Cooney of Galway hurling fame, a grandnephew of Fr John, claims that the cattle, when rescued, were driven to a local farmyard where they were dehorned to make their identification more difficult. They were then taken to a large forestry plantation nearby to conceal their whereabouts for as long as possible.

Further information about the affair emerged during the court case in April when Fr Fahy was tried for obstructing the bailiff in the course of his duty.

Fr Fahy was served with a summons on 11 March by Guard Scanlon from Loughrea to appear in court on 19 March but stated that he would not attend the sitting as he was a republican.

The *Connacht Tribune*, 23 March 1929, reported as follows:

*Summons Against Priest.*
*Alleged Cattle Rescue from Sheriff's Bailiff.*
*Loughrea Case*
The Rev John Fahy CC, Bullaun, failing to appear on a summons at the Loughrea District Court on Tuesday in connection with the charge of obstruction and seizing stock from the sheriff's bailiff at Bullaun a few weeks ago, the case was adjourned to next court on 2 April.

Father Fahy was charged that he did 'at Bullaun, on 25 February 1929, unlawfully rescue from Peter Whelan, sheriff's bailiff and court messenger, two head of cattle, which were taken in execution of decree of the District Court of Justice, entitled the Irish Land Commission versus Bridget Nevin, dated at Loughrea 20 November 1928.'

Guard Scanlon, Loughrea, proved service of the summons on Fr Fahy at his residence at Bullaun.

Supt Doyle, who prosecuted, stated as Fr Fahy did not attend the court it may be necessary to apply for a bench warrant for his arrest before next court, and he applied for the adjournment.

Mr Cahill DJ adjudicated.

Not surprisingly these events did not go unnoticed by Bishop Dignan. Away from the glare of publicity he was in contact with Superintendent Doyle of Loughrea who was the senior Garda officer dealing with the case. On 21 March the bishop attempted to ascertain if a public apology from Fr Fahy would be enough to have the matter resolved before it took its course through the courts. He further undertook 'to assist in having any reasonable demands of the government carried into effect insofar as the criminal aspect of the case is concerned'.

The government was as anxious as Bishop Dignan to resolve the matter while upholding the rule of law. An apology by Fr Fahy from the altar and to the court and a payment by him of £7 14s 10d, the amount levied against him would have brought a conclusion to the case. This is clear from a Department of Justice Memo (26 March 1929).

In order to formalise this arrangement the secretary of the Department of Justice Henry O'Friel went to Loughrea for a meeting with Bishop Dignan. After complex and protracted discussions O'Friel returned empty-handed to Dublin. He reported to his minister that

> owing to Fr Fahy's eccentricity and intractability the bishop was not in a position to give the necessary assurance.

O'Friel, in his departmental submission, elaborates further on his encounter with the bishop:

> He admitted that Father Fahy was unlikely to attend or recognise the court, that it was unlikely he could be induced to apologise publicly or pay the amount of the seizure except possibly through ecclesiastical action of the bishop. The bishop in fact holds a written undertaking from Fr Fahy duly witnessed by two priests in which he said that in obedience to the bishop he would publicly apologise for having broken the law of the land by rescuing etc etc. The bishop however seemed to be a bit uneasy whether he could enforce this undertaking and he certainly left no doubt in my mind that the undertaking was valueless as far as the court proceedings were concerned.

The discussion between Bishop Dignan and O'Friel was quite tetchy at times particularly when the bishop brought up a centuries-old church statute – *privilegium fori* – or benefit of clergy which ensured that priests would not be tried in a secular court except where ecclesiastical approval had been sought and obtained. This edict still formed part of the most recent (1917) Code of Canon Law. O'Friel however countered this claim by stating that the statute had in fact no legal standing according to British law in Ireland before 1921.

Living up to Peadar O'Donnell's assessment of him as having a great gift for leadership and, particularly pertinent in this instance being a fine propagandist, Fr Fahy rejoiced in all the publicity his actions generated. Both he and his bishop felt that the whole affair exposed a possible basis for a church-state conflict, a development which the Cumann na nGaedheal government would wish to avoid.

Uppermost in Bishop Dignan's mind was the fear which he conveyed to O'Friel that if Fr John was ever to find himself in prison he would almost relish the prospect of going on hunger strike which would make a bad situation much worse.

On the thorny issue of church-state relations, Fr Fahy believed that if arrested and imprisoned it would

> definitively expose the Free State as a Protestant state under English rule rather than as a Catholic state which it claimed to be.

With all the behind-the-scenes manoeuvres failing to bring about a satisfactory resolution, the civil authorities felt that the only option now open to them was to let the law take its course. Despite the long-standing tradition of cabinet confidentiality, Fr Fahy claimed to know that the Executive Council voted, by four votes to two, in favour of letting the prosecution proceed.

# CHAPTER SEVEN

## *Arrest, Imprisonment, Trial*

Fr Fahy was arrested at his home in Bullaun on 16 April by Supt Doyle, Loughrea and a party of guards and detectives. He was brought to Loughrea District Court where two charges were preferred against him in connection with the rescue of the two head of cattle from the Sheriff's bailiff. Details of the arrest of Fr Fahy emerge from the following report written by Supt Doyle which he submitted to the Department of Justice.

Co. Form C2.

**Dated at Loughrea this 16th day of April 1929.**

With reference to my report of the 13th instant re above I now beg to report that on this date I took Father Fahy into custody. I went to Bullaun this morning with Sergeant McKeon in my own car, and Sergeant Feighan, Garda Compton and Mulkeen "S" Branch Unit in another car. I arrived at Father Fahy's house about 8.35 a.m. and was admitted by a male servant. I told the male servant to tell Father Fahy that I wanted him. The servant mentioned that Father Fahy was in bed, so I said I would wait until Father Fahy got up. Father Fahy appeared in about ten minutes and I told him I was taking him into custody and read the Bench Warrant to him. He asked if I would wait a few minutes while he was writing a letter to his Parish Priest and getting a cup of tea. I said I had no objection. No one entered the house except myself and Sergeant McKeon, uniformed Force. After about an hour Father Fahy said he was ready and came away quietly with me in my own car. Just before he left his house he said to me that the civil authorities adopted the only logical course in arresting him. He then mentioned that we thought to get the church for us but that it did not work this time. I told him he was mistaken; that we were proceeding with the case until the church intervened.

On the instructions of Mr.Finlay I charged Father Fahy in barracks with (1) obstructing Peter Whelan in the lawful execution of an Execution Order of the District Court, contrary to section 24 of the Enforcement of Court Orders Act 1926. (2) With unlawfully rescuing from Peter Whelan, sheriff's bailiff and Court Messenger, two head of cattle taken in execution of a decree of the District Court entitled the Irish Land Commission versus Bridget Nevin. I gave the usual legal caution. He made no statement.

At the Court Father Fahy adopted the attitude that the Court was an unlawful assembly. When I gave evidence of arrest he asked me what the meeting was and I said "a District Court." He asked then under what authority it was functioning and I refused to answer. He asked me if I used force to bring him to Court. I replied that I took him into custody on the authority of a Warrant. He asked me if I had the permission of the ecclesiastical authorities to arrest. I replied that I informed his Bishop that he (Father Fahy) would probably be taken into this Court by force. He asked then if I knew the penalty, in any independent country, of taking a citizen by force into an unlawful assembly, and on getting no reply, said it was high treason.

When asked at the conclusion of the evidence for the prosecution if he had any statement to make, he made an attack on the payment of annuities. He said that not alone did he admit rescuing the cattle, but that he was proud he had done so. He said that he was out to prevent the robbers from seizing stock to send over money to"robber Winston Churchill." He said it was well known how the Clanricardes, the Ashtowns, and Persses of Galway got the land in the time of William by robbery and murder. He pointed out that the Irish people were under no obligation to pay rent to these people.

Father Fahy was returned for trial to Galway Circuit Court on 3rd June next. He was offered bail, himself in £100 and two sureties of £50 each, but he refused to take bail. At the time of writing Father Fahy is at present in the Presbytery, Loughrea, and the clergy there told me they would do their best to make him accept bail.

(Signed)..... P.Doyle, Supt.

Peadar O'Donnell in *Another Day* adds further detail to Supt Doyle's statement as follows:

> He was held at Loughrea until late in the evening, while ecclesiastics in authority over him and priests devoted to him stormed at him and pleaded with him. In refusing to recognise the court, it followed that he could not be remanded on bail. He left the state no option but imprison him. He was lodged that night in Galway jail. I went on to Galway where I saw his sister, Agnes, and his brother, Joe. They were anxious that having taken this stand Father John should be let follow his own course. 'Father John is a man who always has to stand well with himself,' Joe told me.

A full report of Fr Fahy's court appearance appeared in the *Connacht Tribune* on 20 April.

### Committed For Trial
### Charges Against Priest at Loughrea
### Statement in Court

Before Mr Cahill DJ, at Loughrea District Court, on Tuesday, the Rev John Fahy CC, MA, Bullaun, was charged with having, on February 25, at Bullaun, obstructed Peter Whelan, court messenger, in the execution of an execution order of the district court, and with having, on same date, at Bullaun, unlawfully rescued from Whelan, who was acting as sheriff's bailiff, two head of cattle which had been taken in execution of the decree of the District Court of Justice, entitled the Irish Land Commission versus Bridget Nevin, dated at Loughrea, 20th November, 1928.

Fr Fahy was arrested at his residence at Bullaun on Tuesday morning by Supt P. Doyle and a party of guards and detectives and conveyed by motor to the courthouse, which was crowded during the proceedings. The arrest was a sequel to Fr Fahy's refusal to appear in court on summons.

Mr T. Finlay BL (instructed by Mr R. J. Kelly, State solr) prosecuted on behalf of the State. Fr Fahy conducted his own case.

A. M. Toole, court clerk, produced the order book showing the ruling of the justice at Loughrea on the 20th November, 1928, where a decree for £5 17s. 4d. and costs, £1 11s. 6d., was obtained at the suit of the Irish Land Commission against Bridget Nevin, Ballymurray. The decree in question was issued on foot of that order on January 26 last and bore the signature of the district justice and Mr R.J. Kelly, solr for the plaintiffs.

Raoul Joyce, under-sheriff, gave evidence of receiving the produced decree and directing same to Whelan for execution. In cross-examination by Fr Fahy, Mr Joyce said Whelan was an employee of his. Witness would have had to execute the decree personally if necessary had Whelan been unable to carry out his orders.

Peter Whelan, court messenger, stated that, accompanied by his son and Peter Hudson, the driver of the motor car which conveyed him to Bridget Nevin's farm, he seized two head of cattle, their property, and proceeded to Loughrea. About 350 yards below Bullaun he saw a crowd of men block the road from left to right. Witness and his son came with the cattle towards the crowd and was met on the road by about 20 men and Fr Fahy. Witness spoke to the men but could not say if Fr Fahy heard the words addressed to the crowd. Fr Fahy then took a whip from under the arm of one of the men and, rushing forward, slashed the cattle back past witness in the direction of Bridget Nevin's farm. Fr Fahy spoke to witness and told him not to be foolish – not to take the cattle, that he (Whelan) would not be able to get them. Witness subsequently searched for the cattle but could not trace them and the decree still remained unexecuted. Fr Fahy said he would not mind if the stock were taken for a lawful debt, but he would not allow the stock to be taken for land annuities.

Fr Fahy remarked that Whelan's statement was fairly correct but there were some omissions. There were not 20 men in the crowd.

Mr Cahill, remarking he did not like to interrupt Fr Fahy, pointed out that at this stage he was entitled to cross-examine the witness on the evidence he had given.

Fr Fahy then inquired over what assembly he (justice) was presiding.

'I am presiding over this court,' replied Mr Cahill. – 'Who is responsible for bringing me here?' Fr Fahy asked. 'I thought you knew that,' replied the justice. 'The State is responsible.'

Having complained he was brought up there that morning by force, Father Fahy said every human being wanted to know why his liberties were interfered with.

The district justice said that was what they called a preliminary hearing. It would be his duty if a *prima facie* case was made out to send Fr Fahy for trial before a jury of his countrymen.

Fr Fahy: What is this assembly? – Mr. Cahill: At the present stage you are entitled to examine the witness. You can make a statement afterwards. I do not want to curtail your latitude or liberty at all.

Fr Fahy then asked Peter Whelan if he remembered the question addressed to him before he took the stock and witness answered in the negative. – Did I say – pointing to the cattle – 'Are those for rent?' – Yes. – Then I said 'We are not allowing the British exchequer to rob in this area.' – Witness said he did not remember the remark. – Fr Fahy: You appeared excited and probably do not remember. You were not just to yourself in describing the incident because you took out a gun and pointed it. – Justice: I don't like interrupting Fr Fahy, but it must be question and answer.

Fr Fahy: Did you take out the gun afterwards and point it? – Yes, but it was only an imitation (laughter) – Fr Fahy smilingly remarked they would have taken the cattle anyway (laughter). – In further cross-examination, witness said he did not get the option of telling the truth as to who rescued the cattle or lose his job.

Peter Joseph Whelan, son of the last witness, also gave evidence.

Supt Doyle deposed to the arrest of Fr Fahy at his residence that morning at Bullaun. Witness administered the usual legal caution and defendant made no statement.

Cross-examined by Fr Fahy: You brought me here by force to-day? – I brought you under the authority of a warrant. – Had you the permission of my ecclesiastical authorities to bring me here? – Your ecclesiastical superior, the Bishop,was informed you were being brought in here. – You came by force this morning with policemen, CID men, who, I presume, were armed, and left me without time to acquaint my ecclesiastical superior? – Your superior was told by me personally that you might be brought in here to the court. – If you are a member of the Catholic Church you should know there is a Statute that forbids you to take me by force. – Your ecclesiastical superior was told by me personally that you would probably be brought in to the court. – What do you mean by 'probably'? – That you might not attend voluntarily. – You, the gentleman who brought me here, should know what this meeting is? – This is the district court, held under the Free State Constitution.

Held under what law? – Witness declined to answer. – 'By what law? again queried Fr Fahy, is this – what you call a court – assembled here?' – Witness again declined to answer on the ground that Fr Fahy's questions were not relevant to the case. – 'One thing I know,' observed Fr Fahy, 'it is not an Irish court.'

Remarking again he did not want to interrupt him, the district justice asked Fr Fahy to confine himself to questioning the witness on his evidence. He (Fr Fahy) was at liberty to make a statement afterwards. – Fr Fahy: My liberties are being restrained. This is supposed to be a free country. – Continuing, Fr Fahy said it appeared to him an apparently intelligent gentleman presided over that assembly and he refused to tell him by whose authority it was assembled. – Mr Cahill reminded Fr Fahy he had already been told. – 'Until you answer my question I am in an unlawful assembly,' rejoined Father Fahy. – Mr Cahill replied he was not there to answer questions.

Fr Fahy, proceeding, held the superintendent and others were guilty of high treason against the Irish nation by bringing him into an unlawful assembly held in Republican territory under the jurisdiction of the Irish Republican Government. They had also broken the ecclesiastical laws.

Mr Finlay BL asked the court to have Fr Fahy returned for trial.

The justice said in his opinion a *prima facie* case had been made out against Father Fahy on these two charges and justified him in returning him for trial. Before doing so he asked if Fr Fahy wanted to give evidence or reserve his defence.

Fr Fahy, replying, said he had been brought by force into an unlawful assembly convened by British authority on the soil of Ireland, against the wish of the Irish nation, against the jurisdiction of the lawful government of the country – the Irish Republic. He warned those responsible for bringing him there they were guilty of the greatest of national crimes in bringing a citizen of a free country into an enemy court and holding that court on Republican territory. He considered that an illegal assembly enforced in this country by British law, British soldiers, British Black and Tans. 'I consider,' he proceeded, 'you are all guilty of high treason,' adding, with a smile, he hoped he would be as lenient when the government of the Irish Republic came to deal with them (laughter).

With regard to taking the stock off the bailiff, Fr Fahy admitted the fact he took the loot off the robber that was to be handed over to Winston Churchill. And not alone had he not any regret for his action but felt proud of it, and hoped that a campaign against the robber bailiffs would increase and develop until they were swept out of this island into the sea, and they (people) got possession of their own lands. They knew the descendants of the Norman, Williamite and Cromwellian robbers – such as Clanricarde, Ashtown and Persse – got the soil of this country by robbing and by murdering their ancestors. Referring to the Land Acts proposed by the British government for this country, Fr Fahy said he held, as all decent Irishmen held, that instead of buying back their own lands, the people should take them back and to succeed they had only to cease paying rents for lands of which their forefathers were deprived by loot and robbery.

Mr Cahill asked if Fr Fahy had an application to make for bail and he replied he had not. Fr Fahy was later removed by motor under escort to Galway jail.

Fr Fahy was to spend the following seven weeks in Galway Jail until his trial in Galway Circuit Court on 3 June. The first indication of how he was adjusting to prison life can be gleaned from the short memorandum sent to the Cabinet – The Executive Council – from the Department of Justice.

ROINN DLÍ AGUS CIRT
(Department of Justice)

BAILE ÁTHA CLIATH

20th. April, 1929

OC/137.

Secretary,
to the Executive Council.

With reference to previous memoranda concerning the prosecution of Rev. John Fahy, C.C. Bullaun, County Galway, I am directed by the Minister for Justice to send herewith for circulation to members of the Executive Council for their information a copy of a police report of the proceedings which took place on the 15th. instant. Mr. T.A.Finlay, B.L. conducted the prosecution. The Rev. John Fahy declined to accept bail and he was lodged in Galway Prison on the night of the 16th.instant. His conduct in prison has been satisfactory. He applied to the Visiting Committee for permission to be given assistance for the cleaning of his cell on the payment by him of the customary charge. There is power under the rules to grant to a prisoner awaiting trial such an application. The application was granted; the applicant's contribution being fixed at 1/- per diem. This is normal. It is perhaps of interest to say that it is understood that Mr.de Valera could have on application secured a similar privilege in Belfast Prison on the occasion of his recent imprisonment there but that he did not make any application.

RUNAIDHE.

News of Fr John's arrest and incarceration spread quickly. Understandably it created quite a stir locally and throughout the country. Many local authorities and political groups discussed the issue. Support for the stand taken by Fr John was widespread.

The *Connacht Tribune*, 18 May, included the following:

## FIANNA FÁIL AND FATHER FAHY

At a meeting of the East Galway Comhairle Ceanntar, Fianna Fáil, held in the Foresters' Hall, Ballinasloe, on Sunday, P. Beegan in the chair, the following resolution was unanimously passed: "We condemn the action of the Free State Government in arresting and detaining in prison the Rev J. Fahy CC, Bullaun, because of his action in defending the fundamental rights and liberties of the Irish people. We wish to express our sincere gratitude to Father Fahy for his fine example of heroism ... M. Quinn, sec.

Fr Declan Kelly in his *Images of Ballinasloe* (2007) provides the following information on Paddy Beegan:

Paddy Beegan TD, a native of Oatfield in the parish of Aughrim, was elected to the Dáil in 1932, having joined the Volunteers in 1917 and the South Galway Brigade of the IRA in the battle for independence. Taking the Republican side at the treaty, he was imprisoned from August 1922 until December 1923.

A farmer by occupation, he had joined Fianna Fáil from its formation and was parliamentary secretary to the Minister for Finance at the time of his sudden death, aged sixty-one, on 2 February 1958. He was hugely popular in Ballinasloe. In the by-election caused by his death, his nephew, Tony Miller, was elected TD.

Resolutions, less strident in tone, were passed by County and Municipal Councils seeking his release. The actions of Wexford and Tipperary South public bodies were mirrored across the country.

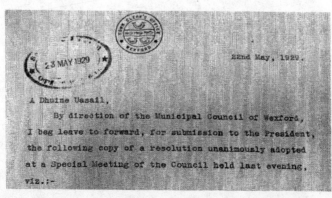

23 MAY 1929

22nd May, 1929.

A Dhuine Uasail,

By direction of the Municipal Council of Wexford, I beg leave to forward, for submission to the President, the following copy of a resolution unanimously adopted at a Special Meeting of the Council held last evening, viz.:-

Proposed by His Worship the Mayor, seconded by
Councillor Bolger, and

RESOLVED "That we request the Government to reconsider
their attitude in the case of Father Fahy, as we
consider that it is very inadvisable to have a clergyman
of any Denomination imprisoned"

Mise, le meas,

*Nicholas Bolger*

Town Clerk.

The Secretary,
President Cosgrave,
Government Buildings,
Merrion Street,
DUBLIN.

---

Comhairle Contdae—Tiobraid Árann (teas)
(County Council)                    (Tipperary S.R.)

Laurence Ryan,
Secretary.

Oifig an Comhairle Contdae,
County Council Offices,

Sráid emmet, cluain meala,
Emmet St        Clonmel

29th May, 1934.

A Chara,

I am directed to submit, for the consideration
of the Executive Council, copy of resolution, as follows,
passed at a meeting of the Tipperary S.R., County Council
held on 28th instant -

Proposed by Councillor James P.Kennedy, seconded by
Councillor Cronin - Resolved - That we, the Members of
the Tipperary, South Riding, County Council call on the
Executive Council to release the Rev. Father Fahy, to
allow him to take his place in the Centenary Celebrations
to be held next month.

Mise, le meas,

*M. Ryan*

Runaidhe.

There was a threat by members of the Finance sub-committee of Galway Co. Council to boycott the celebrations to mark the centenary of the granting of Catholic Emancipation planned for 2 June if Fr Fahy remained in custody. The canonical implications for Fr Fahy now that he came under the ecclesiastical authority of the Bishop of Galway, as a guest of the nation in Galway Jail, got an airing at the same meeting.

The *Connacht Tribune*, 25 May, contained the following report of the sub-committee's deliberations.

BISHOP OF CLONFERT'S STATEMENT
*Sequel to Regrettable Council Discussion*
*Father Fahy's Arrest*
Galway Urban Council, on the motion of Mr Michael O'Flaherty PC, have unanimously decided to take part officially in the celebrations and procession in Galway on 2 June in honour of the Centenary of Catholic Emancipation.

At the meeting of the Finance Committee of Galway County Council on Saturday, Mr Gilbert Lynch (chairman) presiding, Mr M. J. Cooke proposed that the County Council officially attend the procession in connection with the Catholic Emancipation Centenary celebrations in Galway on 2 June. Chairman: Yes, we are the premier body, and I think we ought to be represented officially. – Mr. O'Toole remarked it would be a grand thing to have a Catholic Emancipation procession through the town while they held a man in gaol for doing his duty. 'It is hypocrisy; that is what it is,' he continued. 'You have a priest in gaol just as you would have a hundred years ago. You are not emancipated. The Penal Laws are here as good as ever, and you have got to submit to them.' – Mr Cooke observed he did not wish to have any discussion over it. – Mr O'Toole: Let there be honesty about it. – Chairman: Let us be unanimous if we decide on it. – Mr O'Toole: I will not.

Mr Corbett: I suggest that it be asked that Father Fahy be allowed out for the day to take part in the procession and say Mass before he comes out. – Mr Bartley Lydon seconded. – The chairman asked if there was any seconder for Mr Cooke. – Mr. O'Toole: I will not second him. – Mr Lydon: If Father Fahy be allowed out I will second him.

Mr Kelly said they were going to blame the church for keeping Father Fahy in gaol. – Mr O'Toole: I blame them for half the misfortune in Ireland. – Mr Kelly, commenting on Mr Cooke's resolution, said if they were forced to become Catholics officially it was the last word in this country. – Mr Cooke remarked that was not the point. – Mr Kelly: It is. Are you not able to go on your own to the procession? – Mr Cooke remarked that the Urban Council would attend officially. – Mr Kelly: With great respect, do not bring us as far as that. I think you should be made to withdraw that comparison. (Laughter.) – The chairman said there was nobody to second Mr Cooke's proposition. – Mr Cooke: Perhaps the chairman himself would. – Chairman: I will second it. – Mr Cooke: And have a vote on it. – Chairman: Is there any amendment? – Mr O'Toole: I propose as an amendment that Galway County Council do not be officially represented while there is a priest of the county in gaol. – Mr P. Kyne seconded. – Mr Cooke: Is that an amendment to the resolution? – Mr. Kelly: It cannot. The church cannot be blamed. – Mr Corbett: If Father Fahy is allowed to say Mass in gaol – Mr Kelly: Is he not allowed to say Mass? – Chairman: No, he is not. – Mr Corbett: It may be said it is not a question for laymen to talk about, but we are talking about Emancipation and we have not freedom. In saying this I am as loyal a Catholic as the Bishop of Galway.

Chairman: That raises another question. As Mr Kelly says, he believes in the firm but not in some of the travellers. As far as that is concerned I agree with him. According to the law of the land, if a man is charged with murder he is allowed to be tried by his peers. Father Fahy ought to be allowed the privileges of the church. 'A priest once, a priest ever.' Until a man is found guilty he is presumed to be innocent. – Mr Cooke: Is it the government that has done that? – Chairman: When a priest leaves one diocese and goes to another he is subject to the diocesan authority in which he is residing. What I gather is that the bishop of this diocese refused to allow Father Fahy to say Mass while in prison. That raises the question of Catholic teaching, and as a Catholic I am opposed to that. – Mr Cooke: They have rules and regulations of their own with which we have no right to interfere, and we have no power to interfere. – Mr Kelly: The answer to Mr Cooke is this: We are always talking about freedom and having freedom of thought and if we are not allowed to think about things according to our own views one has not freedom of thought. I agree that in a matter like this we are entitled to our opinions whether the church is right or wrong. If it was a question of faith or morals we would have no right to interfere. – Mr Cooke: I do not like to see this religious discussion arising. It is not a place for it. – Mr O'Toole: Why did you start it?

Mr Cooke: It is the whole country I am talking about. You are taking the small little question of Galway. I am talking about the Catholic Church. – Chairman: Will you withdraw your proposition? – Mr Cooke: I will not. – Mr Kelly: We ought to cut out this of being ultra good Catholics – someone will tell us we are not. – Mr Corbett: I am proposing that we have no objection to take part if Father Fahy is allowed out for the day. – Mr Cooke: I have no objection to that but you should propose it as a separate resolution. Do not move it as an amendment. Mr Corbett: We are not talking on behalf of any party. We are talking as Catholics. – Mr. O'Toole: My amendment is that the county council or any of its subsidiary bodies be not represented because there is no emancipation while there is a priest in jail. – Mr Corbett said the subject was quite in order to touch upon. They could agree to go to the procession as a demonstration of faith but it was also in order that Fr Fahy should be allowed to take part. He would move that as an amendment. He would like to see the procession representative of every element. He himself would like to be there. He would, however, like that Father Fahy be allowed out for the day to take part and celebrate Mass as a good Irish priest.

Chairman: I do not think we could ask that. They would be only too glad to grant it if they thought he would give his word that he would come up for trial. – Mr Corbett: They can do it as well as letting him around the ring. – Chairman: If we are to be represented at all we should have an assurance from the bishop that Father

Fahy will be allowed to celebrate Mass in jail. – Mr. Cooke: are you withdrawing from my motion? Chairman: Absolutely. – Mr O'Toole: If there was less religion and more honesty preached it would be better for the country.

Eventually the following minute was made and it was directed that a copy be sent to the Bishop of Galway: 'The Finance Committee of Galway County Council, discussing the proposal to take part in the Catholic Emancipation Centenary procession which is to be held in Galway on June 2, unanimously decided that the County Council could not take part officially in the procession while Father Fahy, who is detained in Galway jail, is deprived of his faculties.'

Mr Cooke said he would like to see Father Fahy out, but he submitted they had no right to dictate to the church. They were going too far.

In the course of further discussion, the chairman said that if they did not get a reply before that day week the members would not attend officially. The secretary pointed out there were only eight members present and he did not know if the other members of the council would acquiesce in their decision. – Mr. Corbett: You can take it that 24 members will agree with that. – Mr O'Toole: Fianna Fáil, Labour, Cumann-na-nGaedheal, and even the Independents are well represented here.

Mr Corbett: It may be mentioned that as far as the Bishop of Clonfert goes, Father Fahy has full faculties. If invited to a procession in Clonfert diocese we will go. – Mr O'Toole: We will.

That debate and unwelcome publicity generated by Father Fahy's presence in Galway jail brought a sharp rebuke from Bishop Dignan who issued this short hard-hitting press statement:

*Interference With Ecclesiastical Discipline.*
The Most Rev Dr Dignan, Bishop of Clonfert, has communicated the following statement to the Press:

I regret to see from reports in the public Press that certain public bodies are making a pretext of Father

Fahy's position to interfere with ecclesiastical discipline. They are thereby making it more difficult for Father Fahy to give public and full satisfaction for any scandal or injury to religion which may result from his action.

They are also unaware that Father Fahy has given me a signed promise to make a public apology for his action.

Fr. Fahy's case was now a major national news item because Bishop Dignan's statement and the discussions of Galway County Council Finance Sub-Committee were reported not only by the local Galway papers but by the widely read Dublin dailies. The Irish Independent issues of May 20th and 22nd carried prominent articles on this story with headlines such as:

*Imprisoned Priest*

*Galway Body's Action*

*Bishop's Advice to Boards*

*A Recent Resolution*

Supporters of Fr Fahy in the Galway area were obviously intent on keeping his extraordinary situation highlighted in the minds of the people as the following news item in the same issue of the *Connacht Tribune* suggests:

FATHER FAHY'S ARREST
*Pamphlets Posted on Courthouse Doors*
Printed pamphlets dealing with the arrest of the Rev Father Fahy CC, Bullaun, Loughrea, who is at present in Galway jail (having refused to give bail) for the alleged illegal seizure of cattle from the sheriff's bailiff, were posted upon the doors of Galway Courthouse on Wednesday. Similar pamphlets were posted upon the doors leading into the district court where the county council met on Wednesday as the room where it usually sits was occupied by the temporary rating staff. The pamphlets were subsequently removed by the civic guards.

On 11 May Fr Fahy wrote a long letter 'to some person unknown' (later identified as Mary MacSwiney, sister of Terence MacSwiney former Lord Mayor of Cork who in August 1920 had been arrested on suspicion of IRA involvement and who died in Brixton Jail after a hunger-strike lasting seventy-four days). In his letter Fr John

- defended his actions as 'acts of justice and charity'.
- denied the legitimacy of the conquest 'unless the church teaches *ex-cathedra* that Ireland belonged and belongs to England, I will never accept it.'
- denied the right of the Free State to legislate.

Mary MacSwiney and Fr Fahy shared many Republican sentiments. However, unlike Fr Fahy, she was reluctant to embrace the social radicalism of Peadar O'Donnell which as she saw it, 'put class before country'. She had been one of the fiercest critics of The Treaty and her implacable opposition to what it contained ensured that she found in Fr Fahy a close political soulmate.

The substantive public debate on the Treaty began in the Dáil in Earlsfort Terrace on 19 December 1921. Bertie Smyllie, editor of the unionist-leaning *The Irish Times* in describing MacSwiney's contribution on 22 December said that

> She had a quiver full of poisoned arrows and she launched every one of them. Nobody escaped her mordant scorn ... For nearly three hours Miss MacSwiney was eloquent, tearful, ironic, fervent, reproachful, implacable; but bitterness was the driving force behind her every word, and a more unprofitable speech could not be imagined.
>
> To speak for nearly three hours in any circumstances is beyond the powers of most human beings. To sustain such a pitch of bitter fervour as Miss MacSwiney sustained would have been considered impossible, if one had not heard her with one's own ears. The speech was a kind of apotheosis of medievalism. Miss MacSwiney would put the clock back 750 years.

Throughout the 1920s MacSwiney was, like Fr Fahy, as F.S.L. Lyons put it 'adamant for the Republic whatever the cost'.

To republicans like MacSwiney, Countess Markievicz, Grace Gifford who had married Joseph Plunkett in prison the night before he faced the firing squad in 1916, Tom Clarke's widow Kathleen and James Connolly's daughter Nora, it was treasonable even to contemplate recognising the Free State, with or without an Oath.

Fr Fahy shared with those members of Cumann na mBan an absolute unwillingness to compromise on what they firmly believed in and it followed therefore according to Lyons

> that if the Republic was the only lawful government in the country, then they had the right to attack – to shoot down if need be – any traitor who claimed to be exercising authority either in the Free State or in Northern Ireland. They saw themselves, in short, as the soldiers of a perpetual revolution which would end only when all thirty-two counties entered the republican fold.

Fr Fahy sought advice about his situation from Rev Dr Michael Browne, Professor of Canon Law in Maynooth who later became Bishop of Galway. Fr Browne was a close friend of Éamon de Valera and a supporter of Fianna Fáil. He urged Fr Fahy to submit in obedience to his bishop and accept the conditions already agreed as he makes clear in this letter from Maynooth.

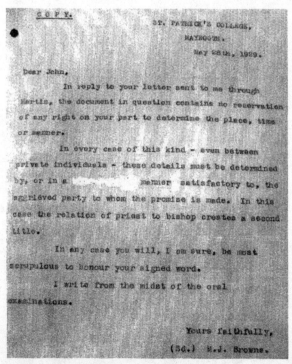

COPY.

ST. PATRICK'S COLLEGE,
MAYNOOTH.

May 28th, 1929.

Dear John,

In reply to your letter sent to me through Martin, the document in question contains no reservation of any right on your part to determine the place, time or manner.

In every case of this kind – even between private individuals – these details must be determined by, or in a ........ manner satisfactory to, the aggrieved party to whom the promise is made. In this case the relation of priest to bishop creates a second title.

In any case you will, I am sure, be most scrupulous to honour your signed word.

I write from the midst of the oral examinations.

Yours faithfully,

(Sd.) M.J. Browne.

The nature of the charge against him and the traditional re-spect accorded to priests in Ireland left many of the prison staff and inmates in awe at this new arrival among them.

Up to the early weeks of May Fr John had a steady stream of visitors. These included Fr Michael Browne, Peadar O'Donnell's wife Lile and Louis O'Dea described in *Another Day* (p. 99) as 'a solicitor, a good Republican and a good neighbour,' who had been chosen to handle the case.

During those weeks in jail Fr Fahy's spirits were high and in Peadar O'Donnell's words (p. 99)

> he certainly made his presence felt in it. His concern for people in trouble made him big brother to all the prison-ers. He was laughter in the grey of their misery. Everybody was courteous to him and he wandered around pretty much at will. One day he spotted a new-comer, a tinker, one of the Wards from Ballinasloe. Father John knew the people of the roads, and the people of the roads knew Father John well. He called the prisoners and warders to halt as they marched past him, and with such sharp authority that he got almost a barrack-square re-sponse. All the ex-soldiers among them rapped the cob-bles and, said the one among the prisoners who told the story to me, 'any old farmer that had a foot in the air, froze it in the air.' Father John addressed the tinker: 'Macaward, Bard to the O'Donnells, it is an evil day for Ireland when I see thee thus. But be of good heart, broth-er. When we achieve our independent Republic, Peadar O'Donnell will restore to you your tribal lands in Tirconail and your great herds of kine, and you will have your flowing robes …' Father John went on to describe the brave world that awaited the tinker. When he paused for breath, Macaward spoke urgently, 'For the love of God, Father John, slip me a chew of tobacco'.

However the pressure of jail life and the seriousness of his situation now began to take their toll on Fr John as Governor Gordon reveals in the letter opposite to The Department of Justice.

The Prison,

Galway.

30. 5. 29.

I beg to report that Revd. M. Browne D.D. Professor of Canon Law at Maynooth College, visited on 22nd instant Revd. John Fahy who is in custody for trial at the Circuit Court to be held in Galway on 3rd proximo. The visit was given in the Governor's Office - not in the hearing of any officer.

Dr. Browne informed me he wished to explain to him as a friend some of the obligations and consequences of his position and that his visit was for that purpose alone.

Father Fahy has refused all letters and communications addressed to him since Saturday 25th instant and informed me he would not see any person, lay or cleric, who might call to see him, and that he was not to be informed if any should call as he would make no exception save in the case of his Solicitor, Mr. O'Dea.

He gave as his reason that he found the strain of his position too much for his nervous system, and wanted absolute rest and quiet until his trial.

He consulted the Medical Officer on 28th instant for neurasthenia and was prescribed rest.

On yesterday 29th instant His Lordship, Dr. Dignan, sent me a letter requesting me personally to give Father Fahy one which he enclosed and addressed to him and sealed. His Lordship's letter he also refused when I took it to him this morning.

I have not opened His Lordship's letter, but have acknowledged its receipt and informed him that it was refused, and asked for further instructions.

I am forwarding with this report seven unopened letters which were received since he notified his intention of refusing letters.

Since his committal he has been otherwise amenable to prison rules and has made no complaint whatever about his treatment.

(Sd.) P. GORDON.

Governor.

Secretary,
Department of Justice.

Neurasthenia was a term coined in the late 19th century to refer to a condition of chronic mental and physical weakness and fatigue. The term was dropped from the Diagnostic and Statistical Manual of Mental Disorders in 1980 and is no longer in scientific use.

From 25 May Fr Fahy's refusal to see any visitors except his solicitor and his unwillingness to accept a letter even from Bishop Dignan marked a noticeable change in his behaviour.

In the days leading up to the trial, Peadar O'Donnell and Louis O'Dea were in regular contact with Fr Fahy who saw no reason why he should deny that he rescued Miss Nevin's cattle from the bailiff. O'Donnell states (p. 100) that

O'Dea and Father John evolved a polished formula and so when Father Fahy was asked how he pleaded, guilty or not guilty, he said to the jury he saw no reason why the judge should not proceed as if they had just found him guilty. The judge interpreted this as a plea of guilty and sentenced Father Fahy to six weeks' imprisonment to date from the day of his arrest.

Peadar O'Donnell is being very modest in suggesting that Fr John and Louis O'Dea alone devised a formula for a successful court appearance. O'Donnell was a highly experienced negotiator and strategist and it is inconceivable that he hadn't a major input into the manner in which the case should proceed.

COPY.                                                      Loughrea
                                                         . 3rd June, 1929.

     With reference to my report of the 16th April, re rescue of
Sheriff's Seizure and arrest of Rev.John Fahy, C.C. Bullaun, I now
beg to report that Fr.Fahy's case was disposed of at Galway Circuit
Court held on this date.

     Fr. Fahy was defended by L.E.O'Dea, Solr., Galway.

     At the opening of the case Mr.O'Dea mentioned to the Judge
that it was Father Fahy's wish to be tried by a Judge without a
Jury.  He mentioned that Fr.Fahy was aware that certain things had
taken place which would tend to gain the sympathy of certain people
and this might make even one Juror not act in accordance with the
oath administered to him.  Fr.Fahy would consider this the greatest
tragedy of all.  Mr.O'Dea then said that Fr.Fahy had instructed
him to say that all the evidence given in the depositions was true.

     The Judge then asked Mr.T.A.Finlay, B.L. what he had to say and
the latter replied that he had no objection to the adoption of the
course referred to by Mr.O'Dea, and that the Judge would accept Mr.
O'Dea's statement on behalf of the accused as a plea of guilty.

     Judge Wyse Power then said that he would accept the plea of
guilty.  He referred to the fact that no personal violence was
offered to the Court Messenger and that this would influence him in
taking a more lenient view of the case than he would otherwise have
done.  He sentenced the accused to six weeks imprisonment without
hard labour, the sentence to take effect from date of Fr.Fahy's
arrest, which meant that Fr.Fahy was then discharged from custody.

     Mr.O'Dea then got up to say that Fr.Fahy had been commanded by
his Bishop to express regret in Court for what he had done in this
case and in obedience to the command of the Bishop he now expressed
such regret.

     Outside the Court a number (about 40) of Fr.Fahy's sympathisers
gathered and when he was going away gave a cheer.  No one from
around Loughrea or Bullaun was present in or near the Court, except
a brother of Fr.Fahy's.

                                                            Supt.

Supt Doyle's report on the trial written immediately after his return to Loughrea Garda Barracks is as follows.

*The Irish Times*, 4 June, reported events in Galway the previous day under these headlines:

RESCUE OF SEIZED CATTLE
FR FAHY'S REGRET

The case against the Rev John Fahy CC, of Bullaun, Loughrea, who was charged with the illegal rescue from Peter Whelan, Sherrif's bailiff, of cattle seized by decree for land annuities, aroused considerable interest in the Galway Circuit Court yesterday. As Father Fahy, when returned for trial, had refused to give bail, he was brought up in custody, but was accommodated with a seat at the solicitors' table.

When the case was called, his solicitor, Mr O'Dea, said: My client instructs me that the depositions are correct, and he desires that this case shall be tried without a jury. He admits that he took the cattle off the bailiff, Whelan, and he is prepared to abide the consequences. His one anxiety now is that no jury would be sworn, for this reason: Various sympathies have been aroused over the question at issue, and my client fears that those sympathies, as well as the fact that he is a priest, may possibly result in even one member of the jury straining in the slightest degree the oath that shall be administered to him. My client considers that that would be the greatest calamity that could happen in this case. His own words to me were of the extremest nature, and show that Father Fahy puts truth before every other consideration. I have explained to him that if he should adopt any attitude other than that which I intend to adopt the danger which he fears so much may occur.

I request, therefore, that this case be dealt with without a jury, and on the same basis as if the severest verdict had been returned by a jury.

Judge Wyse Power sentenced Father Fahy to six week's imprisonment without hard labour, to date from his arrest, which meant that he was immediately discharged.

Mr O'Dea then stated that Father Fahy had asked him most particularly not to plead any extenuating circumstances in the case, or anything that could be interpreted as such. The Most Rev Dr Dignan, the Bishop of Clonfert, had commanded Father Fahy to express regret for his action, as a priest having a vow of obedience to his bishop. His client now obeys this command, and hereby makes such expression of regret.

Father Fahy then left the Courthouse, and as he drove away he was cheered by a number of those in the crowd that had gathered outside.

The widespread publicity generated nationally by this case ensured that every detail of Fr Fahy's activities and well-being while in jail and afterwards was followed closely even at the highest level of government. It is noteworthy that copies of correspondence between Fr Fahy, Bishop Dignan, The Prison Governor and Fr Browne, Maynooth, sent in the first instance to the Department of Justice were then forwarded by Henry O'Friel, Departmental Secretary, to the Executive Council for their consideration.

Ripples of unease from the case continued to reverberate through the Department of Justice and in Government circles in the months following the trial.

The following memorandum from Henry O'Friel to the Executive Council clearly illustrates the extent of routine surveillance and intelligence gathering which was carried out by the security forces on those perceived to be a threat to the State.

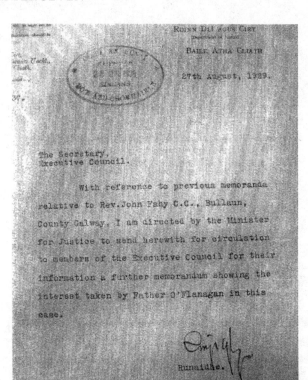

ROINN DLÍ AGUS CIRT
Department of Justice

BAILE ÁTHA CLIATH

27th August, 1929.

The Secretary,
Executive Council.

With reference to previous memoranda
relative to Rev. John Fahy C.C., Bullaun,
County Galway, I am directed by the Minister
for Justice to send herewith for circulation
to members of the Executive Council for their
information a further memorandum showing the
interest taken by Father O'Flanagan in this
case.

Rúnaidhe.

It will be remembered that Rev. John Fahy C.C. of Bullaun,
Loughrea, was charged with illegal rescue from a Sheriff's
officer of cattle seized by decree for land annuities.
Bridget Nevin was the person from whom the cattle were
seized the rescue of which led to Father Fahy's arrest.

It is learned that Father O'Flanagan visited
Nevin's house for the purpose of compiling reports for
American Press. Father O'Flanagan is a journalist for
American papers and some time ago the "New York World"
gave prominence to the case of Father Fahy.

It is also learned that the car in which Father
O'Flanagan travelled to the Loughrea area was driven by
a Doctor Patrick McGuinness of Kinnity, a brother of
Sean McGuinness who, it will be remembered, escaped
from prison.

Fr Michael O'Flanagan (1876-1942) was a priest of the Diocese of Elphin, a Vice-President of Sinn Féin from 1917 and like Fr Fahy he was concerned to have land redistributed. National independence and cultural renewal were at the forefront of his priorities. He was suspended from his ministry in 1918 and opposed the Anglo-Irish Treaty. The description of him as a journalist for American papers may be explained by the following information which appears (p. 178) in Denis Carroll's biography of Fr O'Flanagan:

> For a number of years between 1928 and 1931 Fr O'Flanagan spent several months annually in the United States ... There is no ground for arguing that he used these periods as lecture opportunities to eke out an income, since none was available either from Sinn Féin or from his diocese.

Fr O'Flanagan later supported the Republican side against Franco in the Spanish Civil War. Dr Patrick McGuinness and his brother Seán (known to his family and friends as Jack) grew up in Kilbeggan where their father was a teacher. Jack was a Sinn Féin TD in the 1920s and had been OC 1st Battalion Offaly No 1 Brigade. He was interned with many other 'Irregulars' but with outside help he escaped from Mountjoy with several colleagues and remained a committed republican throughout his life. After the escape he travelled to America dressed as a priest. On his return to Ireland he began to farm on what was a portion of the Locke Estate on the outskirts of Kilbeggan. Ruairí Ó Brádaigh, IRA Chief of Staff, delivered the oration at his funeral.

Jack's brother Dr Patrick was District Medical Officer for the Kinnitty area of Offaly. He was for many years, up to his early death at the age of forty-seven in 1945, director of elections for Fianna Fáil in the Laois-Offaly constituency. And as if to show that political ecumenism prevailed in the McGuinness family, one of Patrick's sons, Patsy who had hurled at Minor, Junior, Intermediate and Senior level for Offaly and had won a county Senior hurling medal with Kinnitty in 1967, stood for Fine Gael in County Council elections in the 1970s.

CHAPTER EIGHT

# The Red Scare

Once the tension and adverse publicity surrounding the imprisonment and trial of Fr Fahy had died down, Bishop Dignan had to deal decisively with his troublesome curate.

After giving the matter most careful consideration Bishop Dignan decided against imposing the ultimate episcopal sanction which would have been to 'silence' Fr Fahy. Having already secured the written promise from Fr John to apologise in court for his actions, the bishop now instructed him that under no circumstances was he to discuss politics if two or more people were present. He also transferred Fr John back to Clostoken as curate.

Peadar O'Donnell unflatteringly describes that ancient parish thus:

> There is a Clostoken in nearly every diocese, a ragged curacy which is a sort of place of punishment for priests who stumble. The people there know that unless the new priest is a fledgling on his first appointment, then he is a poor man under a cloud of some kind. They are civil to the first but they reach out warmly to the second.

There Fr John continued to discharge his priestly duties, while O'Donnell often used the curate's small thatched house as a second office from which he edited *An Phoblacht*, when not working in the paper's head office in Dublin.

But despite the strict conditions and limitations laid down by Bishop Dignan, Fr John regularly held meetings in his house with both local supporters and with groups of men from different parts of the country. They came seeking his and O'Donnell's advice as to how best to respond to the threat of court proceedings against smallholders who had defaulted or were in arrears with their land annuities payments. The activities of different units of the IRA were regularly on the agenda. Permission or refusal for many an operation emanated from that obscure presbytery.

Fr John, for example, arranged through O'Donnell's wife Lile in Dublin that guns from an IRA company quartermaster in the city be made available to a group for a raid on the State Solicitor's Office in Ennis. The intention was to destroy as many documents as they could lay their hands on.

While many serious issues were discussed in the Clostoken gatherings, there were several light-hearted interludes too. During one of Peadar O'Donnell's extended visits to the area, Lord Lascelles and his wife, Princess Mary, visited Portumna where they had a residence. It came to the attention of Fr John and O'Donnell that the local parish priest, Canon Joyce, was fussing over the titled visitors. O'Donnell editorialised in the following issue of *An Phoblacht* under the heading 'Princess Mary's Little Priest'. This did not endear him to the Canon and of course Fr John, by extension, was blamed equally for what was seen as serious disrespect to a much-loved pastor. The matter was made worse by the attempted burning of Lascelles' Irish home.

Fr John and O'Donnell got a frosty reception one day shortly afterwards when they called to a woman who had a son in a religious order. The traditional cup of tea was served with little enthusiasm. The two visitors soon realised that some quick thinking was needed if they were to extricate themselves from a mess of their own making. O'Donnell describes how the visit unfolded:

> 'Did you hear what Princess Mary did with the rosary beads Canon Joyce gave her?' Father John asked the woman of the house. 'I did not,' she snapped. 'Ah well, maybe it's just as well.' Father John and I nibbled at other topics. Our hostess suddenly turned to Father John, 'What did you say about the rosary beads?' 'Ah that, maybe I shouldn't talk about it. The poor things, they don't know any better. Well, it was this way: When they left here they went to Belfast and as they came to the bridge over the Boyne at Drogheda, Lascelles said to his missus: "Have you them things ready?" "In my hand," said she, and as the train entered on the bridge she put her hand out the window and she dropped the rosary

beads into the Boyne.' 'She did not, Father,' the woman gasped. 'She did so,' Father John assured her, 'for I have it from the lips of a man that was in the carriage with them, a cattle dealer from Ballinasloe.'

Bishop Dignan's order to Fr John to refrain from discussing politics must have led to some very amusing situations. In social gatherings Fr John would regularly inform people in his company of those restrictions when a contentious political point arose. His normal routine in such a situation was to initiate a discussion on some aspect of astronomy, a subject in which he was, apparently, reasonably well versed.

From his observations of different units while travelling around the country in the following year evading arrest and organising continued resistance to the payment of the land annuities, Peadar O'Donnell came to form a particularly high opinion, with some reservations, of the Galway groups under Fr Fahy's control. He wrote as follows:

> As it happened I had some little cause to fear arrest then, so I went to earth in Galway, and like many other occasions when I was forced off the main road on to the laneways, I benefited greatly from the experience. I got to know the group around Father John, one by one in their own homes. I shared fireside chats with them in a setting of their neighbours. We met in conference. Looking back on it now I am of opinion that the Galway committees were at once the most advanced in idea, and the best fighting group in the Irish countryside at that time. Their weakness was that they had less pattern of organisation than the Donegal team. They had not the same gift for relating themselves to the people around them; they were commandos rather than a movement.

By his continued political association with Peadar O'Donnell, Fr Fahy was incurring the wrath of most mainstream politicians and senior clergymen at national level. There was a 'Red Scare' in operation.

Anyone advocating radical social and economic alternatives to the conservative status quo, especially in the area of land ownership and wealth redistribution, was invariably branded a

communist and deemed to be taking dictation from Moscow. It
took exceptional courage on Fr John's part to go, like Dr Noel
Browne two decades later, against the tide. Like-minded priests
around this time fell foul of their bishops and life was made
very uncomfortable for them.

Peadar O'Donnell's own bishop in Raphoe, Dr MacNeely,
urged his people to 'pay your rents and don't heed O'Donnell'.
Bishop Fogarty of Killaloe diocese was so concerned with the
mood among the rural community of farmers, large and small,
that he put an additional question into the catechism: 'Is it a sin
not to pay land annuities?' Children preparing for Confirmation
were to be instructed clearly and to answer: 'It is a sin not to pay
land annuities.'

How fraught the times were may be judged from the following series of events as described in *Another Day*. Peadar
O'Donnell conducted an after-Mass chapel-gate meeting in Clare
(deliberately chosen because it was in Bishop Fogarty's diocese,
Killaloe). Of all the Hierarchy, this bishop had been possibly the
most consistent and outspoken critic of republicans and opponents of the Treaty. Throughout the 1920s his condemnations of
these groups became ever more vindictive and intolerant.

In the course of that after-Mass meeting O'Donnell set out to
convey to his audience that he was similar in so many ways to
them 'in background, experience and ideas'. He was preparing
his listeners for a verbal attack on Bishop Fogarty's father who
according to O'Donnell was known among his own people as
tear-'em-down Fogarty, as big a blackguard of a bailiff as was
ever in North Tipperary (Killaloe diocese) and that no man
should blame such a man's son for telling people to pay rent.

Of another man in a somewhat similar situation, O'Donnell's
own uncle had once remarked that

> It does not surprise me, for let me tell you, there was enough
> ignorance in that man's father to poison seven generations.

Later that day O'Donnell held a meeting with a small group
of supporters in Nenagh, where he recounted to those present
some of the comments he had earlier made about the bishop.
Inevitably this was reported back to Bishop Fogarty and
retribution was swift and severe. One of the men at the Nenagh

conference had a son studying for the priesthood in Maynooth. Because the father did not protest against O'Donnell's comments, the son was asked to leave Maynooth and was later ordained in another seminary for the foreign missions. O'Donnell in *Another Day* said that he later 'met that young priest in exile and he heart-sick for home'.

By late 1929 and into 1930 more and more farmers were falling into arrears with the payment of the annuities. The crisis in agriculture worked to the advantage of the movement led by O'Donnell, Fr Fahy and others around the country. Their campaign had been perceived by many as radical, troublesome and even revolutionary. With increasing numbers of medium and even large farmers feeling the economic draught, support now began to flow much more readily in their direction.

A supporter of O'Donnell felt sufficiently optimistic about their campaign that he remarked that 'this is becoming a runaway and the government will have to get out of its way'.

In addition to sending delegates to various anti-imperialist movements across Europe, the IRA leadership spearheaded by O'Donnell, Seán MacBride, Frank Ryan and George Gilmore sent a group in 1930 from the land annuity committee to the Congress of European Small Farmers that met in Berlin. Eventually a number of TDs from across the political divide in Dáil Éireann and many County Councils were now voicing agreement with Fr Fahy, O'Donnell and others involved in the anti-annuities campaign which for much of the 1920s had failed to command anything but the faintest support.

When de Valera and Fianna Fáil came to power in 1932 the whole question of the land annuities came centre stage. One of de Valera's first decisions was to declare that the payment of the annuities to England by the Free State had not been legitimate and that henceforth such payments, amounting to more that £3 million per annum, would cease. He offered to submit the whole question of the annuities to international arbitration but mindful of the disastrous outcome of the Boundary Commission in 1925, insisted that the arbitrators would come from outside the Commonwealth, a demand the British refused to contemplate.

A twenty per cent duty on Irish exports was imposed by the British in retaliation which in turn provoked de Valera to place a similar charge on English coal being imported into Ireland. These and many other retaliatory measures between the two countries became known as the Economic War. It had a crippling effect on many Irish exports. Worst hit was the vital live cattle trade to England resulting in the already low income of many small farmers, especially in the West of Ireland, being reduced even further. Butter and bacon exports were heavily subsidised to lessen the blow of the British duties.

By 1938 both the British and Irish governments were, for different reasons, ready to negotiate a settlement. The rise of Hitler in Germany convinced Neville Chamberlain and his British cabinet colleagues that in the event of a major war erupting in Europe, it would be in their best interests to have a friendly Ireland on their western flank. On this side of the Irish Sea, the Fianna Fáil government was painfully aware of the disastrous consequences that the Economic War was having on the day-to-day lives of so many people in this country.

The Irish negotiators were led by de Valera who on this occasion was determined to be centrally involved 'no doubt recollecting the debacle of 1921'. The main points of the agreement were

- that the British waived their remaining claims on the land annuities and other payments such as RIC pensions amounting to about £100,000,000.
- Britain would return what had become known as 'the Treaty ports' – Berehaven, Cobh and Lough Swilly – and fuel storage facilities at Haulbowline and Rathmullan.

The outcome has been hailed by historians as possibly de Valera's greatest political achievement matching in importance his success in ensuring that this country was spared the devastation which was visited on much of continental Europe during World War II while ostensibly pursuing a policy of neutrality during what we have quaintly come to call 'The Emergency'.

From an Irish perspective the favourable terms of that 1938 settlement, especially the clause relating to the land annuities, owe much to the earlier efforts of Peadar O'Donnell, ably supported in word and deed by Fr John Fahy and many small groups across the country who despite having their efforts initially denounced in the 1920s by church and state as being reprehensible, subversive and even communistic, played a major part in putting that whole issue right at the heart of Irish-British politics for the following decade.

CHAPTER NINE

## An 'Exile' in Kilconnell

Throughout 1930 and most of 1931 Fr John combined his ongoing efforts to abolish the payment of the land annuities with his constant drive to strengthen in structure and numbers the local IRA units in East Galway.

He actively recruited members into the IRA and was involved in efforts to purchase arms and ammunition from soldiers serving in the national army. In September 1931 *The Irish Press* reported that he addressed a secret parade of the local Loughrea unit of the IRA in the following terms:

> I am out for overthrowing any government that would be established in Ireland except the Irish Republican government.

With the prospect of a General Election looming and a change of government looking more likely, the following extracts from a letter Fr. John wrote at this time to Máire Hastings shed some further light on how he viewed the political situation then developing:

> As a worker in the No-Rent Campaign here I wrote a little thing for propaganda purposes but with the reign of terror that is on here we couldn't get any suitable fellows with sufficient manliness to act it.
>
> It seems that Dev is going to get another chance. Whilst I am not a member of Fianna Fáil I hope that he will do the right thing and scrap that so-called Treaty. Otherwise you'll have another bad split – the I.R.A. will not ever accept the Treaty to break the Treaty. That is how we look on it. Neither will the citizens of the Republic agree to bury Ireland for even de Valera. We will not buy our little farms and bits of mountain and bog from a Fianna Fáil government no more than from a British government. On this matter there is a clear and definite mind amongst Republicans.

The Irish Bishops issued a strongly worded pastoral on 18 October in which they condemned both the IRA and Saor Éire which had just been launched with Peadar O'Donnell as one of its main organisers. In the course of the pastoral letter the bishops said that they were greatly influenced by

> the growing evidence of a campaign of revolution and communism which if allowed to run unchecked, must end in the ruin of Ireland, both soul and body.

The bishops in referring further to the IRA stated that it was

> a society of a militarist character whose avowed object is to overthrow the State by force of arms.

Of Saor Éire the pastoral said that it was

> frankly communistic in its aims and determined to impose upon the Catholic soil of Ireland the same materialistic regime, with its fanatical hatred of God, as now dominates Russia and threatens to dominate Spain.

The tone and content of this latest bishops' pastoral was very reminiscent of earlier ones issued by the Irish hierarchy against The United Irishmen in 1798, against The Fenians in 1867 and against Republicans opposing the Treaty as recently as 1922. The Bishop of Kerry, David Moriarty, had remarked while preaching in St Mary's Cathedral, Killarney, on 17 February 1867, against what he termed the 'Fenian Conspiracy' that

> hell wasn't hot enough nor eternity long enough to punish such miscreants.

The common strand running through these pastorals was that the church, as Patrick Murray stated,

> saw itself as the divinely appointed guardian not only of faith but of political morality. Whatever the political issues and political movements from Catholic Emancipation to the end of the 1930s the attitude of the church to those was characterised by one fundamental feature: vigorous opposition to ideas and organisations it could not control.

And O'Donnell in *Another Day* said that despite branding the land annuity agitation and the IRA as communistic, anti-God and generally an affair of blackguards out to destroy the church that more often than not

> the Church-burning, anti-God Reds, when arrested turned out to be neighbours' sons that grew up among them.

That O'Donnell comment brings to mind a somewhat similar one made by another well-known IRA man and writer, Brendan Behan, who, when asked some decades later on a BBC television show 'what was his religion?', famously replied that 'I'm a Communist by day and a Catholic after it gets dark.'

Recalling the vital support he received from members of the clergy in Galway and throughout the country as he went from place to place avoiding arrest, availing of much needed hospitality and transport and attempting to breathe life into the campaign he so doggedly promoted, O'Donnell stated that 'few communists have been so well served by so many priests'.

The October pastoral from the hierarchy declared the methods and principles of the IRA to be 'in direct opposition to the Law of God', and that anyone involved in Saor Éire was deemed to be outside the Christian fold. However neither the contents of the pastoral – read without comment by Fr Fahy at Mass on the appointed Sunday – nor the solemn undertaking given to Bishop Dignan at the time of the court case in 1929 had succeeded in curtailing his ongoing involvement in IRA activities in East Galway.

The local Gardaí remained convinced that Fr John was possibly the most active IRA leader in the area. Their files show that at that time he was

> constantly associating with prominent IRA members, and was frequently seen going around on a motor cycle with civilian cap and overcoat apparently organising for the IRA and other illegal movements

and that he

> spent time in the company of men allegedly committing serious crimes, even with Craughwell's Tom Kenny – the Galway delegate to Saor Eire.

The Gardaí made it clear that they were reluctant to act against Fr Fahy because he was a priest and they further believed that Bishop Dignan's own strong Republican sympathies made it extremely difficult for them to demand that these law-breaking activities be curbed.

By the closing months of 1931 Bishop Dignan felt compelled, whether on his own initiative or from a combination of governmental and hierarchical pressure, to deal once more with Fr Fahy's political activities. On 13 January 1932 he sought an explanation for the *Irish Press* report about the Loughrea meeting from Fr John who submitted the following letter by way of response:

Clostoken
16/1/'32

My Lord Bishop,
I unreservedly and unequivocally deny in whole and in part the following statement which appeared in *The Irish Press* and which was solemnly denied by the person who was declared to have made it: 'At a parade of about 30 men in charge of Kennedy, Sylvester and John Burke on Sept 5th or 6th 1931, Father Fahy CC Clostoken was present dressed in plain clothes. Father Fahy on that occasion made a speech as to the need of training and organising and said he was out for overthrowing any government that would be established in Ireland except a Republican government.'

During recent weeks, My Lord, the police agents of the Free State have given shocking torture to young boys to force them to sign false statements about me. Where torture failed they have offered large sums of money and well paid positions.

With regard to faithfully obeying your Lordship's commands contained in the document given to me by Your Lordship in June 1929, I await any specific charge which Your Lordship may have against me.

I am,
Your Lordship's Obedient Servant
John Fahy CC

St. Brendan's,
Coorheen,
Loughrea.
17/1/32.

Dear Fr. Fahy,

I have received your letter of yesterday in which you unreservedly and unequivocally deny in whole and in part the accuracy of the statements published in the Press concerning your alleged presence at a parade on Sept. 5th or 6th 1931. Of course I unhesitatingly and unreservedly accept your denial.

In my letter to you of the 13th inst. I asked you to state definitely that since June '29 you were not present at a parade or assembly, etc — see my letter to you. There is no question of a specific charge as you state in your letter of the 16th inst. For my own peace of conscience and for other reasons (which I may not mention to you) I would ask you to assure me on your word of honour that you are faithfully obeying the command given you on June 4th 1929.

I am making no charge against you and I did not charge you in my letter of the 13th inst. I do not order you to give me this assurance, I do not ask or demand it under obedience. I am simply making a request of you that you give me in writing your personal assurance that you are obeying in the letter and in the spirit the "Document" given you last June.

Yours sincerely,
†J. Dignan.

Immediately on receipt of that letter the bishop sent the following, inviting a written reply from Fr Fahy.

That in turn elicited this response from Fr John:

Clostoken
18/1/'32

My Lord Bishop,
Immediately after receiving 'The Document' containing your Lordship's command in June 1929, for my own peace of mind owing to the terribly stringent nature of the restrictions therein, I have had a long and thorough consultation with the best qualified canonist that I could find – a professor of Canon Law in Rome and a Doctor of Divinity – and ever since I have acted on his advice. I hereby on my word of honour say that the above statement is true.

Knowing the circumstances prevailing in this country today, My Lord, I realise that the state and other authorities may be causing Your Lordship serious trouble owing to me. I presume to have some understanding of Your Lordship's position.

I assure Your Lordship that I will accept in the best of grace, whatsoever action that Your Lordship in your office as my bishop or otherwise may be compelled to take in my case.

In justice to Your Lordship, I am very anxious that if the state authorities have a case against me they should face the facts themselves and bear their own burden

I am,
Your Lordship's Obedient Servant,
John Fahy.

There is conflicting evidence between some of Fr Fahy's statements and denials in those letters when placed against the intelligence gathered by the local Gardaí.

It is difficult to believe that the bishop was unaware that Fr Fahy had flagrantly disregarded the conditions imposed on him after the 1929 jailing episode. Clonfert is the smallest diocese in the country and it could reasonably be assumed that Bishop

Dignan, whose political antennae were always sensitively tuned, would be fully aware, from a variety of sources, of Fr Fahy's frequent transgressions. The bishop surely knew in advance, the answers to questions he posed to Fr Fahy.

By the following month the tone in correspondence from Bishop Dignan to his rebellious curate strongly hinted that the ecclesiastical millstone was about to grind in earnest.

*St. Brendan's,*
*Coorheen.*
*Loughrea.*
*12/2/32.*

*Dear F. Fahy,*

*I see in "The Irish Press" of yesterday (Thursday) that before the Military Tribunal two men – John Burke and Martin Silke – made statements reflecting on your character as a priest. I wish to enquire into the truth of these statements. Meet me in the Parochial House, Loughrea at 2.30 pm. today (Friday).*

*Yours sincerely,*
*+J. Dignan.*

After what must have been a tense and difficult meeting between the two men, Bishop Dignan demanded that Fr Fahy sign the following statement:

*St Brendan's*
*Loughrea*
*12/2/1932*

*In the presence of God and before my bishop, I solemnly affirm that since June 1929 I have not been a member of any political club or organisation: I have not given any advice, help or suggestion by act or word or writing towards violation of the law or towards prevention of the execution of the law and I was not present at any deliberation of two or more persons concerning any political policy or action.*

*Without any reserve or mental restrictions, I solemnly and truthfully assert that the statements made about me and my (alleged) activities in the IRA and Saor Éire by Col Neligan, John Burke and others before the Military Tribunal now sitting in Dublin were utterly false and without any foundation whatever.*

*I make and sign this statement freely and I allow my bishop to publish it at his discretion.*

*Signed:*
*Witness:*
*February 12th 1932*

Shortly after that encounter Fr Fahy was relieved of his duties as curate in Clostoken and ordered to take up temporary residence in Kilconnell under the direction of the Parish Priest Fr Bowes who resided in Aughrim.

The details of the sanctions imposed by Bishop Dignan on Fr Fahy at that time are unavailable. However it is clear from the following letters that Fr Fahy's active parish ministry was temporarily suspended. Whether he was forbidden to celebrate Mass publicly and refrain from administering other sacraments – *suspensio a divinis* – is unclear. It is significant that Fr Fahy's signature does not appear on any Aughrim and Kilconnell parish records during the months of 1932 when he resided in Kilconnell.

Parochial House,
Kilconnell,
15/4/'32

My Lord Bishop,
I hereby apply again for a mission in the diocese and in doing so I regret having been connected with politics in the past.

I promise that in future I will not take part, private or public, in politics whether local or national.

I am,
Your Lordship's Obedient Servant,
John Fahy

The Parochial House,
Kilconnell
20/4/'32

My Lord,

I have heard from Fr Bowes today that Your Lordship
was not pleased with my letter of application for a mission in the diocese. I wish therefore to say that I promise
to abstain in future from the political activities to which
Your Lordship objects. Needless to say I regret any trouble that I have caused Your Lordship.

I am,
Your Obedient Servant
John Fahy

These letters are markedly different compared to earlier ones
written by Fr Fahy to Bishop Dignan. Gone is the bluster, the ob-
fuscation, the deliberate introduction of political red herrings
and most significantly there is now a clear unambiguous acknowledgement of his earlier involvement in political affairs.
The tone is contrite. He gives every indication that henceforth he
will abandon the political arena and all its associated activities.

These promises of 'good behaviour' in the future do not
seem to have cut much ice with Bishop Dignan at least in the
short term. The bishop would have been painfully aware for example that earlier promises and undertakings by Fr Fahy had
not been kept and he was determined, within limits, to convince
Fr John that he would have to mend his political ways.

Throughout that summer of 1932 Fr Fahy was kept on a tight
episcopal leash with his future in the diocese still officially unre-
solved. He received the following letter in July from Dr Dignan:

Dear F. Fahy,

You will please attend the
Diocesan Retreat beginning on
Monday next at 4 pm. in Esker.
I hope to be able to give you a
Mission immediately after the Retreat.

Yours sincerely,
+J Dignan.

This short letter was noteworthy for at least two reasons. The fact that Fr Fahy got a personal notification commanding him to attend the priests' retreat suggests that while he was still a priest of the diocese, his position at that time was very much under a cloud. However the possibility of a new appointment held out the hope that his temporary isolation from mainstream diocesan life might be nearing an end.

The following letter of 9 September finally brought deliverance for Fr Fahy from what must have been a very anxious and frustrating six months for him.

9/9/22.

Dear F. Fahy,

I am changing you to Ballinakill. You will please report to F. Porter on Saturday, Sept. 17th and take up work in your new curacy on that day. I do hope and pray you will devote yourself exclusively to your work as a minister of God, an alter Christus.

Yours sincerely,

+ J Dignan.

On reading the exhortation in the final sentence the impression clearly emerges that Bishop Dignan was writing more in hope than in confidence and that he was less than convinced that moving Fr Fahy to Ballinakill would finally wean him off his more turbulent political pursuits.

CHAPTER TEN

## The Ballinakill Years 1932-1945

The General Election of February 1932 resulted in Fianna Fáil, led by Éamon de Valera, coming to power for the first time, though not without the support of a much reduced Labour Party. Many republicans and smallholders in the West supported the change of government with varying degrees of enthusiasm. De Valera was understandably not happy governing without an absolute Fianna Fáil majority, a situation he hoped to remedy at the earliest opportunity.

Like many republicans all over the country Fr Fahy was sufficiently encouraged by a number of initiatives undertaken by the new administration to give his support to de Valera at least for the time being. The release of about a hundred IRA prisoners, the decision to suspend The Public Safety Act establishing non-jury courts with military members, which had been enacted following the assassination on his way to Mass on 10 July 1927 of Kevin O'Higgins, Minister for Justice and External Affairs and Vice-President of the Executive Council, and the dismissal of James McNeill as Governor-General suggested that more favourable times lay ahead for republicans.

Throughout 1932 there was widespread public disorder across the country. The Army Comrades Association (ACA) was set up in February to protect Cumann na nGaedheal supporters and party activists from attacks by IRA units. The ACA was, at first, led by T. F. O'Higgins, brother of the late Kevin. By early the following year the association had adopted a blue shirt as the centrepiece of its uniform and it was by that name – The Blueshirts – that henceforth it was known. In July 1933 General Eoin O'Duffy, who had been dismissed as Garda Commissioner by de Valera, assumed leadership of the ACA, a move which undoubtedly hastened its demise. In August O'Duffy's proposed march of the Blueshirts, now called the National Guard, past the Dáil was banned by de Valera. In the following month The Blueshirts (National Guard), The Farmers' Party (now known as the Centre Party) and Cumann na nGaedheal came together to be known as the United Ireland party, shortly to be called Fine Gael with O'Duffy as leader.

From the moment he came to power in 1932 de Valera set out in a most methodical manner to widen what up to then had been his narrow support base among all levels of the Catholic clergy in Ireland. He began as Patrick Murray put it

> to simulate a clerical voice himself, his utterances on the economic, social and educational issues being often indistinguishable in tone and content from episcopal pastorals or even papal encyclicals. He gradually assumed some of the style and function of a lay cardinal.

The Fianna Fáil party and in particular its leader were seen in a new more favourable light from the time in June 1932 when the Eucharistic Congress was held in Dublin. That event, so successfully organised, generated an intense level of religious fervour across the country and as Murray states (p. 262)

> represented one of the most considerable and enduring publicity triumphs of de Valera's career. His ceremonial appearances in the company of Irish bishops and senior churchmen from all over the world in the presence of hundreds of thousands of people marked the symbolic end to the loss of official church approval from which he and his associates had suffered so badly since 1922, both politically and personally and emergence as a Catholic statesman of unexampled orthodoxy.

Professor Dermot Keogh was of the opinion that

> The Eucharistic Congress provided de Valera with a timely opportunity to baptise his synthesis of Republicanism and Catholicism.

By late 1932 de Valera was sufficiently buoyed up by the generally positive reaction to his first year in office that he felt the time was right to attempt to secure an outright Fianna Fáil majority in the Dáil. And so he called an unexpected General Election for January 1933.

Fr Fahy actively involved himself in the election campaign on behalf of Fianna Fáil. It was his deep-seated antipathy to

Cumann na nGaedheal more than his support for de Valera and his party that influenced the political stance taken by Fr John at this time. He travelled extensively in the south-east Galway area in an untaxed vehicle rallying support for Fianna Fáil and appeared on an election platform with de Valera in Portumna as the campaign entered its final week. Little did either Fr John or the members of Lusmagh Pipe Band – Jack Hynes, Johnnie Larkin, Mick Groomes, Michael Gibbons, Pat Quirke, Bill Rigney, Pat Lantry, Bill Troy, Tim Cannon and Paddy Hynes – who led the torch-light procession into Portumna that night, know that they would all become very acquainted with each other on Fr John's appointment to Lusmagh more than a decade later.

De Valera's gamble of going to the country paid off handsomely as Fianna Fáil won 77 of the 153 seats and increased their share of the vote from 44.5 to almost 50 per cent.

Fr John's involvement in that election campaign only months after his appointment to Ballinakill brought a sharp rebuke from Bishop Dignan who then took no further action.

How bishops dealt at that time with priests like Fr Fahy who participated in republican activities varied enormously from diocese to diocese. Had he been ministering in neighbouring Galway, the lenient treatment he received from Bishop Dignan would have been noticeably absent as this from Bishop O'Doherty (formerly of Clonfert) indicates:

16th June, 1933.

To the Clergy of Galway, Kilmacduagh & Kilfenora.

1. "Any priest, secular or regular, in these Dioceses ( Galway, Kilmacduagh, and Kilfenora) who by word or writing or even signs, whether in Tribunali or outside it, expresses to any person the opinion that it is not gravely unlawful to be a member of the I.R.A. or Saor Eire Organisations is 'ipso facto' suspended, and absolution from this suspension is reserved to the Bishop or the Vicar-General, and will be granted only after the imposition of a grave , salutary penance. "

2. " MEMBERSHIP of any of the societies mentioned is to be treated in Tribunali as in the case of any other mortal sin. "

+ Thomas O'Doherty,

Bishop of Galway, Kilmacduagh,
& Apost. Adm. of Kilfenora.

Dr Murphy in his *Stone of Destiny* notes a report in the *East Galway Democrat* 4 November 1933 which neatly highlights the political tensions still evident in presbyteries and parishes throughout the country:

> Later in 1933, Fr Porter PP of Ballinakill, presided at a protest meeting addressed by Paddy Hogan and two other pro-Treaty TDs after shots were fired into the house of Henry Goonan, secretary of the local Cumann na nGaedheal branch, and Fr Fahy, although a curate of the parish, conspicuously did not attend.

During August 1934 Bishop Dignan received an anonymous letter from a group in Achill Island informing him that Fr Fahy had recently spent time with Peadar O'Donnell at the latter's bungalow there. The group claimed to be 'shocked' and 'scandalised' by Fr John's association with Peadar and it was hinted darkly that the pair of them were engaged in subversive activities promoting Saor Éire and the IRA throughout Mayo at that time.

In the light of earlier promises that Fr John had made regarding his intention to shun political controversy, Bishop Dignan felt it prudent to check the veracity of the allegations contained in the letter.

In response to the bishop's query, Fr John wrote a detailed and forceful rebuttal of the allegations and insinuations made against O'Donnell and himself.

Writing from Ballinakill in September 1934 Fr John said that the

> anonymous and scurrilous document sent to Your Lordship from Achill was the concoction of an imported Blueshirt and an emanation of slime! It originated from the anti-Irish prejudices of a member of the family who co-operated in earlier times in the hanging in that area of Fr Manus Sweeney.

Fr Sweeney, curate at Newport, was a rebel who joined the French at Killala. He was hanged in Newport outside his own church on 9 June 1799. By a strange coincidence, Fr Sweeney like Fr Fahy features in the book *Radical Irish Priests 1660-1970*.

Fr John used the occasion cleverly to let the bishop know about his long association and deep friendship with Peadar O'Donnell since his work in Scotland where they cooperated

with others to try and ameliorate the awful housing conditions of the migratory labourers from the West and North of Ireland.

Fr John, in replying to the bishop, also conveyed that on each of his many visits to O'Donnell in Donegal and Mayo he encountered several priests in both counties who were proud to number Peadar among their closest friends. In fact it was made clear that association with O'Donnell was a guarantee of accommodation in presbyteries wherever he went.

Warming to his task Fr. John continued:

In the past we faced the foul music of imperialism openly and fearlessly, and now that I am retired from the conflict, I am quite certain that my comrade Peadar O'Donnell will continue his fight for the dispossessed and noblest element of nations openly, honestly and fearlessly as long as The Good God leaves him his terrestrial existence. Peadar O'Donnell is as good a Catholic as I am and, as long as he remains such and is true to the Land of his Fathers I shall be honored to have association with him.

I have reason to know that some members of the clique responsible for that scurrilous document sent to your lordship, and who have the brazen-faced audacity to sign it "Catholic Action", have recently attended a Protestant function in Achill organized to commemorate the memory of the notorious proselytiser, Nangle. To my personal knowledge

I know of efforts made in Achill by Peadar O'Donnell and his wife Lil and their friends to undo amongst the people some of the evil effects of the proselytisers.

I would not have wearied your lordship with this long letter did I not know that, as regarding our Religion and our Nation you have the noblest intentions, and, as this ugly move has been made I wish to apprise your lordship truthfully and honestly of the circumstances of the case. As regards the charge of scandal I am prepared and willing and anxious to test the case and demonstrate publicly that the charge is false and vile. Also, my lord, I believe that it would be a very good thing for Religion in this country to have such a charge thoroughly investigated and demonstrated. Many of our noblest Catholics have been hurt in recent years owing to their national principles. I believe, my lord, that in similar circumstances in any other country in the world save in our own beloved Ireland, the reaction would have terrible.

I wish to state also that, since your lordship's conversation with me at Esker two years ago

I have not directly or indirectly taken any part whatsoever in politics of any kind. Neither am I a member of any Organization political economic or social. Last week, after seeing Fr. O'Flahery alright, I met Peadar O'Donnell in Dublin. He was going to Tirconaill and I just went with him solely for the trip and to see an old friend of mine there. He called to Achill on some business on the way and that is how I found myself there. I only regret that my short holiday should be the means of causing your lordship much mental pain by having to read the vicious production returned enclosed.

I am,
Your Lordship's Obedient Servant,
John Fahy C.C.

It seems that there was nothing further heard from the 'shocked' and 'scandalised' members of the Achill 'Catholic Action' group, and their shell-shocked condition induced by sightings of Fr John and Peadar O'Donnell outside their usual habitat and range, did not prove to be permanent.

No doubt Bishop Dignan, too, was content to let the matter rest.

That affair confirmed the fact that Fr Fahy was well established on the national political stage and his enduring loyalty to O'Donnell made him a marked man. Of course the great regard in which the Donegal man was held by a minority of highly esteemed Catholic priests around the country also emerges and the absence of a monolithic approach from the Catholic clergy to Celtic communists like O'Donnell becomes very evident.

It finally became clear to Fr Fahy that he would, henceforth, be unable to participate in political or agrarian campaigns that would attract unwelcome publicity on either himself or Bishop Dignan, who in any case was determined not to become embroiled in any further controversies not of his own making.

By 1936 Fr John's thoughts began to turn to the possibility of bringing some semblance of order and unity to farmer representation which up to then was characterised by disunity, fragmentation, class tensions and political infighting both in Galway and throughout the country. After consulting with some close friends he drafted a 'Provisional Programme for the Formation of a Republican Farmers' Party for Galway'. He was very mindful of the fact that farmers did not exercise political or economic clout proportionate to their numerical strength and the essential nature of what they produced.

The National Centre Party, The Farmers' Party and a considerable number of regional and local groupings such as the County Galway Farmers' Association all tried with limited success to further the well-being of the agricultural and farming community. It is difficult to see how a Republican Farmers' Party could have succeeded where so many others had failed. Even its title was not destined to win universal acceptance.

Fr Fahy looked on from the sideline as the next attempt in the West to forge some unity among farming groups took shape with the formation of Clann na Talmhan.

Fr John spent the late 1930s and the war years relatively free of controversy in Ballinakill. He kept beagle hounds for hunting hares and at that time he had a hunter which he called Rory. One of Fr Fahy's favourite pen-names was 'Rory of the Hills'. He often asked people in the locality to rear young hunting dogs for him, a practice which didn't always meet with their approval. But no one had the temerity to refuse his requests. He was widely known for his horsemanship and his advice on 'breaking' young horses was often sought. It seems that Fr John always succeeded in winning over his charges irrespective of how sulky a young hunter might be. He organised a race meeting in Ballymana, Craughwell in 1941 in Grady's field opposite Leonard's shop.

There was a strand in Fr Fahy's personality that rebelled against conformity. He often found it difficult to follow agreed procedures or to submit to a higher authority. This in turn occasionally landed him in difficult situations which, with a little forethought, could have been avoided.

The following sequence of events illustrates that point quite well. Having sought Bishop Dignan's permission to leave the parish for a fortnight immediately after Christmas 1942, Fr John decided, for whatever reason, to absent himself without waiting for episcopal approval.

Within days Bishop Dignan became aware that the shepherd had temporarily abandoned his Ballinakill flock and he despatched the letter overleaf to the presbytery in the foothills of the Derrybrien mountains seeking an explanation.

The reason for Fr John's long absence is unknown and there is no record of how he extricated himself from that latest brush with authority.

The fall-out from that and other minor skirmishes was eventually set aside by Bishop Dignan and probably with some hesitation he finally gave Fr John charge of his own parish two years later.

3/1/'43.

Dear F. Fahy,

You asked my permission to absent
yourself from the parish for a fortnight,
and I have REASON to believe you left
the parish without awaiting a REPLY.

As this course of action is contrary to
the Statutes and as it is very unusual
for a priest to leave his curacy on
St. Stephen's Day for a fortnight, I would
ask you to explain your absence.

                    Yours sincerely,
                       + B Dignan.

CHAPTER ELEVEN

## *Lusmagh 1945-1959*

Fr Fahy was transferred from Ballinakill to Lusmagh in May 1945. The parish of Lusmagh, south-west of Banagher, has as its main boundaries The Shannon, The Little Brosna and The Rapemills/Lusmagh rivers. It is the only parish of Clonfert diocese situated in County Offaly.

In a Lusmagh parish magazine, *The Lusmagh Herb – The Annals of a Country Parish* published in 1982, the then parish priest Fr Tom Kennedy wrote a brief profile of each of his predecessors from 1818 onwards. The following is his note on Fr Callanan, Fr Fahy's predecessor:

Father Richard Callanan (1926-1945) extended the National School in 1931 and the parochial house in 1939 and beautified their surroundings. He carried out extensive repairs to the church and promoted rural electrification. He is remembered with affection and respect. He was transferred to Ballymacward and appointed Vicar General of the diocese.

There were very specific and clearly defined conditions dated 21 May 1945 attached to Fr Fahy's appointment to Lusmagh by Bishop Dignan, the most salient of which were:

1. You are not going as PP and by going you acquire no right whatever to the Parish; if you go I shall in courtesy address you as PP, and, in letters I write I shall address them to you as PP but as there shall be no canonical appointment and no induction, you have in law or in fact no canonical right to the Parish.
2. I shall give you all the powers of a PP; you will have full power to administer the parish, to attend at marriages etc. and no one need know you are not PP.
3. I reserve to myself the right to remove you at any time, if in my considered judgement and prudence, I think it well to remove you. In this regard your status will be that of a CC.

4. You are to shun politics and you are not to take part in public life by acting on Committees of any kind without my written permission.

5. The people of Lusmagh are to be treated in a very civil and gentlemanly manner. Any display of temper, any harsh words, or any attempt to force them will give offence or scandal. You cannot drive them but they are easily led and they will respect and obey you if you prove yourself a really genuine 'ambassador of Christ'. No offence or scandal is to be given them.

6. The Church, school, cemetery and house, are to be maintained in their present excellent condition.

If you prove yourself worthy it is my intention to appoint you PP in course of time.

It is clear from both the tone and content of Bishop Dignan's conditions, that he was laying down very clear markers in the most unambiguous manner possible which were to govern Fr Fahy's administration of the parish.

A formal letter of appointment followed a few days later:

*25/5/45.*

*Dear F. Fahy,*

*I hereby appoint you in charge of Lusmagh parish, and I hereby delegate and give to you all the faculties required to administer the parish, viz. the right to assist at marriages, give Letters of Freedom, etc. It must be clearly understood by you that you are not Parish Priest, yet I give you all the powers of a P.P. in as far as Canon Law will allow me. If at any time you need any special faculties, apply to me and, if I may, I shall be pleased to grant them.*

*You will take charge on Sunday, June 3.*

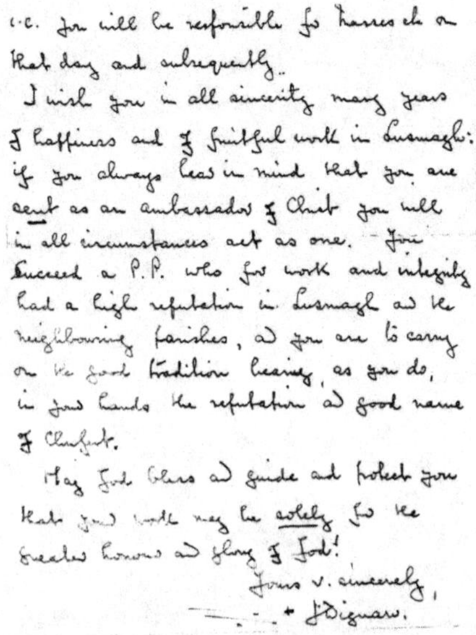

*[Handwritten letter, partially legible:]*

*i.e. You will be responsible for Masses etc. on that day and subsequently.*

*I wish you in all sincerity many years of happiness and of fruitful work in Lusmagh: if you always bear in mind that you are sent as an ambassador of Christ you will in all circumstances act as one. You succeed a P.P. who for work and integrity had a high reputation in Lusmagh and the neighbouring parishes, and you are to carry on the good tradition leaving, as you do, in your hands the reputation and good name of Christ.*

*May God bless and guide and protect you that your work may be solely for the greater honour and glory of God!*

*Yours v. sincerely,*
*+ J. Dignan.*

The repetition and further emphasis in that letter on some of the key conditions governing this appointment lead to the conclusion that the bishop was determined to try to confine Fr Fahy solely to providing for the spiritual needs of his new parishioners.

Further correspondence in August from Bishop Dignan to Fr John is also worth noting.

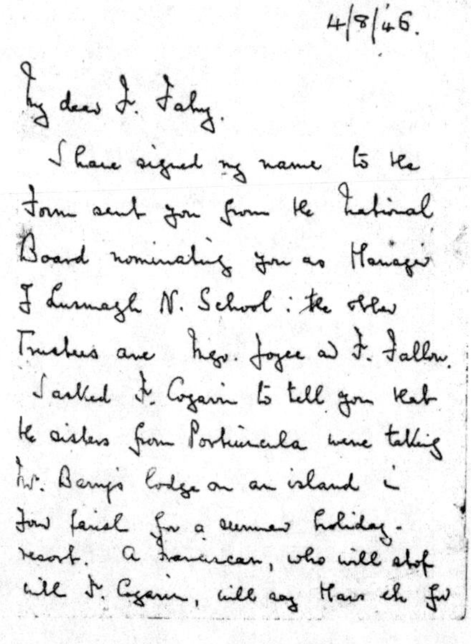

*4/8/46.*

*My dear Fr. Fahy.*

*I have signed my name to the form sent you from the National Board nominating you as Manager of Lusmagh N. School: the other Trustees are Msgr. Joyce and Fr. Fallon.*

*I asked Fr. Cogavin to tell you that the sisters from Portumna were taking Mr. Barry's lodge on an island in your parish for a summer holiday resort. A American, who will stop with Fr. Cogavin, will say Mass etc. for*

It is a coincidence and a peculiar twist of fate that land agitation activities in Lusmagh directed against Bertie Barry, named
in the above letter as the owner of the holiday home to be used
by the Franciscan Missionaries of the Divine Motherhood from
the newly built Portiuncula Hospital, Ballinasloe, would be a
significant factor in Fr Fahy's transfer in dramatic circumstances
from Lusmagh to Abbey fourteen years later.

Fr Fahy's early years in Lusmagh were largely uneventful.
He gave every support possible to his parishioners in difficult
economic times following the end of World War II. An early example of this support was his attendance at a meeting of the
Shannon Tourist Development Association which was reported
in the Nenagh Guardian 26 January 1946. The meeting was convened to explore the possible economic benefits through the development of tourism in the Shannon valley between Athlone
and Killaloe. The report stated that Fr Fahy spoke at length on
the Tennessee Valley project in the US and that he cited the success of the Scots in capitalising on the beauty of their mountains,
lakes and moors.

Lusmagh, with a population of about 450 at that time, was
noted for the amount of beet grown there annually which was
transported from Banagher Railway Station to Tuam Sugar
Factory. That whole process was vividly recalled in a fascinating
piece written by Paddy Kelly in *The Lusmagh Herb* (p. 56).

Most of the farmers in Lusmagh had large families and
small, often fragmented holdings. They were mainly engaged in
mixed farming enterprises producing store cattle, sheep, pigs
and a small acreage of cereal crops in addition to beet growing.

Invariably the women, in addition to child-rearing and domestic duties, contributed handsomely to the household income by selling home made 'country' butter, eggs and poultry.

What is termed today 'off-farm employment' was almost unknown. Industrial employment in Bórd na Móna, the ESB and Bantile, later to become Banagher Concrete, was still some distance away into the future.

Increasing mechanisation gradually contributed to a reduction in the number of farmers' sons and farm labourers being employed on the land. The prospects for many young men and women in parishes like Lusmagh grew more bleak and sadly the emigrant ships to England and America beckoned with unwelcome regularity.

Fr Fahy for the most part avoided public life and shunned politics as directed by Bishop Dignan. He did, however, campaign in a low-key manner to have a bridge constructed over the Little Brosna river at the lower end of the parish. He encouraged the parishioners to embrace enthusiastically the rural electrification scheme which ultimately transformed the face of rural Ireland and regularly contacted politicians when schemes of benefit to the parish were mooted.

A letter written in 1949 by Catherine Fitzgerald, Fr Fahy's housekeeper, authorising him to purchase a new monstrance for St Cronan's church sheds interesting light on religious practice at that time.

With her Kerry-born husband she had kept a boarding house in Oxford for the university students. When she became widowed she returned to her native Lusmagh and lived with her cousin Johnnie Larkin and his family in Gortraven. Catherine was en route to visit her in-laws in Caherciveen when she wrote the following letter to Fr John from her hotel room in Limerick:

Central Hotel
Limerick

14/8/49

Dear Father Fahy,

I have decided to get the monstrance & present it to St Cronan's – or rather; ask God to accept it, for the benefit of my loved ones who have gone to their reward, my parents Thomas & Katie, & think it is great enough gift to include all 4, don't you? furthermore I have sent an order for £70 to my Trustee bank, in favour of your good self. I want to be sensible about it, & ask you to purchase one that you

2 think suitable & good value — (next time you are in Dublin), nor do I want to "spoil the ship for the half penny worth of tar" If you will consider yourself a perfectly free agent in this matter, & realize that what pleases you will please me, & if at £70 you cannot get a nice enough gift, is.ly for Gods acceptance, go to £80 – or £90 or even £100 – I will let you have a cheque for the amount from my current a/c as soon as I know what you have spent!

needless to say all this is absolutely "entre nous," when the time comes the family

can be told - & given a fine the
of it. I want to feel that my parents
& Thomas & Katie's names - are on
the base of the monstrance - Just
written simply on a piece of paper
& stuck underneath, is that
permissable? And am I
asking too much to have
Benediction twice month
once after high mass - &
on the second Sunday
as now. I feel that the
oftener we use the monstra
the greater the benefit to
my loved ones. I hope you
appreciate this - & feel
I am not asking too much

I would hate to over tire you.
I arrived here o.k.
& am enjoying my visit
I leave on Friday - my address
after that date - will be
Co miss It Burns
new St West End
Cahirciveen

I want to thank you for all
the nice things you said
about the family at the
breakfast & all your other
kindly considerations
for them & me. believe me
I am most grateful -
Sincerely yours

As a footnote to the letter, Fr John ensured that Catherine's wishes were met. Her generosity was recorded for posterity when he had the following inscription engraved on the beautifully ornate monstrance which is still used regularly in St Cronan's for all relevant liturgies:

> Presented to St Cronan's Lusmagh by Catherine Fitzgerald in memory of her parents John and Rose Larkin, her brother Thomas and his wife Catherine. Oh Sacrament Most Holy, Oh Immense Love, Oh Sweetness above all Sweetness.

By this time, Dr Dignan's health had begun to deteriorate. Fr Declan Kelly in his diocesan history states that

> Following a heart attack after a Confirmation ceremony in Eyrecourt in the late 1940s Dr Dignan's health began to decline, though he still kept to a robust schedule. The late Fr P. K. Egan recalled him shortly before his death speaking to parishioners in the cemetery in Kiltormer on a bitterly cold day, supporting his increasingly frail body by draping his arms around two large headstones. He died at his residence in Coorheen on Sunday 12 April 1953.
>
> Before he died he insisted that no large monument mark his grave and so he is buried among his parishioners in Mount Pleasant Cemetery, Loughrea. The spot is marked by a small but sturdy iron cross, bearing only his name, title of office and date of death.

Bishop Dignan was succeeded the following December by Bishop William Philbin who for the previous sixteen years had been Professor of Dogmatic Theology in Maynooth.

One of Bishop Philbin's first actions after his transfer from Maynooth to Clonfert was to ratify formally Fr Fahy and three other recently appointed parish priests.

The document of formal collation to the parish of Lusmagh was enclosed with a covering letter.

Coláiste Seosaim Naomta,
Páirc Searrbaile,
Deul Áta na Sluaġ.

9 July 1953

My dear Dr. Daly,

I have only recently got the formulae of conferring parishes printed by Browne - Nolan (I am only now issuing formal collation to the three new parochi I appointed). Hence my delay.

I find the formula makes mention of seal affixed. It is, of course, valid without this, but for completeness sake you might wish to leave back the form & I will send it with seal affixed.

With all good wishes,
Yours very sincerely,
+ W. Philbin.

Various land improvement schemes were actively promoted in the late 1940s and 1950s by the Department of Agriculture. Reclamation and drainage works were very much in evidence across the country. Grants became available for a wide range of activities all designed to make the land of Ireland more productive and the farming community more prosperous.

The money for all this work, known as the Rehabilitation Project, came from Marshall Aid and was overseen by James Dillon, Minister for Agriculture. His objective was to reclaim up to a million acres of land mostly in the western half of the country at £10 per acre.

Fr John led by example and was determined to upgrade the quality of the land attached to the parochial house as the following document illustrates.

## LAND REHABILITATION PROJECT.

Regd. No...R/19/2181...

Land Project Office,
............Church St.,
...................Tullamore.
13th. June, 1957.

Dear Sir/or Madam Rev. Fr.

The Minister for Agriculture approves of the carrying out by you of the improvement work described in the attached specification(s) subject to the conditions stated below.

The work should be completed by........15th. July, 1957,........ As soon as possible thereafter and provided the work has been carried out to his satisfaction, the Minister will make a cash grant to you of £    6  :  0 : 0.

The land to which the lime and fertilisers (if specified) are to be applied is indicated overleaf.

Yours faithfully,

Rev. Fr. John Fahy, P.P.,                    ..................................
                                                      District Officer.
Lusmagh,
Banagher.

Checked by:- *I. Culloty*

## CONDITIONS.

1.  The decision as to whether the scheme of work specified has been carried out in a satisfactory manner shall rest with the Minister for Agriculture.

2.  The Minister reserves the right to reduce the grant, or withhold it completely if, in his opinion, the work done is unsatisfactory or is not in accordance with the specification(s).

3.  The Minister will not be liable for any damage to any property or person arising out of the work or the carrying out thereof.

4.  The decision of the Minister in all matters relating to the Project shall be final.

[OVER

Name of Occupier....Rev,.Fr,.John.Fahy.P.P........... County.Offaly........

Townland (s)..............Shelbourne......,........,.............. O.S. No..29,..(7.)..

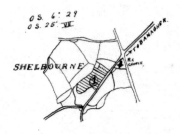

---

**Instructions re Spreading of Lime and Fertilisers.**

.As.the.grant.does.not.exceed.C5.per.st,.acre.no.lime.and...........

..phosphates.need.be.applied.....................................................

AN ROINN TALMHAÍOCHTA.

LAND REHABILITATION PROJECT.

SPECIFICATION.

File No. R/19/2381.....  Name of Occupier.........Rev. Fr. John Fahy, P.P.

| Field No. | Index | Length in perches, or area | Description |
|---|---|---|---|
| I. | | | Uproot and remove all scrub from field and trim back fences. |
| | | | Lift and remove all stones from field and fill in cavities. |

At that time there were over twenty acres of good land in parochial hands. Fr John always kept a number of dry stock and of course his beloved hunter Simon, his pride and joy. In this enterprise he was regularly assisted by local man Bill Kelly and by neighbouring farmers and their sons as the need arose. In an era when there was little emphasis on education, boys from the National School were frequently withdrawn by Fr John from the principal Mr Flynn's room to pick stones or potatoes, foot turf or move the cattle or perhaps drive them to the fair in Banagher. The existence of this active service Flying Column made up entirely of boys from the senior classes was a constant source of worry for Tom Flynn because in the event of an unannounced inspector's visit, the discrepancy between the actual attendance and that recorded in the Roll-Book would quickly become apparent. Whatever about tackling the school principal, not too many inspectors would relish the prospect of locking horns with a manager whose disposition and reputation were known far beyond the confines of Lusmagh.

CHAPTER TWELVE

## The 'Irish Development Corporation' Saga

During 1956-57 Fr Fahy was involved with a small group of priests and a successful Irish-American businessman Mark Neville in attempting to set up an Irish Development Corporation (IDC) with the aim of assisting in the economic recovery of the country.

In this undertaking, Fr John and Neville, who had been a much-decorated US Marine Commander during World War II, were linked with Fr Mark Mimnagh (Ardagh & Clonmacnoise), Fr John Dore (an Oblate priest), and two brothers, Monsignor Thomas and Monsignor Patrick Temple, natives of Shannon-harbour, Banagher and serving in the Archdiocese of New York. Fr Dore and the Temple brothers were widely known for their strong republican leanings.

Fr Mimnagh spent two years at this time in the US gathering money for a new church in Abbeylara, Co Longford where he was then a curate. He was National Organiser for Muintir na Tíre in 1954 and would later serve in St Rynagh's Banagher parish 1960-1968 where he helped to resolve some industrial disputes. He was also the driving force in establishing St Rynagh's Hurling Club from a number of smaller units within the parish.

Fr Dore from Shanagolden in Limerick, a noted mission preacher all over the English-speaking world and possessed of unlimited energy, was the recipient of many awards for his out-standing work in collaboration with Fr (later Bishop) Eamon Casey among the Irish community in London in the 1960s.

The Temple brothers had studied in All-Hallows College, Dublin before completing their training in Dunwoodie Seminary, New York prior to ordination in 1913 and 1914. Both men regu-larly visited their family in Shannonharbour and maintained a loyal and lively interest in the land of their birth. Of Monsignor Thomas, the *All-Hallows Annual* 1956 stated that:

... he was always in the forefront when Ireland needed friends, he always assisted every worthwhile Irish cause, his voice and pocket-book were always at Ireland's disposal, his great desire was to see his beloved Ireland completely free.

Mark Neville drafted a 17-point National Plan for the revitalisation of many aspects of Irish economic and social life, central to which would be the establishment of a steel mill and shipyard on the West coast of Ireland. It was envisaged that this would be 'a joint venture of government and citizenry' and 'with her own iron and steel industry Ireland would then construct a fleet of 200-300 modern cargo vessels over a period of ten years'.

Further on in this grandiose plan it was suggested that 'the beef and packing industry might use a new look profitably'. There would be an extensive public works programme initiated, preference for all positions should be given first to married men, then to men engaged to marry. Every effort would be made to encourage single persons to marry – a recurring theme in Fr Fahy's pastoral work.

Other hopes held out in the plan included the following:

Home or village industries such as handicrafts of various categories should be nurtured and developed;

All surplus farm commodities such as fruits, berries, vegetables should be canned for export;

Reforestation of all barren land should be pursued without delay under a public works programme. Paper mills should be founded in order to manufacture this vitally needed commodity;

Freezing facilities to be installed on fishing vessels;

Farm life should be brightened by a tremendous effort to modernise each and every home with electricity and up-to-the-minute plumbing facilities;

A separate house, apartment or simply more living room space should be provided where practical to every Irish homestead. This would provide the son of marriageable age a separate domicile in which to establish a family;

A National Defence Act should be passed whereby all youths should serve at least 6 months active basic military duty and 3-5 years in a reserve capacity;

There should be a strengthening of aids to Irish business and farming by means of favourable taxation or even monetary assistance. At the same time foreign participation in the economy of Ireland should be greatly discouraged. Ireland is geographically as well as numerically too small to absorb any influx whatsoever either on her farms, her shops or her industry. Extra taxes on foreign elements should be invoked without delay.

This last point is classic 'economic nationalism', so favoured by Fr Fahy even at a time when the groundwork was being laid for what would become the Anglo-Irish Free Trade Agreement of 1965, followed by accession to the EEC in 1972.

Fr Fahy was entrusted with the task of selecting a site for the proposed steel works. Before long he claimed to have located an area extending to nearly 1000 acres in the Inverin area of Connemara overlooking Galway Bay. Fr Dore was working on finances and organisational matters.

A 'Certificate of Incorporation' for the IDC was drawn up as a legal instrument to give effect to its aims under Irish law. It was intended to include Joe McGrath of Irish Hospitals' Sweepstake fame, noted racehorse trainer and formerly Minister for Industry and Commerce in the 1920s as a director, in addition to the original group including Fr Fahy.

The preamble to the Certificate of Incorporation was as follows:

> Aware of the long years when the liberty and aspirations our Nation and our People cruelly suffered from an alien foe, when only the ancient and lively Catholic Faith of our Forbears, and the great courage of our Race along with an invincible hope kept alive an unquenchable thirst for knowledge, justice, and freedom under the Divine Benevolence of God, to shape our own destinies, do we United People of Ireland, long deprived of the God-given right, even to this day, to work for our mortal well-being, as well as in the past of freely working for our immortal salvation; recognizing the inalienable right of everyone to work in honor and dignity for the proper provision of roof and bread and raiment, both for the individual and for those whom we are charged under God to protect and cherish, do we therefore THE UNDERSIGNED IRISH PEOPLE, hereby proclaim our desire to form a corporation pursuant to Article _____ of the Stock Corporation Law of Ireland, and do hereby make, subscribe and acknowledge this certificate for that purpose, as follows:-
>
> First:- The name of the proposed corporation is THE IRELAND DEVELOPMENT CORPORATION.

Mark Neville's main proposition was that the Irish Republic would obtain a gift of two hundred million dollars from the US government; one hundred million to be used in constructing the steel and iron foundry and twenty million to be spent in getting the shipyard established.

Business and political contacts were made with Mr Taft, US Ambassador to Ireland and his successor Mr McLeod and with Miss Edna Kelly, US government Congresswoman in charge of Foreign Aid, who was briefed about the proposed IDC during visits to Ireland and by her staff in Washington.

The protectionist and isolationist mindset evident in the plan discouraging foreign investment in Ireland was running counter to thinking in the Irish Department of Finance and in the highest government circles from the early 1950s. The historian Roy Foster said that

> by 1955 economic expansion with foreign capital was becoming the accepted wisdom among all parties. The coalition government of 1954-57 first opened up the question of Ireland's admission to the International Monetary Fund and The World Bank.

T. K. (Ken) Whitaker, the influential head of the Department of Finance and the ex-protectionist Seán Lemass would drive that policy with great vigour from 1957 onwards.

The fate of the IDC would be determined by events outside this country. By early summer of 1957 US taxpayers were very concerned about their own economic well-being and positively alarmed at what they were hearing about scientific advances in Russia which would culminate shortly in the launch of the Sputnik satellite by the Soviets.

Americans were also up-in-arms about their government's worldwide 'Give Away Programme' which meant so much to developing countries like Ireland.

Not surprisingly these factors ensured that the IDC proposals had withered before they had time to take root where it mattered most – in the US State Department.

Even by the values prevailing today, the figures quoted in the IDC documentation and the anticipated employment which would be generated seemed overly optimistic. Viewing the project through a mid-1950s lens it was difficult to avoid the conclusion that an air of unreality permeated the entire proposal.

By summer 1957, Fr Fahy was nurturing the idea of setting up an organisation – 'Ireland for the Irish' – which before long was to become more widely known as 'Lia Fáil'. This development launched him briefly once more on to the national political stage, a move that ultimately would exact a high personal cost from him.

CHAPTER THIRTEEN

## The Original Lia Fáil

The Lia Fáil was an ancient symbol of Irish nationality. According to Dr Brian Murphy, it derived its name from the inaugural or coronation stone on the Hill of Tara and was brought there by the Tuatha de Danann. It was claimed to be the stone 'that roared under the feet of each king that took possession of the throne of Ireland.'

The 19th-century antiquarian George Petrie described the Lia Fáil as

a large obeliscal pillar-stone made of granular limestone and standing vertically less than five feet above the ground. Its original site was at the Mound of the Hostages, probably lying horizontal but it was moved to its present site and upright position in the Rath to mark the graves of the 1798 rebels killed nearby.

Writer and nationalist, Derrinlough, Offaly native William Bulfin believed the 'Lia Fáil' to be 'a symbol of the nation's indomitability'.

The followers of Fionn mac Cumhaill were called the Fianna of Fáil. Professor Eoin MacNéill, Gaelic scholar and first Professor of Early and Medieval Irish History at UCD designed the Volunteer cap badge with the letters FF incorporated in it and Éamon de Valera chose the name Fianna Fáil for his new party in 1926. Dr Douglas Hyde, our first President, had used the Lia Fáil as a 'symbol of national rebirth' in the early years of the Free State when he named a new UCD Irish journal after it.

Not surprisingly, Fr Fahy felt strongly that the new organisation he was about to set up would also be the embodiment of all that was best from our long and troubled history.

So, not to be outdone by Hyde, MacNéill or de Valera, he too decided to invoke that ancient symbol of Irish nationality – the Lia Fáil – and call his new movement after it.

# CHAPTER FOURTEEN

## *Birth of Fr Fahy's Lia Fáil*

Lia Fáil was set up at a meeting presided over by Fr Fahy in Lusmagh school after evening devotions in St Cronan's church on 1 November 1957. The social and economic circumstances prevailing locally and nationally at that time and his disillusionment with politicians of all the main parties, after thirty-five years of self-government, provided the impetus for Fr John to take this initiative.

Census figures for the five-year period 1951-1956 reveal that the population of the country fell to its lowest level in centuries to 2,898,000, with emigration running at 45,000 annually.

With the population steadily falling and the National Debt having increased from £190,000,000 to £370,000,000 between 1952 and 1957, the challenge facing this country was truly daunting. Even our ability to cope with independence was being seriously discussed and questioned.

People highlighting these facts were vilified and portrayed as 'purveyors of doom and gloom'. The politicians found it infuriating to see people like Bishop Lucey of Cork, Bishop Murphy of Limerick and Archbishop Walsh of Tuam availing of Muintir na Tíre meetings, past pupils' reunions and Confirmation ceremonies to stress the gravity of the problems confronting the Irish people and demanding proper services for our emigrants, many of whom were poorly educated and ill-equipped for life far away from home.

The following notes in Fr Fahy's handwriting recall that meeting of 1 November and its aftermath.

*Birth of Lia Fáil.*

*On November 1st 1957 the people of Lusmagh, Banagher, Offaly, held a Meeting at Lusmagh to discuss the problems of emigration and unemployment. The parish priest Fr. John Fahy presided at the meeting.*

'Francis Kelly, Lusmagh was secretary. From that Meeting Lia Fáil was born.

It was the unanimous opinion of the Meeting that it was a matter of vital and urgent necessity for the survival of the Irish People in Ireland that the ~~question~~ problem of the 'Land of Ireland' be tackled and solved immediately. When we got our own government in 1921 this was the first problem that our rulers should have tackled and solved. Through ignorance, incapability, treachery and treason our politicians not only neglected their duty to the Irish People in this matter but

allowed, and are [2] still allowing foreigners, English, Dutch, Germans etc etc, to come in and purchase the best land of our country. Ireland is being reconquered through the Bank of England! A new Plantation is taking place! Irish boys and girls are being shipped out of Ireland more than under Cromwell, whilst Englishmen and other aliens are being 'planted' on the best land of Ireland.

To counteract and undo that horrible treachery of our politicians the Meeting at Lusmagh launched a Movement called "Ireland for the Irish". The secretary had the following leaflets printed containing the aims of the ~~new~~ Association:

# "IRELAND FOR THE IRISH"
## ("I. FOR I.").

"The Ireland for the Irish" Association was launched in Lusmagh, Offaly, November 1st, 1957, when the following Provisional Committee was appointed:

PRESIDENT: Fr. John Fahy, P.P., Lusmagh.

SECRETARY: Francis J. Kelly, Newtown.

TREASURER: Frank Larkin, Stream.

COMMITTEE MEMBERS: Patrick Kelly, Tim Bennett, Denis Kelly, Martin Sullivan, Paddy Groomes, Kieran Donegan, William Killeen, etc.

### PURPOSE OF ASSOCIATION.

1—To secure that all the lands and sources of wealth in Ireland be preserved for the Irish people.

2—To make it illegal for any alien to purchase any land, property or source of wealth in Ireland.

3—To have annulled forthwith all sales of land, property and sources of wealth to aliens contracted since the establishment of the Irish Republic.

4—To have the 1924 Land Act annulled. This Land Act was ordered by Lord Middleton to secure the British Garrison in the lands they had plundered from the Irish people.

5—To divide the land of Ireland amongst the young men of Ireland.

6—To limit private ownership of land, giving forty acre farms of good land to each man, as long as young men have to emigrate from the countryside.

7—To reinstate the dispossessed Irish people on the good soil of Ireland from which their fathers were driven by the robber-invaders who are in possession still of most of the good land of Ireland.

### GOD SAVE IRELAND.

"M.T." Birr.

// 

# FIRST OBJECTIVE

## —OF—

## " IRELAND FOR THE IRISH "

♣

**50,000 YOUNG MEN ON THE LAND IN TWELVE MONTHS**

**and**

**100,000 YOUNG MEN AT PRODUCTIVE EMPLOYMENT**

♣

Our Lady of Victories strengthen us.

---

"Midland Tribune" Office, Birr.

# " IRELAND FOR THE IRISH "

## Under the Patronage of Our Lady of Victories.

### I

The first article in our programme is: "To secure that all the land and sources of wealth in Ireland be preserved for the Irish people."

The land of Ireland is the chief, and only, means of living for the vast majority of the Irish people. It is our primary source of wealth; it is our greatest and most vital economic treasure; it is the basis of our national life; on it our existence as a people depends.

The first duty of our native Government when, in 1921, it took over the adminstration of the greater part of our country, was to tackle the problem of the land of Ireland and solve it, as it should have been solved, for the Irish people. The position, as regards the land of Ireland, when our native Government took over in 1921 was this: as a result of a series of invasions by organised robber-hordes most, almost all of the good soil of Ireland was possessed by the descendants of the robber-invaders. The native Irish people were a dispossessed nation in their own country. The vast majority of our native Irish people were still on the mountains, in the bog-lands and on the poor, barren, rocky soil where the Norman, Cromwellian and Williamite robber-invaders drove them and banished them. In the rocks of Donegal, in the Rosses and the Frosses, for instance, along the Western seaboard of Mayo, Connemara and Galway, in Achill, Costelloe, etc., a dense population with cottages as thick as they could stand where there was no visible means of sustenance; so in Clare, so in Kerry, and so along the heather-line of the Galtees, and of the mountains of Cork, Carlow and Wicklow. On the other hand, in unnatural contrast, the rich land of Ireland was an uninhabited ranch; the best land of Ireland stretching from the plains of Boyle to Dublin Bay, and from Letterkenny to Clonmel, was the most sparsely populated part of the country; as far as the native Irish people were concerned these were de-populated areas; the descendants of the land-robbers, the British Garrison, with their castles and mansions, their vast demesnes and huge ranches were still there in possession of all the good soil of our country; the Jacobite, Cromwellian and Williamite planters still held the best land of Ireland.

As regards the land of Ireland that state of affairs was both *unjust* and *unnatural*:. *unjust* because a robber can *never* acquire a just title to robbed goods; the land the invader held was land acquired by robbery. It was *unnatural* because, in God's divine plan the population should be densest where the soil is richest; the Creator designed that his creatures dwell where He provided the best means of sustenance for them.

*Now, the very first act of our native Irish Government should have been to put back the dispossessed Irish people on the good land of Ireland from which the robber-invaders had driven their forefathers.*

Did our native Government do that? No, alas no! Our politicans looked after themselves, abandoned the dispossessed Irish people, and left the bodach his loot. For thirty-five years the politicians and their friends and camp-followers have so battened on our people that to-day we, as a race, are in danger of extinction. Not only did they criminally fail the Irish people by leaving the robber his loot, but—treason and treachery most foul—at the robbers' bidding they passed legislation to secure that the robber would hold his loot for ever ! ! ! That was what the 1924 Land Act, called the Hogan Act, but really the Lord Middleton Act, did!

*It was one of the greatest acts of treason ever committed against the Irish people.* It gave tenant right to the British Garrison, to all Cromwell's and James' planters, to the Williamite marauders, to all graziers, ranchers, grabbers, etc. We hope that the Irish people will join us in demanding the immediate annullment of that treasonable Act.

## II

The second aim of "Ireland for the Irish" is: "To make it illegal for any alien to purchase any land, property or source of wealth in Ireland."

*To have this legislation passed is a matter of vital and urgent importance for the Irish people.* English, Dutch, Germans, Jews, Orange Freemasons and latterly *Russians* are buying the best soil of our nation! *Our politicians are treacherously helping and sanctioning this diabolical treason against the dispossessed Irish nation!* In any other free country politicians would be hanged, drawn and quartered if they were guilty of such treason against the citizens. Our politicians should be strung from the lamp-posts, and left strung from them, for presiding over and sanctioning such perfidious treachery. May Our Lady of Victories strengthen us to undo that foul treachery.

De Valera says the amount of land purchased by aliens is exaggerated. We have reason to know that quite recently 150,000 acres of the best soil of our country was bought by foreigners. Ours is a small agricultural country where every perch of good arable land is of inestimable value. De Valera dined in Trinity College last (Autumn) year on the eve of the day on which Trinity College purchased 800 acres of the best soil in County Louth! Was it to consecrate the purchase that he put on his white vest and went there on the vigil of the Feast? We acknowledge Ireland's indebtedness to De Valera: he fought gallantly to hoist our flag; he had the moral courage to stand up to John Bull in the council chamber; he undid for the greater part, the surrender of the Treaty; as Ireland's representative amongst the nations of the world he gained honour, respect and prestige for our country; unfortunately, he either knows absolutely nothing about managing our national economy, or else he doesn't care a straw whether Ireland is bled to death, reconquered, raped and the Irish people exterminated. What use a man fighting for a country if, later on, he connives at that country's destruction?

By the laws and Constitution of France, and of all independent countries, no aliens are allowed to purchase land or property. Our second aim is to have such legislation enacted by our Government immediately.

Our third aim is to have all sales of land, property and sources of wealth to aliens contracted by aliens, since the Proclamation of the Republic in 1916 annulled forthwith.

Our next objective is to give forty-acre farms of good land to the young men of Ireland. Fully conscious of its import we make the following claim: *If the politicians hand us over the Government for one twelve months we guarantee that,, without a penny extra cost to the nation, we will put 100,000 young men on farms of land, and put another 100,000 men at productive employment.* All we ask to do that is control of the Government for twelve months. We issue that challenge to the politicians fully cognizant of all that it implies.

Have the politicians the patriotism to accept our challenge?
Or, will they emulate Pontius Pilate and hold their jobs?

Whilst young men are forced to emigrate for a living we would put a ceiling of one hundred acres to the amount of land any farmer may own.

Having reinstated our people in their God-given patrimony, the land of Ireland, we aim to tackle the next most vital problems confronting the nation—employment, the development of our natural resources, etc.

# *Ireland For The Irish*

## YOUNG MEN OF IRELAND

## ATTENTION

# FIRST YEAR PLAN

**100,000 YOUNG MEN ON 40 ACRE FARMS.**

**100,000 YOUNG MEN AT PRODUCTIVE EMPLOYMENT.**

**The Land Is There — The Work Is There.**

## IRELAND IS YOURS

### JOIN

## LIA FAIL

**(Land and Industrial Army of Ireland)**

**—AND—**

## TAKE OVER YOUR COUNTRY

With 'The First Objective' documents and posters ready for distribution, attention began to focus on setting up a structure across the country which would bring the various groups sharing a common goal together under the Lia Fáil banner. The provisional National Executive of Lia Fáil which was appointed when these various land-associations came together consisted of the following members:

| | |
|---|---|
| President: | Eamon Ginnell |
| Vice-president: | Frank Kelly |
| Chairman: | Barney Kelly |
| Secretary: | Denis Kelly |
| Treasurer: | Tom Kavanagh |
| Committee Members: | W.H. Milner |
| | Dick Power |
| | Michael Shaughnessy |

Parish, District, County, Provincial and National units were agreed. Between them, it was planned that these interdependent groupings would develop, co-ordinate and implement policy under the management of the National Executive.

The following membership oath was drafted by Fr Fahy and is reproduced here as it appeared in his own handwriting.

Recruits Oath
to
Land-Army:
"With full knowledge of the origin, leadership and purpose of Ireland's Land-Army, I, of my own free will, offer myself as a recruit to that Land-Army, and, I solemnly promise to submit myself herewith to the Orders and Discipline of that Army."

Fr John also composed and circulated a litany at this time which he called the 'Working Farmer's Prayer'.

## Working Farmer's Prayer.

From The Dáil
From Ignorant Politicians
From Incapable Politicians
From Treasonable Politicians
From Fine-Gael
From Fine-Gael Toadies
From Fianna-Fáil
From Fianna-Fáil Toadies
From Fianna-Fáil 'Yes-men'
From Labour Mandarins
From the Mulcahy Gang
From the Hogan and Higgins Gang
From the De Valera Gang
From the Ryan Gang
From the Lemass Gang
From Childers and the Church Body
From Dillon's Big Mouth
From English Invaders
From the Land-Commission
From English Syndicates
From Real-Estate Agents
From all Land Grabbers
From all Land Sharks
From Gombeen-Men
From Graft
From Political Nepotism
From Jobbery
From High Salaries

From Big Mouths
From Long Necks
From Big Bellies
From Big Arses

From Wholesale Anglicisation
From Wholesale Demoralisation
From Plague of Talkers
From Plague of Parasites
From Death by Mechanisation
From Dictation by Tinkers and
          Corner-Boys
From Upstarts and Chancers
From Game-Fans and Gamblers
From Rackets and Racketeers
From Political Gangsters
From Radio Eireann
From the Sunday Press
          AMEN.

*SAVE IRELAND, O LORD.*

The litany accurately reflected Fr John's total despair and his lack of respect for the politicians who in his view were responsible for the stagnation evident in so many strands of Irish society. While the criticism of those inhabiting the political world was predictable, somewhat more perplexing are the references to various body parts from which he wished to save Ireland.

For example, did the sight of a long neck always remind him of de Valera? Did the mellifluous tone and oratorical brilliance of James Dillon drive him to resent those he judged to have big mouths?

Who had Fr John in his sights when he railed against those in the political establishment who were generously endowed fore and aft? Some great Irish minds of the last half-century have failed to provide a credible explanation for that particular conundrum!

Fr Fahy realised by Christmas 1957 that Bishop Philbin had become aware of the plans to launch Lia Fáil on the national stage. He wished to gauge how the bishop felt about such developments. An exchange of correspondence between the two men ostensibly dealt in some detail with thoughts Fr Fahy had about a pamphlet he was preparing on the idea of a 'Christian Republic'. Fr John used the opportunity to inform Bishop Philbin what he had in mind about Lia Fáil. It is clear that the bishop was unimpressed with the prospect of Fr Fahy being involved in situations far removed from and possibly in conflict with his priestly work. It is equally clear from the following two letters that Fr Fahy seems to have conveyed to Bishop Philbin his readiness to reserve his energy exclusively for his pastoral efforts.

ST. BRENDAN'S,
LOUGHREA.

5 February 1958

My dear Dr. Fahy,

Thank you for your kind letter on receipt of my own : also for the printed sheets from "Christian Republic". I am now returning these with the earlier sheets and also the letters which you sent me earlier.

I think you are wise to feel that the burden of what you were thinking of undertaking would be extremely heavy and also extremely difficult for a priest, as well as being very controversial. I gather that the clergy in Limerick do not support the groups in question there — at least the first group who wrote to you: I think they prefer to work in their own organizations. There is always the difficulty of keeping such movement from going to extremes and arousing a kind of general land-greed — although one can of course see the undesirable developments that people like yourself deplore from unselfish reasons. I believe you will be a happier person and that your own priestly work — including educational developments of which I have heard — will benefit by your taking the withdrawing attitude which you support in these troublesome fields. With every good wish, I remain,

Yours very sincerely, + W. J. Philbin

ST. BRENDAN'S,
LOUGHREA.

13 February 1958

My dear Father Fahy,

Thank you very much for your nice letter. Indeed I have never doubted your good will and readiness to follow my suggestions. I hope and believe that God will bless and prosper all your pastoral efforts and that your good work in Lusmagh will continue to meet every success.

I remain,
Yours very sincerely,
+ W. J. Philbin

The tone in both letters is remarkably similar to that expressed by Bishop Dignan nearly thirteen years earlier when Fr Fahy was first appointed to Lusmagh. In both instances Fr John is encouraged to focus exclusively on his pastoral duties and to use his great energy solely in the service of the parishioners in his care. In both cases too, it has to be said, the bishops write more in hope than in confidence.

During the months following the setting up of Lia Fáil, the energy of its leading lights, including Fr Fahy, was concentrated on the need to put a strong, workable and energetic organisational structure in place in the counties most responsive to the message emanating from Lusmagh.

Meetings were held, at which policies were discussed and plans began to take shape. All this activity was conducted in a low-key manner and not likely to attract attention or publicity.

By this time the Irish Land Commission had substantially scaled down its land redistribution work, which of course was its core activity. The Republic's finances were by now in a most perilous state, and a range of government policies which for over twenty years favoured larger farmers was likely to ensure that the Land Commission's reduced role would continue for the foreseeable future. The inexorable decline in the number of small holdings under forty acres since independence and the intensification of that decline from the ending of World War II heightened the sense of disillusionment of Fr Fahy and those who had held out hopes of a vibrant, expanding, prosperous rural Ireland. Those hopes had most famously been articulated by de Valera himself in his celebrated St Patrick's Day broadcast in 1943 which included the following, often misquoted, passage and with which he launched that year's General Election campaign:

> The Ireland which we have dreamed of would be the one
> of a people who valued material wealth only as a basis of
> right living, of a people who were satisfied with frugal
> comfort and devoted their leisure to things of the spirit;
> a land whose countryside would be bright with cosy
> homesteads, whose fields and villages would be joyous
> with the sounds of industry, with the romping of sturdy

children, the contests of athletic youths, the laughter of happy maidens; whose firesides would be forums for the wisdom of serene old age. It would, in a word, be the home of a people living the life that God desires that men should live.

Officially de Valera delivered the famous address on the feast of the national apostle to mark the fiftieth anniversary of the foundation of the Gaelic League.

In commenting on it Professor Joe Lee said that

The invocation of divine authority on this occasion serves to disguise the fact that much of the broadcast was an election speech masquerading in the guise of a festival homily. A general election had to be held within three months.

He added that the address was

A classic combination of the spiritually sublime and the electorally mercenary.

As the post-War era rolled on, de Valera's dream looked less likely to materialise with each passing year. Lee concluded that

There would be fewer and fewer 'sturdy children' to romp in a wasting society. There would indeed be 'contests of athletic youths' – on the building sites of Britain, where 'McAlpine's God was a well-filled hod'. Not only would emigration soon reach levels unprecedented in the twentieth century, but Ireland would boast the highest rate of female emigration of any European country between 1945 and 1960.

CHAPTER FIFTEEN

## *The launch of* Lia Fáil *– The paper*

The first issue of *Lia Fáil* appeared in August 1958 – price three-pence. The masthead for each of the ten issues carried the title *Lia Fáil* with two sub-headings as follows:

*Organ of the Land and Industrial Army of Ireland*

and in brackets underneath

*(Under the Patronage of Our Lady of Victories)*

In the months prior to the launch one of the details to be settled was the question of deciding on a publisher. Eventually it was narrowed down to a decision between the *Westmeath Independent* and *The Longford News*, the latter finally being chosen. The local Lia Fáil secretary Margaret Kelly – who had succeeded her husband Francie, now national vice-president – stated in a note to Fr Fahy at that time 'that the *Longford News* are dearer but will print stiff stuff.'

Some of Father John's 'stuff' would indeed be very 'stiff'. This would become increasingly evident as each new issue of *Lia Fáil* rolled off the printing press in the following eighteen months. That the *Longford News* was chosen to print the *Lia Fáil* paper was not too surprising. Its owner and editor Vincent Gill was in some respects like Fr John, an anti-establishment figure. Gill himself wrote most of the articles in the *Longford News* and when he occasionally found himself short of material, he simply made up a few stories to fill the gap. Just as Fr John didn't spare the politicians, Gill didn't make life easy for some of the well-heeled denizens of Longford and its hinterland.

On one occasion, according to Hugh Oram (*An Irishman's Diary, Irish Times,* 7 September 2010)

he wrote an account of a large wedding in the Travelling community and said it had been attended by the President and every member of the diplomatic corps. When he was reporting on any big society wedding in Longford, he reversed this procedure and listed all the members of the

Travelling community as having been present. Yet another time, he reported on a past pupils' reunion dinner at St Mel's College, naming everyone he knew from Longford who had ever been detained in Mountjoy, describing them as having attended the function.

Gill produced the paper in his cottage by the Royal Canal in Longford until he decided to retire in 1974 when he sold the paper for £12,000 to Albert Reynolds who remained as proprietor for the next five years. In addition to writing the copy, Gill sold the ads, printed each week's edition and travelled the county in his van 'packed with a dozen of his cats and dogs, stopping at every pub to sell copies of his paper'.

In somewhat similar vein, Fr John bought a small second-hand Baby Ford van to deliver the *Lia Fáil* newspaper as each issue became available. Paddy Doyle from Mount Temple, later to settle in Cloghan, attended most of the *Lia Fáil* meetings in Lusmagh presbytery with Barney Kelly and was asked by Fr John to drive the van and distribute the paper to outlets all over the country. Initially the response to Paddy's sales pitch was encouraging but as shopkeepers – particularly those of the Fianna Fáil persuasion – gradually became aware of the editorial line being pursued, the task of maintaining a viable sales and distribution network became increasingly difficult.

Themes varied in minor ways from one issue of *Lia Fáil* to the next. But overall there were great similarities both in the topics covered and in the way they were presented. The inactivity or inability of the Irish Land Commission to take over large farms and estates for division among small farmers, the duplicity of politicians in general with special venom being reserved for de Valera, Childers and Lemass, the economic and social disintegration of many rural communities and the occasional spark of resistance being lit here and there around the country by *Lia Fáil* supporters or like-minded activists formed a nucleus of articles around which each issue revolved. Jews, Freemasons, foreigners, Protestants and particularly their Representative Church Body, were all denounced with unrelieved severity by Fr Fahy.

On the political front he claimed, in the September issue (No. 2) that if *Lia Fáil* had control of the twenty-six counties for five years 'it would blast the border out of existence' and he went on to describe how this would be done. It would

- Make emigration illegal;
- Recall our young people who have emigrated;
- Train the manhood of the nation in military service;
- Harden and equip our Army and Garda Síochana;
- Spend ten million pounds organising and training our race abroad for war on the British empire;
- Spend further millions organising an underground army all over the world for the final onslaught on that piratic empire;
- Follow the old principle – England's difficulty is Ireland's opportunity – and watch for the fatal hour, then the 1916 Rebellion would only be a pin-prick to the Lia Fáil rising. At a given signal an army of experts would sabotage the British empire, destroy her atomic-power plants, her airforce, her navy, her war potential, etc.

There is scarcely a nation or people on the earth that England has not robbed, murdered, pillaged and looted.

While our imperial army, in co-operation with those world allies would be blasting the British empire all over the world our Irish army and air force (equipped with atomic arms) would cross the Border and give the Orange mob what they have been looking for for a long time.

If Dev and his toadies think that Irish chivalry is dead he is making a hell of a mistake. The young Irish lads hurling themselves at the might of the British empire in a gallant attempt to remove that border should make him change his thoughts.

A fraction of the millions spent by the dastard politicians during the last 35 years on jobbery, graft, nepotism etc, would have organised, trained and equipped with up-to-date atomic small arms etc, an Irish imperial army capable of blasting not only the border imposed by England on our country, but the whole monstrous edifice of the British empire. We Irish are as big an empire as the British, if we would only organise ourselves as zealously to fight for justice as she does for injustice.

Despite the rabble of toadies that are keeping the political dastards in power, the young men dying on the Border give proof to the world that Irishmen have still preserved their ancient chivalry.

It is clear from Fr Fahy's last sentence that he was fully behind
the IRA Border Campaign which had begun on 12 December
1956 and would continue intermittently until 26 February 1962.
Because of this campaign, de Valera and the new Fianna Fáil
government elected after the March 1957 general election rein-
troduced internment the following July. Among those interned
in the Curragh Military prison was Ruairí Ó Brádaigh, who had
been elected a Sinn Féin TD for Longford-Westmeath on an ab-
stentionist ticket. Ruairí confirmed that a consignment of *Lia Fáil*
papers was sent to the internees as each new issue came to hand.
He also stated that while the internees were always delighted to
see Fr Fahy attacking senior government ministers, they were
less happy with his unrelenting criticism of the Representative
Church Body of the Church of Ireland.

Bishop Lucey of Cork who had recently delivered the homily
at the Mass celebrating the centenary of St Michael's Church,
Ballinasloe, had his words denouncing the evils of emigration
quoted extensively in issue No. 2 of *Lia Fáil*.

Fr John was obviously buoyed up also by the support he received from priests like the noted Republican Fr Thomas Burlage
PP, Mountmellick, and Fr Philip McGahey PP, Castletown-
geoghan, Co Westmeath who was actively mobilising his parishioners to press to have the vast estate of Captain Boyd-Rochford
of Middleton Hall divided among the local small farmers.
'Westmeath! With joyful hearts we salute thee!' was Fr Fahy's
concluding exhortation to all involved in that particular struggle.

Aliens were warned in each issue of *Lia Fáil* that 'The Irish
people object to your buying Irish land.' On a number of occasions lists of foreigners who had recently bought land were printed.
Addresses and size of the properties purchased were also listed.

According to Fr Fahy the ownership of the good land of Ireland
before *Lia Fáil* was set up 'was based on murder, robbery, plunder, confiscation, apostasy, treason, speculation, gambling, a
process aided and abetted in his view by this 'auctioneering
company' which he 'advertised' in the February issue.

Extensive coverage was given in a number of issues to what historian Tim Pat Coogan called 'a confused programme of Monetary Reform.' The articles on Monetary Reform were written by Fr Sweetman and W. H. Milner. Milner, a farmer from Walsh Island, Portarlington, had been involved with Séamus Lennon's Irish Monetary Reform Association and was at one time Offaly County secretary of the Irish Farmers' Federation.

Milner's fertile imagination nourished a succession of conspiracy theories which invariably pictured Ireland being over-run by Freemasons, Jews, Aliens, and all with the support of incompetent, corrupt native politicians.

It is clear from the following letter that he was active in *Lia Fáil* and that he was well-versed in the business of attracting attention to ideas and movements which cried out for the oxygen of publicity.

> "Weston"
> Portarlington.
> 5th Dec. '58.
>
> Dear Father Fahey,
>
> Article for December were posted, sorry for being so late. I stayed at home from threshing to-day to get it finished.
>
> It is hard for me to judge dispassionately but I feel I have broken the matter down to a simple form. At least I tried it on two boys, 9 and 11 years and they seemed to get a good grasp of what it was about.
>
> Don't think me presumptuous, I speak in all sincerity.
>
> Your display cards are not big enough, or spectacular enough. We need larger posters outside the shops, with sensational catch-cries which should vary with each issue, the public go for the sensational and ignore the logical.
>
> For example instead of saying "Milner writes on Monetary Reform", say: "Money destroyed by the million" Read Lia-Fáil on

sale locally. It will be quite possible to pick something sensational out of some article in the paper. I suggest the Monetary Reform article because of its continuity, I hope it will run for a long time yet, Of course they are only suggestions. I was toying with the idea of putting up posters throughout the country in an effort to keep the sales up. The few papers you send here would not be sold but for the fact that I use a little elbow grease myself.

You also need publicity on a national scale. The Sunday Independent and the Sunday Press go into most homes in Ireland, and even go overseas. Could you organise a few people in your own circulation area to start a correspondence in these and perhaps other papers. Let someone write attacking the monetary articles, then someone else Reply defending the issue, gradually let the others come in, for attack and defence in an effort to start a hot and prolonged controversy. The name Lia-Fáil and Banghee should come quietly into the picture — but not in such an obvious way that the papers will realise we are getting

cheap advertisement. In this way the public will get your name and address, and if the writers are good, it should excite public curiosity and incidentally boost sales, which is the equivalent of putting over your policy.

As far as I am concerned I do not care what they say, so long as it is said in a clean manner. The F.F. incident in Limerick should make good material, there is always a good chance of exploiting opposition of this sort to bring grist to your own mill.

Le buidheacht 7 beannacht,

W. H. Milner.

Fr John extolled the merits of the ancient Brehon legal code of land usage in Ireland which according to him prevailed from pre-Christian times to the Norman invasion. He stated that under the Brehon Laws

the land was loaned by the people to the individual and when the individual no longer needed it, it was resumed by the people. In no case was the title parted with, and in no case did the title vest in any individual. The Chief Prince or King who was elected by the people got pasturage on the land under the same law as the people got it … On the death of the Prince or King the land they had the use of lapsed to the owners, ie the people.

Fr John, in declaring that it was time to reinstate the Brehon Laws in relation to land ownership in twentieth century Ireland, invoked two men occupying very prominent positions in the pantheon of Irish heroes, St Patrick and Michael Davitt.

Apparently our national apostle after converting our forebears

blessed and consecrated their Brehon code of laws as being in perfect consonance with, and conducive to, the Christian way of life.

Fr Fahy circulated the following update, signed 'John Ireland', for members at a meeting in Lusmagh presbytery to mark the first anniversary of the founding of Lia Fáil:

" As soon as the ...... leaflets stating the aims of "Ireland for the Irish" got around, correspondence from all parts of Ireland poured into Lusmagh. Political and social organizations, societies, clubs and individuals wrote approving of the association and requesting membership of it. For years isolated groups in various counties had been agitating to have estates and ranches divided by the Irish Land Commission: there was "The Kildare Land-Division League", the "National Land Settlement League" functioning in Limerick, and the South and in Mayo, the "Bennekerry Land-Division Club" in, Carlow, the "Land for the People League", in Westmeath and many other similar groups. Under the leadership of "Ireland for the Irish" all these *hand-associations came together, agreed to a common policy, formed a Provisional National Executive and called the new movement — "Lia Fáil".*

*Lia Fáil's first objective is to put the young men of Ireland on the good land of Ireland. It will concentrate all its energies on that problem until it is solved.*

*To date, Lia Fáil is firmly rooted in eleven counties. Now that it has its own Paper all the Irish people will soon be told what its policy is and how it means to carry it out.*

*May this generation not pass away before Lia Fáil's vision comes true — the laughter of Irish children filling the soundless void that today stretches from Cavan to the Knockmealdowns and from Drogheda to Boyle."*
                                                                         *John Ireland.*

'John Ireland' was one of Fr Fahy's most frequently used pen-names.

By early 1959 two items were high on the nation's political agenda and both were centred on the then Taoiseach Éamon de Valera. He was chosen by Fianna Fáil to contest the forthcoming Presidential election as Seán T. O'Kelly's tenure in Áras an Uachtaráin was coming to an end. Dev and his cabinet decided to hold a referendum, hoping to abolish the well-established voting system of proportional representation in favour of a 'first past the post' system, on the same day in June as the vote to elect O'Kelly's successor.

Not surprisingly, Fr John used the pages of *Lia Fáil* to persuade his readers to vote in favour of Dev's opponent General Seán MacEoin TD Longford-Westmeath. This might, at first glance, seem surprising as MacEoin was a prominent member of Fine Gael, but his outstanding record as an IRA leader during the War of Independence when he became affectionately known as the 'Blacksmith of Ballinalee' helped to gain him Fr John's support in the race for the Park.

There was also another factor which helped to consolidate this alliance. It would appear that the government had been actively considering withholding 'Public Notice' advertising from the *Longford News*, presumably because as publisher of *Lia*

*Fáil* it was directly involved in the nakedly anti-Fianna Fáil rhetoric emanating from its pages. Its controversial editor Vincent Gill had obviously enlisted the help of his local TD MacEoin to prevent this move, which would have resulted in a substantial loss of revenue for such a small printing house. Seán MacEoin's letter in reply to Gill's representations confirms that old bonds of friendship existed between the General and Fr John.

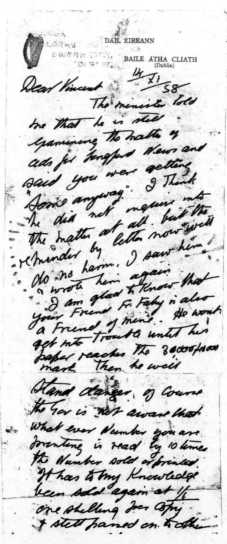

*readers. This of course will offend the narrow minded ministers who believe strongly in the the 'Punitive' action in an indirect way*

*Yours*

*Seán Manton*

The following passages from the February 1959 issue of *Lia Fáil* convey a sense of the coverage of the contest as viewed by Fr John.

## Reasons Why De Valera Should Not Be President

BECAUSE:

1 He is an Alien;

2 He is of doubtful legitimacy (questioned in the Dáil);

3 He split the Irish race in America;

4 He split the Irish people at home;

5 He caused the Civil War;

6 He has banished more Irish people out of Ireland than Cromwell did;

7 He fights with the British Forces to maintain partition;

8 He is establishing a New Plantation of Aliens in Ireland;

9 He is a notorious public perjurer;

10 He is a notorious anti-cleric;

11 His Satanic lust for Power motivates every act of his life;

12 He has consolidated the partition of our country;

13 He has enriched and augmented the British Garrison in Ireland;

14 He has made an Englishman who is Chairman of the Protestant Church Body, Minister for Lands;

15 He is the 'darling' of the British Garrison;

16 He is the 'darling' of Trinity College;

17 He is the 'darling' of the Freemasons;

18 He is the 'darling' of the New Invaders;

19 He is the 'darling' of the Protestant Church Body;

20 He is the 'darling' of the British Government;

21 He is the father and leader of all the 'suckers' and toadies of Ireland;

22 He is duplicit;

23 He is a shameless political dodger;

24 He has been a complete failure as a political leader;

25 He is the "most malignant man in all Irish history" (JOHN DEVOY);

And so on ad. lib.

WHO WILL VOTE FOR DE VALERA FOR THE PRESIDENCY?

All the Aliens, all the Protestant heretics, all the British Garrison, all the landlords and Freemasons, and all the yes-men, toadies and suckers of Ireland.

From 1 to 9 are indisputable historical facts.

Re 9: For six years he refused to take the Oath of Allegiance to the King of England. When he had either to leave public life or take the Oath, he took the Oath —and then he said it was not an oath. Neither jugglery nor lies could have evaded that public legal official oath. Dev swallowed it. The fact that he said he didn't proves him a perjurer.

Re 10: He showed his anti-clericalism in 1922 when he led a Civil War in the country and opposed 'unto blood and tears' the mandates and official pronouncements of the Irish hierarchy. He would do the same tomorrow if their Lordships condemned his policy.

Re 11: John Devoy summed up Dev—"Rule or Ruin"

Historical facts and events can testify to all the other reasons.

## REASONS WHY THE IRISH PEOPLE SHOULD VOTE FOR SEAN MacEOIN

BECAUSE:

1 He is an honest-to-God Irishman of our own flesh and blood whose father and mother we knew;

2 He is a noble son of our race true to faith and fatherland;

3 He is one of Ireland's bravest soldiers;

4 When De Valera was in America splitting our race and destroying their political power, Sean MacEoin was making England's Black and Tan murder gang bite the dust in historic Ballinalee;

5 MacEoin is straight, honest and Irish; De Valera is duplicit, cunning and alien; etc., etc., etc.,

Our advise to all Irishmen who have preserved their self-respect and have a spark of patriotism in them is: If Dev and his gang are much longer in control here they will leave you without a home or a country! For your own self-respect, and for Ireland's sake, NO MATTER WHAT PARTY YOU BELONG TO, don't confer the highest honor of the State on a political gangster who is demoralising our people, banishing our race, and selling our country to aliens.

★ All communications to: The Secretary, Lia-Fail, Newtown Lusmagh, Banagher, Co. Offaly.

★ Sean MacEoin in 1922, shortly after his release from the condemned cell in Mountjoy. The Truce saved him from the hangman's noose. Since that memorable day he has given unselfish and devoted service to the nation

On 17 June, de Valera was elected President but his proposal to abolish Proportional Representation was rejected by the electorate.

Fr Fahy's involvement in the *Lia Fáil* newspaper was obviously causing concern to Bishop Philbin as the following letter reveals.

ST. BRENDAN'S,
LOUGHREA.
26 February 1959

My dear Fr. Fahy,

I am enclosing a communication I have received by this morning's post. It contains a copy of a publication of which I had seen no issue until now, though I had heard mention of it. I am sending you the whole communication that reached me — it amounts to an anonymous letter, a kind of document one does not normally attach much attention to. However in view of certain rumours that you are associated with the paper in question I would be glad to have your assurance, either that you have not been writing for *it, or that for the future at any rate you will not write for it. You will be aware of the stipulations of Canon Law which make it incumbent on me to ask for such an assurance. E.g. Canon 1386,1g I repeat that I shall be satisfied with a simple assurance on your word to one effect or the other above-mentioned. (Under "writing for it", for example, would be included writing per alium, also editing – the "moderari" of 1386.)*

*With every good wish,*

*I remain,*

*Yours very sincerely,*

*+ William J. Philbin.*

It was unlikely that the bishop suddenly became aware of Fr John's extra-curricular journalistic output. The surprise is that he left it so late to contact him. After all, the newspaper had been published monthly (except December) since the previous August. It is very probable that the outrageous personalised attack on de Valera as the presidential candidate in that February edition prompted the anonymous letter to Bishop Philbin and in turn his belated communication to Fr Fahy.

Fr Fahy's response bore a striking resemblance to the manner in which he dealt with similar requests in the past. Whenever he was caught in a tight ecclesiastical corner Fr John's *modus operandi* was to fall back on a well-rehearsed formula of words which saved his bacon temporarily on a few previous occasions. The ploy usually involved him making a full apology for past misdeeds and offering a firm promise not to offend in future.

However, Fr. John's firm purpose of amendment in matters relating to land and politics was never very firm as events up to then and indeed subsequently were to prove!

His reply to Bishop Philbin was as follows:

St Cronan's
Lusmagh
March 1st 1959

My dear Lord Bishop,
I wholeheartedly and unreservedly give your Lordship the assurance you require that I will not for the future either personally or *per alium* write anything for the journal *Lia Fáil*.

In giving this assurance, I am glad to put your Lordship's direction above any sentiment, ambition or urge I may have either nationally or socially.

I am not a member of the committee in charge of the paper or The Movement. If your Lordship wishes to know the names of those who edit and run that paper I can get them and send them to you.

As I feel that it is distasteful to have to deal with a matter of this kind I really regret any unpleasantness for which I have been responsible.

I really regret it and humbly apologise to your Lordship for it.

I thank your Lordship for the considerate way you have dealt with it.

I am,
Your humble servant
Seán Ó Fathaigh.

Notwithstanding Fr John's assertion that he was 'not a member of the committee in charge of the paper or The Movement', it was to him that Vincent Gill of the *Longford News* sent this receipt following payment for printing the early issues of *Lia Fáil*.

HARBOUR ROW. LONGFORD. CO. LONGFORD
PHONE: 342

# THE LONGFORD NEWS

Published Every Saturday. Over 60 Agents
in Counties Longford, Westmeath, Leitrim,
and Roscommon. Largest Local Sales.

January 16, 1959

Received from Rev. Fr. John Fahy, P.P., Lusmagh, Offaly, on behalf of Lia-Fáil, the sum of £160 in payment for printing all issues of Lia-Fáil to date, with thanks

Vincent Gill

Gill
Jan. 16, 1959

The final issue of *Lia Fáil* (No. 10), which is not dated, was published about September 1960 over a year after Fr Fahy's departure from Lusmagh. It outlines a scenario in which all the aims and objectives of *Lia Fáil* had been brought to fruition.

The new *Lia Fáil* government had

> sealed off the country, abolished the constitution and legislature, established a constitution suitable to our country, made laws people could understand, cut the link with sterling, froze the banks, established a new monetary system, made emigration illegal, introduced compulsory military service, settled 500,000 young men on good lands, abolished the Gardaí, Civil Service, embassies, and had put those employees who were surplus to requirements to work at drainage, land reclamation, turf production and afforestation.

Later it emerges that Fianna Fáil

> were tried for crimes against the nation, found guilty and condemned to death. De Valera and his ministers were hanged and their corpses were left dangling in Dublin as a warning to political adventurers, and soapbox politicians, landlords, alien-planters, ranchers and large landowners who opposed forcible resettlement were similarly dispatched.
>
> England issued a threat of war, but the *Lia Fáil* government dared the 'Whore of Babylon … do your damnedest'. It rearmed with planes, nuclear submarines and nuclear small arms. When the *Lia Fáil* government smashed the border and removed partition the English government withdrew its threat.

This new Ireland now led by *Lia Fáil* and inspired by the idealism of a few 'Old Guard Incorruptibles' would be a country which had

> Wheat growing into the very suburbs of Dublin. The Midlands studded with farmhouses, the Plains of Kildare, Meath, Louth, Longford, Limerick, The Golden Vale dotted with homesteads and teeming with life.

Villages, halls, churches, schools, filling the landscape. Everywhere like fairies on green carpets, children, joyous and colourful, playing on the village greens. Old folk enjoying the sun; men working in the fields – and what fields! Bush fences, ditches and scrub – all cleared away, not a perch of wasteland … Wheat, corn, root crops, vegetables and fruit. Such apples, pears and plums. Hives everywhere and factories in the fields. A network of canals and railways in the making.

That 'new Ireland' seems remarkably similar to what Fr John's arch-enemy Dev had envisaged at his 1943 election campaign launch.

The last two issues of *Lia Fáil* – Numbers 9 and 10 – were published after Fr Fahy had moved to Abbey. In both issues readers were advised that all communications were to be addressed to Portarlington, Offaly, as by then W. H. Milner, a close ally of Fr John, had assumed editorial responsibility. Fr John, however, continued to write articles for the paper until it ceased operations.

## CHAPTER SIXTEEN

## *Some reaction to the* Lia Fáil *newspaper*

Not surprisingly there were widely divergent views aired as the
various issues of *Lia Fáil* became available. Letters published in
the paper, as one might expect, were uniformly positive and
supportive in tone for what *Lia Fáil* was attempting to achieve.
Some were signed with names and addresses included. Others
had pen-names attached such as 'a lover of Ireland,' 'Father of
Five,' 'Small Farmer,' and 'Landless'. It is not inconceivable that
Fr John wrote some of these himself. The following letter is fairly
typical of correspondence received by the editor which understandably was not accorded any space in the newspaper:

> The Editor
> *Lia Fáil*
> Newtown
> Lusmagh
> Banagher
> Offaly
>
> Dear Sir,
> I have read the October '58 copy of your paper *Lia Fáil*,
> and I have come to a conclusion after reading it from
> cover to cover that the Editor, that's you, is suffering from
> an acute brain disease.
>      This paper is fantastic. It is ridiculous, it is the notes of
> a madman. God forbid that the so-called *Lia Fáil* organisa-
> tion ever get any standing in this country or we will have
> to call on a H Bomb to kill us quick or suffer the slow
> death of starving at their hands.
>      Would this organisation stop emigration? They certain-
> ly would but how is something I'd rather not think about.
> No-one can stop the Irish emigrating, it was their nature to
> roam since time began and they will keep on emigrating.
>      Why does this organisation scorn Éamon de Valera,
> one of the world's finest statesmen? Why didn't they
> meet him at the last General Election. They would get one
> vote I know – the Editor of that fanatically created paper

or should I say that heap of ridiculous jealous lies and self-created scandal called *Lia Fáil*.

So now let us hear no more of this – 'The Land of Ireland for the people of Ireland.' The land of Ireland was always with the people of Ireland, for all the good they did with it, and don't print fantastic stories like 'Westmeath Farmers prepared to fight to have land divided'. They wouldn't fight for all Ireland and I'm sure they wouldn't fight for a few hundred acres because they lack a quality which every soldier must have – guts.

Before signing this I am as staunch an Irishman as anyone in *Lia Fáil*.

Signed: Anxious Observer

In *The Irish Times* there was a far more penetrating critique of the aims and ideals of *Lia Fáil* which followed the publication of the September 1958 (No. 2) issue of the paper. The writer, having briefly touched on the aims of *Lia Fáil* in a general way, then went on to disagree in most emphatic terms with the article 'Back to the Brehon Laws' by John Ireland (Fr John) as follows:

That is modest stuff compared to the land remedy, which is summarised in the headline *Back to the Brehan Laws*, supplemented by a reference (twice) to the Divine Law.
The writer clearly knows nothing whatever about the Brehon Laws (properly *Feinechus*) and quotes stuff which is quite wrong from a book by Michael Davitt. Professor D. A. Binchy and myself are the only people in Ireland who are informed on this subject.

Before the invader came, the land of this country was not owned by 'the people' but by native despots, and its letting (often also the letting of cattle and sheep) was recognised and regulated under Feinechus. A saer-letting was reasonable enough if the tenant behaved himself and did not object to a ciss or rent that was of the rack variety. A daer-letting was a primitively tyrannical sort of transaction, making the lessor a serf or slave, having to find security for the use of the land and to face such imposts as having crowds of soldiers quartered on him. It's deplorable that this Army should issue orders of the day with no notion as to what it is talking about.

Professor Dáibhí Ó Cróinín (Roinn na Staire, NUIG) suggests that this piece may have been written by Myles na gCopaleen in his 'Cruiskeen Lawn' column.

After the publication of the eighth issue of *Lia Fáil* (June 1959) and the widespread publicity in the national press and radio which resulted from the events in Lusmagh, Banagher and Tullamore, the initial enthusiasm and support for the organisation began to wane. Typical of the fall-off in support was the following short note received by the Secretary in Lusmagh at the time.

Cadamstown
Birr
Co Offaly

Dear Sir,
I am enclosing £3 for papers. I am asking you not to send anymore as the people won't buy them. I also sold about six of the last ones.

They say it is no use when it ended in Banagher the way it did.

Yours truly,
J. Coughlan

This next letter appeared in *The Midland Tribune*, 20 June 1959. It is clearly from a most irate Fianna Fáil supporter:

Letter To Editor
### The New "Patriots"

Dear Editor, — Recently in the Midlands we have had a campaign of hatred and malice, mixed with religion, politics, monetary reform and land that really "beats Banagher."

The character assassins in their scurrilous campaign have, apart from De Valera, singled out and blackguarded our present Minister for Lands and Fisheries, Erskine Childers, exactly the same as his father, that martyr of '22, was also blackguarded.

Childers is not a Free Mason, neither are any of his family. He is not Chairman of the Protestant Church Body and even if he were let Sinn Fein and "The United Irishman" tell us of their Wolfe Tone policy of substituting the 'Common name of Irishmen in place of the denominations of Protestant, Catholic and Dissenter."

Childers father. God rest him. died holding a Crucifix blessed by a Republican priest. and the Rosary which had been in the dying hands of Cathal Brugha.

May God forgive those new 'patriots' who have sprung up recently to defame the names of our great Republicans, be they Protestant o Catholic.—'IRISHMAN.' Banagher 12/6/'59.

CHAPTER SEVENTEEN

# Lia Fáil – *Direct action*

The first mention of direct action at national level by *Lia Fáil* occurred in the *Irish Farmers' Journal* of Saturday 29 March 1958 when it reported on a case which had come before the High Court concerning a disturbance on a farm in Co. Mayo.

In the course of the proceedings it was stated that Francie Kelly, Lusmagh, was the *Lia Fáil* member who had organised the event. The *Journal* reported as follows.

Irish Farmers' Journal, Saturday, March 29, 1958 *p.3*

## Land Commission gets injunction against Mayo farmers

AN application of the Irish Land Commission for an injunction to restrain 17 men from trespassing on 411 acres of land owned by the Commission, at Hollymount, Co. Mayo, until April 14th next, was granted by Mr. Justice Teevan in the High Court.

Mr. Micks, S.C., for the Land Commission said that the land, which had been owned by the Nally Estate, had been acquired by the Land Commission.

The defendants, with the exception of one man, were all local farmers, and that man was one of the national executive of an organisation called Lia Fáil, and came from Banagher, Co Offaly. Another of the defendants had communicated with the local sergeant of the Civic Guard and informed him that he proposed with other associates, taking over the Nally Estate at noon on February 28th. last, stating that the Land Commission had ignored local representations in regard to the division of the land. The following day this man and about 100 persons assembled at the Nally Estate.

There was a certain amount of talk, and it was agreed that nothing should be done for a week if the Land Commission replied to local representations within that time.

On March 7th, this man and

about 200 others assembled at the estate and proceeded to allot land to certain local persons. Then they started to drive stock off the lands, belonging to grazing tenants. The Superintendent of the Civic Guard intervened and prevented any further trouble. Since then, the lands had been nationally divided among certain people, and picketed. That could not be tolerated by the Land Commission.

In an affidavit to the Court, Supt Michael Kealy, Claremorris stated that 'on 7 March about 200 farmers marched in procession to the lands behind a tricolour carried by Mrs Margaret Kelly, Lusmagh, Banagher. When the procession halted Patrick Crowe (local Mayo Farmer) made a speech in the course of which he said "we are now going to divide the estate under the authority of *Lia Fáil* as we are long enough waiting for the Land Commission to act."' He told those present that Francie Kelly was from the National Executive of *Lia Fáil* and that Mrs Kelly, his wife, was secretary of that organisation.

He (Mr Crowe) also produced a letter which he had received from the Land Commission stating that local applications for land would be fully considered but that any interference with the property would render such applicants ineligible for consideration. Patrick Crowe said it was the reply of a hundred years ago; 'it was like the old man telling the little boy to be good and he would get sweets the next fair day, maybe.'

Supt Kealy concluded that with about 140 of those present 'Patrick Crowe and Francie Kelly went on to divide the land.'

Following the granting of an injunction to the Land Commission until 4 April the case came before the High Court again.

The *Tuam Herald* 19 April opened its account of the resumed sitting as follows:

Sixteen Mayo farmers who were said to have been 'led astray' by an organisation known as *Lia Fáil* gave an undertaking in the High Court on Monday, that they would not in future interfere with the running of a 411-acre farm at Hollymount, held by the Irish Land Commission.

The Mayo men were represented by Mr O'Malley BL (instructed by Mr Seán Flanagan Solr TD). Francie Kelly was not present in court and was not represented.

Low-key organisational matters concerned Fr Fahy and *Lia Fáil* both in Lusmagh and around the country in the following twelve months. It was very much a case of 'the calm before the storm'.

## CHAPTER EIGHTEEN

# *Lusmagh and Fr John make national headlines*

On May Day 1959 – Fair Day in Banagher – a series of events began to unfold involving Fr John and his supporters which would, over the following couple of months, leave an indelible mark on all concerned. The parish of Lusmagh would be thrust temporarily from obscurity to prominence in the local and national press, in Dáil Éireann and in local courthouses and its much-loved priest would involuntarily be heading for 'pastures new' long before the dust had settled on that rural idyll.

The eighth issue of the *Lia Fáil* newspaper had a banner headline across its front page – *Lia Fáil Divides Land* – and the first article by Fr John opened as follows:

Around this time, Fr Fahy was interviewed by Eric Waugh, a journalist with the *Belfast Telegraph*. Waugh's article published on June titled 'The Seeds of Wrath in Éire Land' contained the following passage which sheds further light on the events of the morning of 1 May:

At 6.30 on a Friday morning, three weeks ago, five young men arrived at Newtown with three tractors between them. Despite the weather ('Sure it was the wettest morn-ing that ever came from heaven') the men had ploughed one and a half acres of the field opposite Mrs Killeen's cottage within a couple of hours and planted it with wheat for the use of herself and her two sons.

The newly-planted field is part of a fifteen-acre farm which is legally the property of the Land Commission. Its last occupant, Mr Patrick O'Leary, moved three weeks ago to a fifty-acre holding given him by the Commission in a neighbouring townland.

'They're fairly early farmers in Lusmagh,' mused Mrs Killeen as she looked down the field. In her cottage she has the deed of ownership given her by *Lia Fáil*, the or-ganisation the young ploughmen represented. The deed is the first the organisation has issued.

'They asked me to give the operation the official bless-ing of the church,' said Father Fahy, 'and I blessed the seed they were sowing. This is the first land division, but there'll be many, many more ...'
And with a belligerent inflexion in his voice he added: 'In my opinion no one will ever possess that land but the widow and her family who have got it from *Lia Fáil*.'

Father Fahy, now 65 and a former chaplain on the run with the IRA brigades of 1921 is in a fighting succession. His personality, too, reflects the loyalty to the Gaelic tra-dition found among many of the older folk in the remoter Southern communities.

His family background, for three generations, has been one of close implication in agrarian violence dating to the agitation led by Davitt and O'Brien in the 19th century. His position now is obviously one of considerable influence.

Later that day the group turned their attention to the farm of Frankie Barry at Cogran, a couple of miles away. The *Midland Tribune*, 9 May, which comprehensively dealt with these and subsequent events, takes up the story as follows:

They then moved to nearby lands, drove off about 32 cat-tle that were grazing there, ploughed 'a scrape' in one of the fields, and when Gardaí from Banagher who had got notification of the cattle being on the road came out to return the animals, they refused to allow the Gardaí to go ahead, attempted to prevent, forcibly, the animals being driven back on to the land, and eventually were arrested.

Recently the Land Commission when dividing up the Ryan Estate at Rath allocated to Mr Patrick O'Leary, Lusmagh, a section of this land. Mr O'Leary was the owner of about 20 acres at Lusmagh.

*Cattle Driven Off*
The land from which the cattle were driven is owned by Mr Francis Barry, Banagher (a retired London County Council official) and the cattle which were grazing on it are owned by his brother, Mr Albert Barry, Banagher (Rate Collector for Offaly County Council).

*Gardaí Arrive*
When the Gardaí arrived to replace the cattle on the lands on Friday afternoon, five men took up positions on a narrow bridge and refused to allow the cattle to pass. With the men, armed with sticks, at one side, the Gardaí at the other and the cattle in the middle, an impasse was reached.

Reinforcements of Gardaí from Birr, under Inspector J. O'Leary, Sergt J. Flaherty and Sergt J. Kearns, arrived in a short time, and after consultations in which the men, after being warned of the consequences of their attitude, refused to give way, two of them were arrested and taken to the Garda Station.

The remaining three held out, and were arrested after they had tried to drive the cattle away off the lands again when the Gardaí succeeded in getting them into the roadside field. They were subsequently taken to the Garda Station also.

Fr Fahy, *Lia Fáil* and the Paddy O'Leary and Frankie Barry farms featured very prominently in a six-page 'Memorandum for the Government' (5 Bealtaine 1959) subheaded 'Land Agitation' which was submitted by Erskine Childers, Minister for Lands, to the Government at the weekly meeting of the Cabinet. As well as providing statistics on agitations and acquisitions, the memorandum sought to refute *Lia Fáil* claims about the widespread purchase of land by aliens and estimated that the circulation of *Lia Fáil* newspaper was 2000-3000 approx. The document went on to state that

> In the Minister's view, the left wing extreme nationalist element represented by Sinn Féin and *Lia Fáil* exists in many areas but to what extent he is uncertain. The only partial antidotes are those offered by Macra na Feirme, Muintir na Tíre and by the acceptance of the programme for economic expansion.

The minister sought the advice of the Government on steps, if any, required to deal with *Lia Fáil* and concluded that 'The Minister for Justice (Oscar Traynor) will no doubt have observations to make on the law and order aspect of the agitation.'

Later that evening the five men were charged as described in the following morning's *Irish Independent:*

## MEN CHARGED AT BANAGHER

At a special court in Banagher Garda Station yesterday, before Mr. D. Ryder, P.C., the following were charged with obstructing the Guards in the execution of their duty: **Denis Kelly,** Newtown: **Noel Moran,** Ashgrove: **Brendan Killelen,** Newtown: **John J. Kenny,** Cogran. and **Patrick Glynn,** Gortraven. They were remanded in custody to Banagher Court next Thursday. It was stated that the men refused bail.

The charges, it is understood, arose from incidents connected with local land disputes.

At 8 p.m. a crowd gathered outside the Garda Station where the men were detained awaiting transport to Mountjoy. A number of men entered the barracks yard and the men who had been detained came out with them.

There was a parade through the town in which a banner representing Lia Fáil was carried

A large force of Gardaí has been drafted in from surrounding districts and under the direction of Inspector J. O'Leary, Birr.

*The Irish Press*, 9 May carried this account:

> In the course of the afternoon before the special court sitting, relatives of the men had called to the Garda Station with food and clothing for the accused.

The court sitting took place at 6.30 p.m. when the men were charged 'that they did unlawfully and wilfully resist and obstruct Inspector J. O'Leary, Sergt Flaherty, Kerins and Coll, Gardaí Hyland, Joyce, Ivory, McGee, Harrington, Kehoe and Cox, members of the Garda Síochána in the execution of their duty contrary to Section 38 of the Offences Against the Person Act 1861.'

At about 7 p.m. John Kelly, Michael Kelly and Patrick Killeen called to the Garda Station. They were admitted and after a short while succeeded in jamming open the door of the cell where the men were confined. John Kelly gave a prearranged signal to the crowd of about a hundred which had gathered outside.

Some persons in the crowd succeeded in opening the gate leading to the yard. The prisoners got out into the yard where Sergt Coll attempted to get them back. One Garda managed to get a chain on the gate outside but it could not be kept closed.

... the situation was completely out of the control of the Gardaí. They were completely outnumbered. The men got out onto the road and a parade was held in the town.

The five detained men with others got into a van and drove out to Mr Barry's farm, where two Gardaí were on duty. They warned the Gardaí but told them that they would do them no harm. They entered on the land and drove off the cattle again.

On the following day, Saturday, 2 May, six Lusmagh men, John, Michael and Francie Kelly, Jim Glynn, Paddy Killeen and Tom Moran, all brothers of the men who escaped from Banagher Garda Station the previous evening 'were arrested and charged with the forcible rescue of the prisoners'. After a brief Court hearing all six were removed to Mountjoy in three Garda cars under heavy escort to appear in Tullamore District Court the following Friday (8 May).

The *Sunday Independent*, 3 May had a prominent front page article headed 'Banagher's five rescued men still at large', with an opening paragraph as follows:

Where are the five missing prisoners forcibly released from Banagher Garda Barracks? This was still the big query in Offaly last night following yesterday's removal to Mountjoy of six men charged with forcibly rescuing the five from police custody on Friday night.

In fact the five missing men attended 8.30 a.m. Mass on that Sunday morning in St Cronan's Church, Lusmagh.

The *Irish Press* on Monday, 4 May dealt at some length with the appearance of the men at the previous day's Mass.

These are extracts from the article which was headed:

# Neighbours to take care of missing men's farms

NEIGHBOURS are to look after farming operations on the holdings of the five young Offaly men who, on Friday night, left Banagher Garda Station, where they were being held following a clash with Gardai in a cattle incident earlier in the day.

This was decided at a meeting of over 100 parishioners in the schoolhouse of their home area, Lusmagh, last night. No developments in their search for the men were reported up to last night by local Gardai and reinforcements.

The five men attended early Mass in their parish church at Lusmagh, two miles from Banagher, yesterday morning.

Still in the working clothes they were wearing when arrested on Friday afternoon they were greeted warmly in the church yard after Mass, had a discussion with relatives and neighbours, and walked away to an unknown destination. They had told members of their families that they intended to stay "on the run."

Their Parish Priest, Very Rev. J. Fahy spoke to them for several minutes before their departure.

Yesterday evening it was believed that the five men, all in their twenties, were still in the Lusmagh area, being supplied with food prepared in the neighbourhood.

In Banagher, where there has been considerable uneasiness since agrarian incidents began early on Friday there was sign of anything in the nature of an all-out search for the men.

A full report on the incidents has gone to Garda headquarters in Dublin and it is believed that the local force are now awaiting a directive from Dublin.

It is clear that Garda Headquarters in Dublin was stung into action by the open attendance at Mass of the men who had been rescued from Banagher Barracks on Friday. The inability of the Gardaí to locate the missing men was also exercising the members of the Government. And so plans were hatched by senior

Gardaí throughout Monday, 4 May, in great secrecy, to carry through what they called 'a search and snatch' operation in the Lusmagh area at the earliest opportunity.

The *Evening Herald* of Tuesday, 5 May devoted almost the entire front page to the Garda initiative.

The main heading was 'Dawn Swoop on Residence of Parish Priest'. In the top left hand corner of the page was a photo of Fr John in his plaid dressing gown and pyjamas standing at the door of his house after the raid. There were also photos of plain-clothes and uniformed Gardaí in front of the parochial house and of others standing on the roadside beside the squad cars used to bring the fifty or so Gardaí from Dublin Castle. It was confirmed that the raid was planned in such secrecy that the detectives only became aware of their destination when they were already embarked on the journey to Lusmagh.

This report was written by James McGuire, *Herald* Staff Reporter.

In a lightning dawn strike from Dublin Castle this morning six squad cars of Metropolitan Gardaí raided the house of Very Rev John Fahy PP, the sixty-four-year-old Parish Priest of Lusmagh, Banagher, Co Offaly, in search of the five prisoners forcibly rescued from Banagher Garda Station on Friday.

Fifty police, including numerous plain-clothes men in six black limousines, guided by two squad cars from Birr, swept into the Lusmagh parish shortly before 5 a.m. as dawn was breaking.

The raid was led by Chief Superintendent M. Mooney, Portlaoise and their first stop was on the road leading to the parochial house. The house is about thirty yards back from Lusmagh Cross, where the church faces four converging roads.

While one detachment of Gardaí kept watch at the cross, about thirty police and plain-clothes men entered the grounds of the parochial house and surrounded the two-storied building. Meanwhile two of the other cars fanned out into the area to start a series of searches in houses in the district.

Once a cordon had been thrown around the priest's house, Chief Superintendent Mooney and a police sergeant rapped the heavy brass knocker on the white front door. This was at 4.53 a.m.

A light came on in the upper left-hand window of the house, and after a space the sergeant knocked again, while a knot of Gardaí stood staring up at the window.

4.55 a.m: The head and shoulders of the parish priest appeared at the window. He called out 'Hallo, police. Do you want to come in?' Chief Superintendent Mooney then said 'Yes, I have a warrant.' The priest then said 'All right, I'll be down' and withdrew from the window.

### Door opened

4.57 a.m: The front door of the house opened and Father Fahy was seen in his plaid dressing-gown and pyjamas. There was a short consultation between himself and the Chief Superintendent and then the police officer entered the house. The door was left open and several other uniformed Gardaí entered behind the Chief Superintendent who was dressed in plain clothes.

Lights began to spring up in the house as police commenced a search of the various apartments.

5.01 a.m: The priest appeared at the doorway and led officers out to some out-offices in the grounds.

5.03 a.m: Father Fahy re-appeared and went back into the house with the Chief Superintendent and both remained in close conversation in the doorway.

5.06 a.m: The Chief Superintendent departed and the door was closed.

### Consultations

5.14 a.m: The entire body of police moved back down the short gravelled drive to the entrance to the parochial grounds and there were a number of consultations.

5.24 a.m: There was a sudden dramatic development when the priest flung up his bedroom window and called out 'I have a message for the Chief Superintendent.'

Chief Superintendent Mooney immediately left the car in which he was seated and walked alone back into the house. He was met at the door by Father Fahy and both re-entered the house.

5.29 a.m: The Chief re-appeared and joined his men. By this time the other squad cars had returned to the roadway outside the house, and after a brief meeting five of the Dublin cars and the two Birr cars made off back into the parish.

Apart from the dramatic nature of the raid on Fr Fahy's house, a question arises as to who tipped off the *Evening Herald* about the operation. It was very strange that a reporter and a press photographer were outside the parochial house waiting before dawn broke for the arrival of the Garda cavalcade. Fr John also knew about the Garda plans well before the pre-dawn knock on his front door. And he relayed this information to the men 'on the run' who by then were in Cloghan Castle, a mile away.

Another point worth pondering – not directly related to the raid – is the fact that Fr John was able to acquire so speedily a copy of the Memorandum brought to government by Erskine Childers dealing with *Lia Fáil*. Any such document is supposed to be totally confidential and classified and is usually put into the public domain after a thirty-year embargo or longer.

There were obviously serious concerns in the Fianna Fáil government about how to deal with the threat posed by *Lia Fáil*. Several ministers still serving at that time were veterans of the War of Independence and The Civil War and would have shared many of Fr John's intense republican ideals in their earlier days. Clearly they would have been dismayed at the vituperative monthly outbursts in his newspaper against them. But somebody very close to the centre of power in Dublin was not ready, just yet, to betray him. Clearly there was tension between Oscar Traynor, Minister for Justice, and Erskine Childers (Lands) in the Government over the affair. The Garda raid was deliberately leaked to the press beforehand to make sure of publicity.

*The Irish Times* 6 May report of the Garda raid included the following points:

The only occupants of the house when the raid took place were Father Fahy and his 84-year-old housekeeper Mrs Catherine Fitzgerald.

Last night all rifles of the Lusmagh company, FCA, were collected by an Army officer in a van. There is a strong company of FCA in Lusmagh parish, and the missing men are members of this company.

In an interview with an *Irish Times* representative Father Fahy said: 'Since these young men started the land war, not one of them has entered the parochial house or grounds, and I am delighted to see young men determined upon getting a living in their own country. I approve of what the men do to get a living in their own country. Foreigners are coming in while our young men sleep in Birmingham rooms.'

Fr Fahy also said that he told Chief Superintendent Mooney that arrangements were being made for the Human Rights Commission of the United Nations to look after the interests of the five young men.

The following statement was issued to the press after the dawn raid on Fr Fahy's house.

*Statement re Raid on Parochial House, Lusmagh*
I am instructed to give the enclosed document to the press which proves where the responsibility for the raid on Fr Fahy's house at Lusmagh really lies.

The secret Cabinet meeting which this document records was held on Monday 4 May, the day before said raid.
Mr Childers, who is a Freemason, ordered de Valera's Minister for Justice to raid and search Fr Fahy's house. This accounts for the celebrations in the lodges over their great victory. De Valera being President of the Cabinet has the chief responsibility. He cannot dodge this time. This document published shows that Traynor must have been offered as a scapegoat.

*Lia Fáil* is thoroughly aware that Freemasons are past masters at assassinations which they call removals.

If through the discovery of this document which proves that de Valera and his government are controlled by Freemasons one single member or friend of *Lia Fáil* suffers, *Lia Fáil* will hold every Freemason in Ireland responsible but the first and chief Freemason to pay the price will be the Englishman Childers.

Signed:        *Chief Intelligence Officer*
               *Lia Fáil*

This statement was written in Fr Fahy's own handwriting.

The Guards and detectives immediately followed up their search of Fr Fahy's house with a thorough examination of nearby Cloghan Castle, the other likely location where the missing men might hide. There was clear evidence – fresh food, rope ladder, remains of a fire – that the men they sought had recently departed. The main doors of the castle had been securely nailed to prevent any sudden entry.

It was, no doubt, a source of satisfaction to Fr Fahy that these Lusmagh men, for however short a period, occupied Cloghan Castle. This once great O'Madden stronghold – the only one East of the Shannon – had recently been sold by Major Whitford to Major Bowes-Daly who at that time lived in Tanganyika (now Tanzania) prior to taking up residence in Lusmagh. The ancestral Bowes-Daly 'seat' had been at Dunsandle, Loughrea for some centuries up to 1954, a fact not calculated to endear him or his ancestors to Fr John.

The five men on the run had stayed first with Fr Fahy before moving to Cloghan Castle. From there they were transferred across the Shannon to Eyrecourt where they spent the next couple of days.

Pat Glynn and John Joe Kenny were then taken to the home of Peadar and Lile O'Donnell at 176, Upper Drumcondra Road, Dublin, while Noel Moran, Ben Killeen and Dinny Kelly were driven to Barney Kelly's house at Mount Temple, Moate. They slept each night during that part of their odyssey in the home of Jack and Margaret Killane, near neighbours of Barney Kelly and his family. The Killane's were not thought by the authorities to harbour republican sympathies. During their stay in Mount Temple, the lads helped the Kellys with farm work.

The three Dublin dailies, *The Irish Press*, *The Irish Independent* and *The Irish Times* and the two evening papers *The Herald* and *The Evening Press*, and of course Radio Éireann (there was no Irish television at the time) all gave extensive coverage to the raids on both the parochial house and the castle.

# CHAPTER NINETEEN

## *Bishop Philbin gets involved*

Bishop Philbin was keeping a close watch on events unfolding in Lusmagh. On the day after the raid, he dispatched Fr O'Callaghan, Adm St Brendan's Cathedral, Loughrea, and Diocesan Secretary, bearing the following letter to Fr Fahy and demanded an immediate reply. It is clear that the bishop had been made aware of Fr Fahy's intention to close Lusmagh National School on the following Friday to facilitate the greatest possible turnout in support of the parishioners who were due to appear in court on that day.

St. Brendan's
Loughrea.
6 May 1959.

My dear Father Fahy,

    A s you will have noticed, a good deal of the publicity concerning the Lusmagh land incidents and the release of the prisoners from custody has given the impression tha t these activities have your support and encouragement. Seve ral representations to this effe ct have been made to me and in particular it has been said that when you visited the men deta ined in barracks on the charge of interfering with the police you expressed approval of what they had done and told the police they might make a note of this.

    From our corre spondence of January 1958 I had taken it that you were not to be involved in agrarian movements of this kind, the objections to which I had stated from the social and moral angle as well as for the reason that they would in certain manifestations at least be in conflict with the pastoral obligations of the priest. In the present circumstances in particular I would have to regard it as a serious matter if my belief that you had withdrawn from such movements were not well-founded.

    I am still not accepting that you are involved as publicity and rumour suggest. Nor do I believe, though this has been put to me, tha t you have any intention of taking such a step as closing Lusmagh School on Frida y in order to facilitate a demonstration, or of being yourself involved in any demonstration, or of organizing one.

    But I am bound to call your attention to the fact that even slight indications from you will in the present circumstances confirm the wide impression that you have been the influence behind all that has been done, and things have been done which are in conflict with C atholic moral principles. I must ask you to give no reason to have it thought that you are supporting these developments, and not to support them. As some rumours concern possible proximate developments, I must ask you to reply to this letter by the bearer, or if you prefer this to come to Loughrea to see me.

      I remain,

      Yours very sincerely,

      + william J. Philbin.

Fr John's reply bore a striking resemblance to other earlier responses when he found himself caught in awkward situations with his diocesan superiors.

St Cronan's
Lusmagh
6th May 1959

My dear Lord Bishop,
I have kept the assurance given Your Lordship in 1958. I have no position in the *Lia Fáil* organisation.

I will not close Lusmagh School on Friday nor will I organise any demonstration. I did tell the people My Lord, that I would go to Tullamore with them on Friday but I will not go there now.

I will comply with your directions re supporting the Movement from today.

I assure Your Lordship that I will fulfil and obey directions you feel obliged to give.

Your obedient servant
John Fahy

Fr O'Callaghan returned to Loughrea with that reply for the bishop who immediately sent the following brief note back by post to Fr Fahy as an acknowledgement. It was a classic of its type – courteous, succinct and authoritative:

St. BRENDAN'S,
LOUGHREA.
6 May 1959

My dear Fr. Fahy,

Thank you for your letter delivered to me by Fr. O'Callaghan, and for the assurances it contains.

I notice that in the Irish Times of today, and also in the Evening Herald of yesterday there are reproduced what purport to be interviews given by you to representatives of those papers. This is prohibited by Canon 16 of the Tuam Statutes.

I remain,
Yours very sincerely,
† W. J. Philbin.

What Fr John thought of the Tuam Statutes in general or of Canon 16 in particular does not seem, unfortunately, to have survived in written form.

Bishop Philbin who was a native of Kiltimagh, Co. Mayo, was by nature and training very different to Fr Fahy. He had been appointed to Clonfert in 1953 in succession to Bishop Dignan after years of distinguished service in Maynooth. But while Bishop Philbin and Fr John both wished to see the Land Commission far more active in the acquisition of large holdings for redistribution, their views diverged sharply when it came to ways of encouraging the Commission to get on with its task.

Writing about Bishop Philbin in his beautifully produced *Meadow of the Miracles, a History of the Diocese of Clonfert,* Fr Declan Kelly refers to a series of pamphlets which the bishop wrote in the 1950s. The best known one was titled *Patriotism* (1958) and ominously for Fr Fahy, one of its conclusions was that

> In spite of many excellences, love of one's fatherland does not impart automatically the stamp of rightness to all that is undertaken in its name.

Bishop Philbin also warned in that pamphlet that

> where emotions take the lead, reason, the proper guide of conduct, is often suspended and we are apt to be led into excess and errors.

Bishop Philbin was transferred from Clonfert to Down and Connor in 1962 and went on to be widely acclaimed for his contributions during Vatican II.

A number of points in the bishop's first letter to Fr Fahy and in the reply taken back to Loughrea by Fr O'Callaghan are very puzzling.

How Bishop Philbin could write despite 'the several representations' made to him and the widespread publicity created around 'the Lusmagh land incidents' that he was still not accepting that Fr Fahy was involved, is difficult to take at face value.

It is equally puzzling when Fr Fahy declares that he had no position in *Lia Fáil* and that he had complied with directives issued the previous year by Bishop Philbin. His promise 'to fulfil and obey directives' henceforth would once again be put to the test within a matter of days.

CHAPTER TWENTY

## *The search continues: Dáil debate*

The search for the missing Lusmagh men intensified but they continued to evade capture. The *Irish Times* 7/5/1959 reported that

> Meanwhile, telegrams, letters and messages of goodwill are being received from all over the district by the Very Rev John Fahy PP, whose house was raided by a special party of guards from Dublin at dawn last Tuesday. Among telegrams and reports received today was one from the National Students' Council in Dublin, which read: 'We back you in your fight against tyranny, congratulations.'

*Visit from TD*

Many personal visitors included the Very Rev James Canon Earley PP, Ferbane, class-mate of Father Fahy in Maynooth. He conveyed greetings from well-wishers in South Offaly. Mr O. J. Flanagan TD paid a visit early and told reporters afterwards that he 'was disgusted' at the police raid on the parish priest's house.

Mr Flanagan gave notice in the Dáil yesterday that he would ask the Minister for Justice if he would state why the parochial house at Lusmagh was raided; if he is aware that there is no evidence whatever to justify this raid; and further if he was aware of public uneasiness as a result of the raid.

Uniformed police kept watch at a dance held in the town last Tuesday night at which there was a big crowd.

Farmers yesterday completed sowing a beet field for 75-year-old Mr Henry Glynn, who has one son in jail and the other on the run.

Oliver J. Flanagan (Fine Gael, Laois/Offaly) was widely regarded on all sides of the political divide as one of the most assiduous constituency workers to have ever been elected to Dáil Éireann. He was determined to cause as much embarrassment to the Government and to earn as much political capital as possible from these events in his own electoral area.

It's perhaps relevant to point out that when Oliver J. (as he was commonly known) was first elected to the Dáil in 1943 one of his main policies was centred on monetary reform, a concept which fifteen years later greatly exercised some contributors to the *Lia Fáil* newspaper.

Dr Varley in *Galway – History and Society* states that

> Monetary reform aimed at destroying Freemasonry and through state regulation of the money supply, to lay the basis of a Christian social order, along the lines envisaged by Pope Pius XI in *Quadragesimo Anno*.

It is worth noting that Flanagan often objected to outsiders (or aliens as Fr John called them) being allowed to purchase substantial farms in Ireland. For example in a Dáil debate in November 1949 he called the purchaser of an estate in his own county Laois who was from Scotland 'a monster … who comes plundering through the country as Cromwell came'. The terminology is not terribly dissimilar to that found in the *Lia Fáil* paper. Oliver J. Flanagan made some inflammatory speeches particularly in his earlier political days which he later came to regret in the course of wide-ranging interviews with historian Tim Pat Coogan.

On the following pages is a transcript of the exchanges between Deputy Flanagan, An Ceann Comhairle, the Minister for Justice and others in a Dáil debate on 12 May.

**Dáil Éireann - Volume 174 - 12 May, 1959**
**Adjournment Debate. - Raid on Parochial House in Offaly.**

**An Ceann Comhairle:** It may help discussion on this matter if I
indicate at the outset that, for reasons obvious to those who
understand the position in the area, nothing falls for discussion
here except the raid on the house of the parish priest.

**Mr. O.J. Flanagan:** That is all that is referred to in the questions.
Earlier to-day I asked the Minister for Justice if he would state why
the parochial house at Lusmagh, Banagher, Offaly, was raided by a
large force of the Garda on 5th inst.; what evidence was adduced
to justify the raid and, further, if he was aware of public uneasiness
as a result of the raid.
The second question addressed to the Minister asked if it was a
decision of the Government to instruct the Garda to raid the
parochial house, what prompted this action and if what was sought
was found. I addressed these two simple questions to the Minister
because of the seriousness of the position, the great public
uneasiness caused and the most unusual character of the raid. The
Minister replied that Father Fahy's house was visited by the Garda
Síochána because they had information confirming—mark you,
confirming—reports widely circulating in the locality that the men
whose escape from lawful custody had been effected with force
were being harboured there. The Minister went on to say: "I take
full responsibility for what was done."

Not alone is this a most unusual action on the part of the
Government, not alone is it unusual in character, but it is of the
greatest possible consequence to every citizen. The sanctity and
privacy of the home are something to be cherished and defended.
Within 30 yards of the Catholic [1943] Church in Lusmagh Father
Fahy resides. He is a beloved and respected parish priest who
discharges his saintly duties with piety, zeal and vigour. The only
other occupant of the house was his 84 year old housekeeper, Miss
Fitzgerald.
In the silence of the night, just as dawn was about to break, there
arrived from Dublin a large force of the Garda, made up of 50
police and numerous plain clothes men, most of them armed with
revolvers, in six black limousines. They were guided by two squad
cars. At 4 a.m., just as dawn was breaking, they stopped at the
Catholic Church at Lusmagh. Some of the plain clothes men, armed
with revolvers, dropped off at the Catholic Church and proceeded
on foot to the residence of Father Fahy. Up the avenue of the
parochial house there walked between 50 and 65 police. In the
silence of the small hours of the morning the aged parish priest
was knocked up. He looked out to find, with horror and dismay,
nothing less than an army of uniformed and plain clothes police
armed with revolvers. His house was surrounded. He inquired what
was wrong. He was told the men were police. With kindness and
courtesy, he said he would not detain the gentlemen; if they
wanted admission to his house they were free to come in. He
admitted them to his house. No less than 40 armed police piled in.

They searched every room and apartment, disturbing from her slumbers the aged housekeeper.

This may be a cause for laughter on the Fianna Fáil benches. An 84 year old housekeeper being disturbed and the parish priest having to conduct a force of Gardaí through every room in his house may be a cause for laughter to some people. We have the photographs here and in those photographs we see 22 police approaching the avenue.

**An Ceann Comhairle:** I do not think the photographs should be referred to in this discussion.

**Mr. O.J. Flanagan:** I shall not refer [1944] to them then, Sir. The evidence is here. Now, the police found nothing. When interviewed after the raid Father Fahy said: "I showed the police over the house. They examined the place and the out-offices, the garage, the back of the house, and every part of it. I told them that none of the boys had stood in this house or on these grounds since any trouble commenced in the area."

My reason for protesting in this matter is because of its character. Would it not have been possible for the Minister for Justice to have sent the Garda to Father Fahy in the day-time? Would it not have been possible for the Garda to have told Father Fahy then: "We are going to search your house. We have a warrant to do so"? Could they not have searched the house in broad daylight and not waited until the middle of the night or until dawn was breaking? There was nothing to stop them searching the house in the day-time.

We have been told that the Minister for Justice had reliable information that Father Fahy was practically a proven felon, that he was harbouring "wanted" people. Is it any wonder that every parish priest and every curate blushed with shame, with horror and indignation on discovering that the Government refused to trust a parish priest—a parish priest who would have given them any information they wanted and would have told them that his house was not a place for harbouring those required under the law? He would have shown them the same courtesy and willingness to inspect his house in the day-time as he did in the middle of the night. He had nothing to hide.

I think the Government made a bad slip. This was a foolish action. It was a disgraceful act on the part of the Government. It would have been bad enough had it been just a parishioner of Father Fahy's that was concerned. It is almost incomprehensible that the parish priest should have been disturbed by armed police at 4.50 a.m. That is something against which protest must be made in this House. It is something against which [1945] every citizen should protest. It is something against which every citizen should rise up. The criminal law makes a distinction between day and night. If a man enters a house in the day-time he can be charged with breaking and entering. If he enters a house at night, he is charged with burglary.

The Minister accepts full responsibility. He accepts full responsibility for this kind of conduct. He accepts full responsibility, first of all, for wantonly disturbing the rest of a parish priest, and, secondly, for the manner in which this raid was planned and carried out.

I am reliably informed that a conference took place in the Department of Justice and that the Chief Superintendent happened, by accident, to be in Garda headquarters on the same day. He was not familiar with conditions in the district but was invited to take part in this conference. I am also advised that members of the Garda Force, with 36 years' police experience, shrewd and sensible men, were not even consulted or even called to the conference with the Department of Justice on this matter.

I am reliably informed that another senior officer of the Garda Síochána advised against raiding Father Fahy's house as being unwise and not sensible, but the decision was taken and I am told that this is the first time, and contrary to all proper police procedure, that this extraordinary act on the part of the Government and the Minister for Justice has occurred. It has brought forth great anger and disgust from the people, and a certain amount of grave unrest. If this has happened to Father Fahy, it could happen to any other citizen as well, and the result has been that it has brought forth very serious criticism.

I may say that the method and planning of this raid is something that has proved great discourtesy to the Church in this country. It has proved that even the decent members of the Garda Force have been driven to do work which was distasteful to them and which they knew was wrong. This is the first time we have had an incident of this character since the [~~1946~~] house of the late Bishop of Killaloe was raided by the Black and Tans.

**Mr. K. Boland:** There were a couple since that. The Deputy had better check up.

**Mr. O.J. Flanagan:** A raid on a parish priest's house——

**Mr. Galvin:** What happened in 1929?

**An Ceann Comhairle:** Order! The Deputy should be allowed to speak without interruption.

**Mr. Coogan:** Remember Hungary.

**An Ceann Comhairle:** The Deputy should keep to the incident itself and not draw parallels.

**Mr. O.J. Flanagan:** If this incident took place in China, in Russia or in Hungary, protest would be made. A protest was made in this very House by the Fianna Fáil Party against the treatment and arrest of Cardinal Mindszenty and Cardinal Stepinac. Members of the Fianna Fáil Party, including the Taoiseach, voiced protests, as did every Catholic and Christian throughout the civilised world, but here we have, in a Catholic and Christian country, a supposedly Catholic and Christian Government sending down squads of police in the dead of night to carry out a raid on the home of a parish priest. I rise to protest in this House as a Catholic Deputy and on behalf of every Catholic in this State.
*(Interruptions).*

**Mr. O.J. Flanagan:** Deputies may laugh——

**Mr. Moloney:** And the Knights of Columbanus thrown in.

**Mr. O.J. Flanagan:** This is not the first time the Knights of Columbanus have been criticised in this House.

**Mr. Moloney:** It will not be the last.

**Mr. O.J. Flanagan:** I want to protest against this incident. I want to protest in the name of every decent [1947] person in this country who dislikes police raids in the dead of night. What has happened in the case of Father Fahy is something which should not happen, and I trust it will not happen in the future. It has left uneasiness in every home in the country and it has left insecurity as to the privacy of the home. We have no guarantee that similar police raids will not be carried out on the homes of other citizens who, Fianna Fáil may think, deserve the same treatment as Father Fahy. Does it not look stupid and silly when nothing was found? There were no grounds for the report, no grounds for the rumour, no justification for the raid, and the raid was entirely unworthy and unnecessary. The Government blundered and they should apologise to Father Fahy and should inform their secret service that they were at fault and that there was no truth whatever in the report which the police received.

I shall wind up by asking for a fuller explanation of this conduct from the Minister for Justice and by asking the Government to give a fuller explanation. I may say that it has left great uneasiness because it is believed that what has happened to Father Fahy may happen to the Bishop of Cork or anybody else.

**Mr. Galvin:** Did your Government apologise in 1929 when they imprisoned him for three months?

**An Ceann Comhairle:** The Minister for Justice.

**Mr. Galvin:** They did not apologise in 1929.

**Mr. Coogan:** Go to China.

**Minister for Justice (Mr. Traynor):** It is not unusual for Deputy Flanagan to exaggerate and on this occasion he has grossly exaggerated or has tried to exaggerate the facts. I could answer the Deputy with a great deal more freedom if it were not for the fact that to deal fully with this matter might prejudice the fair trial of charges which are or will be before the Courts. The men whom Garda were seeking [1978] had been in lawful custody under a Peace Commissioner's warrant.

**Mr. O.J. Flanagan:** I do not wish to interrupt the Minister——

**Mr. Traynor:** It is better that I should say nothing——

**Mr. O.J. Flanagan:** The Minister has explained——

**Donnchadh Ó Briain:** Keep quiet.

**An Ceann Comhairle:** Order!

**Mr. Traynor:** It is better that I should say nothing about how they ceased to be in such custody. The Garda received information confirming reports which were circulating widely in the locality, that the men were being harboured in the residence of Very Rev. John Fahy, P.P., Lusmagh. There was no adequate reason to doubt the correctness of this information, because Father Fahy was openly associated with those men and, indeed, had made no secret of it. He had, in fact, been seen and heard by the Garda congratulating them on the actions for which they had been arrested and on which charges were being brought against them. It was imperative, therefore, that the Garda should visit Fr. Fahy's house with a view to effecting their arrest if the men were there. They would have failed in their duty if they had not endeavoured to have these men restored to lawful custody.

There has been criticism of the hour at which the visit was made, but if it had been made when Fr. Fahy was attending to his priestly duties, or when people were about, I have no doubt that it would be said that this was done on purpose so as to embarrass the parish priest as much as possible, and of course, in view of what had happened some days previously, the Garda had to reckon with the possibility of a breach of the peace, the likelihood of which was lessened by an early visit. I repeat I take full responsibility for the action taken.

**Mr. O.J. Flanagan:** Shame, shame.

The Dáil adjourned at 10.50 p.m. until 3 p.m. on Wednesday, 13th May, 1959.

This was vintage Flanagan, wringing every last drop of political advantage from the opportunity presented. Parts of his contribution can only be described as unintentionally funny and at times even hilarious.

Fr John at that time did not fit the image of 'the aged parish priest'. He was still jumping ditches and stone walls with The East Galway Hunt. He hadn't the cut of a man about to receive the President's £5 Centenarian Bounty from Seán T. O'Kelly.

According to Deputy Flanagan, Fr Fahy innocently inquired from Chief Superintendent Mooney, Portlaoise 'What is wrong?' We are meant to believe that the reason for the strong Garda presence was a complete mystery to him. He certainly didn't think on that May morning that Mooney and his men were in Lusmagh to listen to the dawn chorus in Cloghan Castle wood.

Comparing the systematic oppression and denial of human liberties and the ruthless suppression of religious practice in communist-dominated China and Russia to the search of Fr Fahy's house was in the words of Justice Minister, Oscar Traynor, 'somewhat of an exaggeration'.

The two Cardinals, Mindszenty in Hungary and Stepinac in Croatia (then part of the greater Yugoslavia), had been through Stalinist show trials and had been subjected to horrific torture in vain attempts to crush them in body and spirit. Fr John's case wasn't quite like that.

And as for Oliver J. becoming apoplectic over 'every parish priest and curate in the country blushing with shame, with horror and indignation', no doubt most of these good men managed to recover eventually to live full and rewarding lives.

Fr Fahy likened the many raids carried out at that time in Lusmagh by guards and detectives to the activities of the Black and Tans, as he reported in the July 1959 issue of the *Lia Fáil* newspaper.

*The Irish Press* 12 May 1959 in a report headed 'Re-arrest of three men' noted that

> Three of the five Lusmagh men missing since they left Banagher Garda Station on May 1 were rearrested by gardaí yesterday. They were apprehended when cattle were being driven from Mr. Frank Barry's farm at Cogran. It was the third occasion on which cattle were driven off those lands during the past fortnight.
>
> Later, the three men – Denis Kelly, Newtown; Noel Moran, Ashgrove, and Brendan Killeen, Newtown – appeared before District Justice McGahon at Tullamore Court, where depositions against six other Lusmagh men were in progress, and they were remanded in custody until Friday.
>
> The two other men still being sought by the gardaí are John Joe Kenny, Cogran, and Patrick Glynn, Gortraven.

A second piece in *The Irish Press* on the same day reported as
follows:

**FIVE OFFALY MEN ARE SENT FOR TRIAL**

AT a Special Court in Tullamore yesterday, District
Justice Hugh McGahon returned for trial, to Birr
Circuit Court on July 14 next, five of the six Lusmagh,
Offaly, men charged with the forcible rescue of five
neighbours from Banagher Garda Station ten days
previously. They were allowed bail.

Informations were refused in the case of the sixth man,
James Glynn. The five returned for trial are: John
Kelly, Michael Kelly and Francis Kelly, brothers; Patrick
Killeen and Thomas Moran.

The men arrived in Tullamore from Mountjoy Jail at 10.30 a.m.
escorted by two squad cars. On the way through the town they
waved to the local people, who, with an air of expectancy, had
been lingering along the main street. At the courthouse the men
were taken in by the back door.

Many cars drove into Tullamore about 10.45 a.m. carrying
farmers, friends and relatives of the men from the Lusmagh
area. They had met at Lusmagh Cross at 10 a.m.

With many Tullamore people they crowded into the courthouse just before eleven o'clock and by the time the court proceedings got under way more than 100 people filled the court-
room.

Justice Hugh McGahon who presided over the sittings of the
District Court which dealt with the *Lia Fáil* cases made a number
of conciliatory remarks from time to time. He cleverly linked the
case of the men who rescued their friends from Banagher Garda
Barracks with the hope that the men on the run would give
themselves up and hasten a final resolution to the whole affair.

For example, when the question of bail for the six rescuers
arose at the end of a hearing on 9 May, the Justice refused the
application but said he would consider the request at the next
court hearing in a few days time. He went on to say that this case
was inextricably bound up with the missing five and that if they
gave themselves up 'that would prove a decisive factor in his
consideration of bail'. He concluded his remarks on that occasion by saying that he hoped his comments 'would be conveyed
to the escapees before the court sat again'.

At a District Court sitting two weeks later when three of the five recaptured men were bound to the peace, Judge McGahon said to the men, 'All I want from you is an undertaking to keep the peace. There may be other means of ventilating your grievances than the driving off of cattle.'

Dinny Kelly said that 'they had never used any violence towards the police. What they had done was done as a protest against the ineptitude of the Land Commission.' Concluding that day's sitting Justice McGahon offered the opinion that 'it was to the credit of the defendants that they had brandished their sticks at the cattle and not at the police and he believed that what had occurred originally was in the nature of a demonstration rather than an act with criminal intent. When the attempt was made to rescue the men there was no evidence that the present defendants had assaulted the Gardaí. They had availed themselves of the opportunity to escape.'

Significantly, the Justice said he had his own opinion about the second attempt to drive the cattle off and it was 'open to an interpretation other than that it was a mere repetition of the previous offence'.

It was quickly becoming clear from the available evidence that the state, while determined to uphold the primacy of the law of the land, was equally keen to resolve the whole affair in a manner which would not inflame local passions any further in Lusmagh or indeed further afield.

Politically, of course, de Valera, the presidential candidate, and his Government were anxious to ensure that their carefully planned election and referendum campaigns would not be derailed over an issue that they felt lacked widespread support.

Three days after the Tullamore sitting of the District Court where Noel Moran entered a bond to keep the peace for two years, the matter relating to Dinny Kelly and Ben Killeen was finally resolved in Kilbeggan Court. Overleaf is the report of those proceedings which appeared in the *Irish Times* on 27 May.

Pat Glynn and John Joe Kenny who had been rearrested on 2 June in fields near their home refused to take bail at a special court in Banagher Garda Station before Kieran Kenny PC. They appeared in custody, according to the *Irish Independent* 13 June 1959, at Tullamore 'on charges arising out of incidents at

Banagher on 1 May when with three other men they escaped from custody. District Justice McGahon adjourned the cases to Thursday'.

## TWO BANAGHER MEN IT GO TO PRISON 27/5/59
### Refuse to sign bonds

AT Kilbeggan Court yesterday, two of the three men from Lusmagh, Banagher, who pleaded guilty at Tullamore District Court last week to charges connected with driving cattle in the area, told District Justice McGahon that they were unwilling to enter into a bond to keep the peace for two years. They were sentenced to 21 days' imprisonment.

They explained that they considered entering into the bond would mean backing down on the protest they made on May Day when a herd of cattle was driven off the land of Mr. Frank Barry at Lusmagh.

The two men, Denis Kelly and Brendan Killeen, with another man, Noel Moran, had pleaded guilty at Tullamore to obstructing the police at Lusmagh and later at Banagher police station and to an amended charge of escaping from custody on May 1st. They were sentenced to 21 days' imprisonment and given a suspended sentence for the same period on the other charges provided they kept the peace for a year. At Tullamore court they were bound to the peace for two years and directed that they enter into a bond of £100 each, with one surety of £100 to keep the peace. The justice added on that occasion that if they failed to keep the peace they could be brought up for sentence at any time. He said he considered it better than a suspensory sentence because they would not know what sentence the court might then give.

The legal representatives of the defendants at Tullamore stated, after an adjournment, that the men would enter into the bond. The surety was forthcoming for Noel Moran; in the case of the others the matter was adjourned to Kilbeggan Court yesterday.

### "BACKING DOWN"

When the case was called, Denis Kelly—as spokesman—said that they had decided that entering the bond would mean that they were backing down on the protest they made on May Day. They were not entering on the bond.

Mr. Niall McCarthy, for the prosecution, said that it was not in any way suggested by police that the land agitation was general. "It is known to be formented by a group or person who has not been before the Court on any occasion," he said.

Justice McGahon said that, in the circumstances, he considered he had given the defendants every opportunity to avoid prison sentences by entering into the bond to keep the peace.

Denis Kelly — We appreciate what you have done. It is a matter of principle with us.

Mr. McCarthy—Might I request that the other defendant speak for himself?

### TO SERVE TERM

The justice said that it was his business that the peace in the area should be kept. He appreciated that it might be a matter of principle with the defendants. The only way he could keep the peace was by imposing sentence in respect of each of the charges of 21 days with hard labour on each defendant. In respect of the first sentence, it would have to be served now. The sentences on the other charges would be suspensory and would not be enforced if each of the defendants kept the peace for a year. If they broke the law in the period they would have to, be served.

Kelly asked if he could address the Court, and the justice refused, saying that his function was to administer justice. He could only conclude that anything Kelly would say to the Court would be by way of propaganda.

When Kelly attempted to speak, the justice told him that he was represented by eminent counsel at the previous hearing and they had said everything that might be said. Anything further Kelly might have to say could be said in the market square and meeting places of the country which were open to him.

Kelly—On May Day we took action—

Justice—Please obey my order.

Kelly—We will have a day in the market square.

The next case was called and Kelly walked over to a press table and told reporters: "We are carrying out the policy of Lia Fáil, as it has been proclaimed."

At the special court in Tullamore the two men, according to *The Midland Tribune*, 18 June 1959, again refused bail and 'accordingly the Justice returning them for trial at Birr Circuit Court in July remanded them in custody and they were removed under strong Garda escort'.

There were further remands both in this case and in the one concerning the five charged with the rescue, to the Central Criminal Court in November when all seven pleaded guilty to having obstructed Gardaí in the execution of their duties and to being a party to an escape from Garda custody of two of them.

Suspensory sentences, a direction to enter bail and an obligation to keep the peace for twelve months were imposed. *The Midland Tribune*, 21 November 1959, noted that 'All seven men offered an apology in court to John Francis Barry, Banagher from whose lands cattle had been driven and promised to treat him in a neighbourly spirit in future. Supt McCague said that all the men who were farmers' sons were of excellent character and hard-working. Mr Justice Teevan said that these decent young men were led into this agitation. He was pleased to be assured by Supt McCague that the agitation had now subsided and was forgotten and all was peaceful.'

Some of the other noteworthy local incidents associated with *Lia Fáil* agitation at that time included the burning of a hayshed and its contents belonging to Bertie Barry and the burning of the thatched house recently vacated by the O'Leary family who had moved to a Land Commission farm in Rath, between Birr and Kilcormac.

Dr Murphy, drawing on a confidential source stated that *Lia Fáil* had planned to blow up Bertie Barry's house at Invernisk, Shannongrove, located off the Banagher–Eyrecourt road and that it had obtained the necessary explosives. However, he states 'someone informed the authorities and the plan was foiled.'

## CHAPTER TWENTY-ONE

## *Carnival Time*

The 1959 two-week-long Banagher Carnival, arranged for the purpose of raising funds for a swimming pool, was due to run from Sunday, 24 May to Sunday, 7 June. The usual core ingredients for a successful parish extravaganza were arranged in the months and weeks leading up to the start of the festivities which were outlined in this programme of events in *The Midland Tribune* 16 May:

BANAGHER BANGS AGAIN !

**BANAGHER 1959 CARNIVAL**

SUNDAY, MAY 24th—SUNDAY, JUNE 7th

Opening with Water Ski-ing Exhibition on the Shannon 2.70 p.m
Sunday, May 24th.

*C.I.E. CRUISER ST. BRENDAN AVAILABLE FOR TRIPS*

McCORMACK'S CARNIVAL AMUSEMENTS

CATERING BY LADIES' COMMITTEE

DANCING IN HYNES' MARQUEE 9—1

Sunday, May 24th—Earl Gill. Admission: 6/-
Tuesday, May 26th—Kevin Woods. Admission: 5 -
Thursday, May 28th—Ralph Sylvester. Adm.: 5/-
Friday, May 29th—Ciaran Kelly. Ceili and Old Time.
Admission: 4/-.
Sunday, May 31st—Johnny Butler. Admission: 5/-.
Tuesday, June 2nd—Donie Collins. Admission: 5/-.
Wednesday, June 3rd—Earl Gill. (Final Night Old-
Time Waltz Competition). Admission: 4/-.
Thursday, June 4th—Chick Smith. Admission: 5/-.
Sunday, June 7th—Johnny Pickering. Monster Ceili.
Admission: 5/-.

Look out for details of Soap Box Derby Thurs., May 28th.

Also Children's Day, Fancy Dress Parade and Step Dancing,
Sunday, May 31st.

Final Parade, Industrial and Agricultural, Sunday, June 7th

*RAFFLES NIGHTLY IN THE MARQUEE.*

The official opening of the carnival on this occasion would not be performed either by the local Fianna Fáil TD Kieran Egan or by the recently appointed parish priest Mgr Francis O'Donohoe. Instead the invitation to launch the eagerly anticipated event was extended to someone who in the eyes of Fr Fahy constituted with de Valera and Lemass the unholy trinity responsible for most of the ills and woes of Ireland, none other than The Minister for Lands and Fisheries, Erskine Childers TD.

Fr John was furious when he heard about the ministerial invitation and set about reducing its impact on the opening-day attendance. He drafted the following leaflet and arranged that an adequate supply be printed in time for distribution by young people from Lusmagh in the neighbouring parishes of West Offaly and East Galway before the carnival opening.

# Freemason Carnival

## CHILDERS
### A FREEMASON
### A HERETIC
### CHAIRMAN OF PROTESTANT
### CHURCH BODY
#### INVITED TO OPEN
*Banagher Carnival*

##### AN INSULT TO CATHOLICS
##### AND IRISHMEN OF OFFALY

## BOYCOTT THE
## CARNIVAL

Fr Fahy's fierce denunciations of the event from the altar and elsewhere met initially with some support, particularly from his own parish. The carnival committee responded by issuing complimentary tickets to a number of young Lusmagh people for various dancing attractions and by the end of the first week resistance began to crumble. It was now very much a case of the spirit being willing but the flesh being weak as the magnetic attraction of Banagher's version of the Ballroom of Romance gradually proved irresistible to the full-blooded Romeos and Juliets of Lusmagh.

The Gardaí eventually established that the carnival boycott leaflets were supplied by a Portarlington-based printing works. *The Midland Tribune* reported that

> arising from the Garda visit to the printer, proceedings
> will be instituted against the owners.

The carnival committee had some of the most prominent Fianna Fáil activists in the area among its members. They had read the extreme anti-Fianna Fáil material which had been published monthly since the previous August in the *Lia Fáil* newspaper. There can be little doubt but that the choice of Mr

Childers to do the honours in Banagher on that occasion was anything but a haphazard one.

Among the local worthies present on the platform which had been set up on the Shannonside Town Park for the official opening ceremony were Kieran Egan TD, Kieran Kenny, a long-serving member of the Fianna Fáil National Executive and Jim Fanning, Proprietor/Editor of *The Midland Tribune*. Fanning also had strong links with Fianna Fáil and would later be nominated by that party to serve on the RTÉ Authority. In the following issue of *The Midland Tribune* (30 May), Mr Fanning gave extensive coverage to the previous Sunday's official opening and, rubbing further salt into Fr Fahy's wounds, quoted the speech delivered by Mr.Childers in full. The report claimed that

> The town was thronged for the occasion, business was brisk in ice-cream and refreshments, and besides the great number of motorists there were myriads of cyclists pouring in from every road. The local Gardaí were reinforced to meet with the traffic problem and Gardaí were on point-duty at every crossing.

Why Fr Fahy singled out Erskine Childers for such personalised attacks is difficult to explain. Admittedly the minister had said since being appointed to the Department of Lands that the state could not make sufficient funds available to redistribute enough land to meet the needs of all smallholders. He had little time for what he called 'tough action groups'. 'The Land Commission', he stated, 'will not be coerced by any kind of agitation whatever – peaceful or otherwise.' Mr Childers resisted *Lia Fáil* pressure to break up certain large holdings. According to Terence Dooley in *The Land for the People* the minister said that 'the employment lost would far outweigh the social advantages of their acquisition.'

This was enough to alienate and enrage even further Fr Fahy and his followers. But the minister's father, also Erskine, had been one of the most unyielding republicans opposed to the Treaty, a consideration that seemed lost on Fr John.

Writing about Cumann na mBan and its fiery leader, Countess Markievicz, the historian F. S. L. Lyons (p. 455) stated that it was fiercely, even virulently, republican, and followed closely the line taken during the Treaty debates by such speakers as Kathleen Clarke, Mary MacSwiney and Erskine Childers. For this reason it was christened by the wags the 'women and Childers party'.

During the Civil War Childers was captured, court-martialled and executed.

Fr Fahy's attempted boycott of the carnival heightened the already tense atmosphere in Banagher and Lusmagh. Two of the five Lusmagh lads who had escaped from custody in Banagher Garda Barracks were still free. There was a huge increase in Garda activity in the area since the incidents which had begun on May Day.

Both areas were staunch Fianna Fáil strongholds. At the by-election in Laois–Offaly in 1956, caused by the death of Bill Davin (Labour), Lusmagh voted, according to the tallymen, 161 to 8 for Kieran Egan, the Banagher-based candidate who easily won the seat. There surely was many an occasion when long-term Fianna Fáil supporters, active in or supportive of *Lia Fáil* and Fr Fahy, experienced great difficulty in attempting to reconcile totally conflicting viewpoints. And finally it should be borne in mind that Banagher and Lusmagh were and still are interdependent and share so many commercial, family and sporting links.

Defiant to the last, Fr John claimed in the July 1959 issue of *Lia Fáil* (No. 8, p. 2) that the carnival in Banagher had run at a loss:

# Ill Timed Carnival Lost £1,000

A CARNIVAL in Banagher which opened with a ceremony by the Minister for Lands, Erskine Childers some weeks ago was boycotted by the people of the area. The failure of the carnival is said to have cost the Fianna Fail sponsors about £1,000 of a loss.

The carnival was ill timed. It came at a period when the district was in a ferment and when some of the most indefatigable workers for Lia Fail were being harried and arrested.

The people of Lusmagh and Banagher showed their sympathy for Lia Fail and their contempt for Childers and his land policy by staying away from the carnival. It was an effective gesture and will teach the fun promoters to think twice before inviting an enemy of the landless men and the impoverished farm workers down to officiate again.

Perhaps it is appropriate to conclude this chapter about the Banagher Carnival and the claims made by Fr Fahy about Erskine Childers in the 'boycott leaflet' by quoting the following passage from a long letter written by Aindrias Ó Caoimh, the Attorney-General, dated 23 July 1959 to Bishop Philbin regarding aspects of events which had recently unfolded in Lusmagh:

The Minister for Lands, Mr Childers, was invited to open the Carnival. I enclose a copy of a Garda Report on an attempted boycott of the Carnival, and also dealing with the publication of 'posters' very defamatory of Mr Childers. While the truth of the defamatory remarks would be immaterial, it may be worth informing your Lordship that Mr Childers is not a Freemason nor does he happen to be a member of the Protestant Church Body, and that while he is, it is true, a member of the Church of Ireland, his wife is a Catholic and his marriage, which was celebrated in Paris, was attended by a representative of the Archbishop of Paris. The child of the marriage is being brought up as a Catholic. I would expect no less of Mr Childers as an honourable man, but others may not be aware of his full and ready compliance with his pre-nuptial undertaking.

(*The 'child of the marriage', Nessa Childers, graduated in Arts and Psychology from Trinity College, Dublin. She qualified as a Psychoanalyst and in 1993 she set up and lectured on an MSc course in Psychoanalytic Psychotherapy in TCD.*

*Today she is a member of the European Parliament [Labour] representing Ireland East [Leinster] constituency.* – J.M.)

*1. John Fahy, Birroge, Kilnadeema, Fr John Fahy's father.*

Séaġan Ua Fáṫaiġ, Cluain Ḟeaṛta

*2. Fr John Fahy ordination photo 1919*

3. *Fr John(right) and his brother, Fr Martin Fahy, outside St Brendan's Cathedral, Loughrea, before the hunt set off, 1938.*

4. See Bishop Dignan's letter to Fr Fahy 4th August 1945, shortly after his appointment to Lusmagh. 'The Nuns' House' used for many years as a holiday home by the Sisters from Portiuncula Hospital. It is located on the Lusmagh (Offaly) side of the Shannon and was photographed from the Galway side at the quay wall at Meelick beside Treacy's house and farmyard. The recently inaugurated walking route – The HyMany Way – between Meelick and Ballinasloe begins at this location. The house was built by Tom Madden, Eyrecourt, in the 1920s for Tom and Pat Colohan who farmed the adjoining land. Bertie Barry acquired the farm after the death of the Colohan brothers in the late 1930s.

5. Fr James Cogavin PP, Eyrecourt, and Fr John Fahy in the procession from St Rynagh's Church, Banagher to the new Vocational School, September 1953. Sean Moylan TD, Minister for Education, is second from right at back.

6. Pictured at the blessing and official opening of Banagher Vocational School, September 1953. L-R: Canon James Earley, Ferbane, Fr Patrick Masterson, Banagher (partially hidden), Dr James McNamee Bishop of Ardagh and Clonmacnoise, Fr John Fahy and altar servers Oliver Moran and myself, Jim Madden. I subsequently served as Principal of this school.

7. Major Denis and Mrs Bowes-Daly with their daughter and dogs in front of the castle where the Lusmagh lads spent some days after leaving Fr John's house in May 1959.

# EVENING HERALD

VOL. 68. No. 706.  Dublin, Tuesday, May 5, 1959.  PRICE TWOPENCE

# DAWN SWOOP ON RESIDENCE OF PARISH PRIEST

**EXCLUSIVE PICTURES**

## Big Co. Offaly search for rescued men

*From JAMES McGUIRE, Herald Staff Reporter*

IN A LIGHTNING DAWN STRIKE FROM DUBLIN CASTLE THIS MORNING SIX SQUAD CARS OF METROPOLITAN GARDAÍ RAIDED THE HOUSE OF VERY REV. JOHN FAHY, THE 64-YEAR-OLD PARISH PRIEST OF LUSMAGH, BANAGHER, CO. OFFALY, IN SEARCH OF THE FIVE PRISONERS FORCIBLY RESCUED FROM BANAGHER GARDA STATION ON FRIDAY.

Fifty police, including numerous plain-clothes men in six black limousines, guided by the squad cars from Birr, swept into the Lusmagh parish shortly before 5 a.m. as dawn was breaking.

The raid was led by Chief Superintendent M. Mooney, Portlaoise, and their first stop was on the road leading to the parochial house. The house is about 30 yards back from Lusmagh Cross, where the Church faces three converging roads.

*Very Rev. John Fahy, P.P., at the door of his house after the raid.*

*The scene in front of Father Fahy's house this morning during the Gardaí raid. The police in the doorway are interviewing Father Fahy.*

## SPRING SHOW OPENS

Shimmering satins and the champagne sparkle in the air spin the live-day R.D.S. Spring Show and Industries Fair a real spring-like start at the flower-decked Ballsbridge grounds to-day.

*(shown on Page Two)*

## Boy was found wandering

A boy who apparently before Garda Croughan in the Children's Court...

## Door opened

## Consultations

## Were stopped

## Examined place

## Searched rooms

## Reported staying in castle

## Trouble over land led to shooting

### Window forced

### Rifles withdrawn

## University paper banned

## Stock car promoter charged

*Paris says...*

that Suits are Softer and Lighter this Summer!

*Lovelle's*

### WEATHER

*The Gardaí leaving (after the raid on Father Fahy's house, this morning, with Chief Supt. Mooney, far right, in plain clothes.*

*"I prefer the Western call but he keeps falling off."*

*9. Fr Fahy pictured in Abbey with his Irish Wolfhound, Bran.*

10. *Photo taken at the wedding of Tom Fahy (Fr John's nephew) and Maureen Rooney in 1961. L-R: Fr. Kevin Burke, Pat Fahy, Canon Mitchell, Tom and Maureen, Kathleen Rooney, Fr John.*

11. *Pictured in June 1967 after the blessing of the renovated church of St. Cronan, Lusmagh were L-R: Fr John Fahy, Abbey, Bishop Thomas Ryan (Clonfert 1963-1983), Fr John Glynn P.P., Lusmagh and Monsignor P.E. MacFhinn UCG.*

12. Pictured in 1968 at the wedding of John Holohan, Abbey and Frances Killeavy, Tullamore. L-R: Fr Sean Murray, Portumna, Fr John Fahy, Fr Gerard Holohan ODC, Clarendon St, Dublin, Fr Bannon P.P., Tullamore and Fr Philip McGahey P.P., Castletown-Geoghegan, Co. Westmeath. Fr McGahey was closely associated with Fr Fahy in campaigns to have large estates divided among smallholders. He was regularly in attendance for court appearances by members and supporters of Lia Fáil and donated the proceeds from dances which he ran to support the Lia Fáil cause.

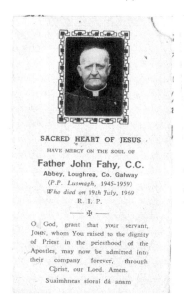

SACRED HEART OF JESUS

HAVE MERCY ON THE SOUL OF

**Father John Fahy, C.C.**

Abbey, Loughrea, Co. Galway

(P.P. Lusmagh, 1945-1959)

Who died on 19th July, 1969

R. I. P.

—— ✠ ——

O God, grant that your servant, JOHN, whom You raised to the dignity of Priest in the priesthood of the Apostles, may now be admitted into their company forever, through Christ, our Lord. Amen.

Suaimhneas síoraí dá anam

GO SDEANA DIA TRÓCAIRE
AR ANAM AN

Athar Seán Ó Fathaigh

Mainistir Chinéil Fhéichín,
Baile Locha Riach

(S.P. Lusmagh, 1945-1959)
a fuair bás 19 Iúil, 1969

R. I. P.

A Dhia, a thug dó do sheirbhíseach, Seán, bheith ina shagart aspalda, tré ghrádam sagairt a bhronnadh air; deonaigh dó, impímid, bheith i gcuideachtain na naom', go deo tré nár dTiarna, Íosa Críost. Amén.

Suaimhneas síoraí dá anam uasal.

13. In Memoriam

14. Pictured is a group from the Lusmagh/Meelick area in Abbey Churchyard on the day the new headstone to Fr Fahy was unveiled by Ruaidhri Ó Brádaigh in 1970. Back L-R: Annie Gibbons, Paddy Sullivan, Nell Brennan, Bridie Killeen, Kitty Ambrose, Stephen McGarry, Ben Killeen, Kathleen Sullivan, Colm Birmingham, Patrick Whelan, Margaret Sullivan, Mary Whelan, Seamus Kelly. Front L-R: Brendan, Ethna, Micheal, Concepta and Gerardine McGarry.

*15. Mrs Nora Cooney, Bullaun, Loughrea, niece of Fr Fahy pictured in 2009 at a family celebration.*

16. Hurling Heroes. The six Cooney brothers from Bullaun, sons of Nora and grand-nephews of Fr Fahy, pictured in Croke Park on St Patrick's Day 1993 with the Tommy Moore Cup after their club Sarsfields (Bullaun/New Inn) had beaten Toomevara in the All-Ireland Club final. The previous year they had won their first title after victory over Kilmallock. All six played in the 1992 final. Jimmy had retired by 1993. Standing L-R: Joe, Brendan, Peter, Michael. Front L-R: Jimmy and Pakie (Capt.).

17. Tom Fahy, a nephew of Fr John, and his wife Maureen pictured at their home in Roo, Craughwell in 2010.

*18. Two photos of Peadar O'Donnell (1893-1986).*

*19. 'Bishop of the Land War' Dr Patrick Duggan, Bishop of Clonfert (1871-1896). The GAA sportsfield in Ballinasloe is named after him.*

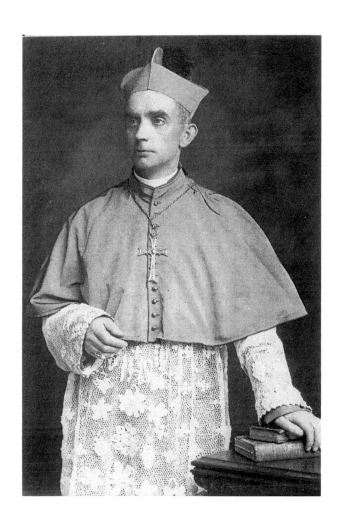

*20. Dr John Dignan, Bishop of Clonfert 1924-1953.*

*21. Dr William Philbin, Bishop of Clonfert 1953-1962.*

22. *Ruaidhrí Ó Brádaigh and his wife Patsy, pictured at their home in Roscommon in 2010.*

23. Mrs Margaret Kelly, Lusmagh, one-time secretary of Lia Fáil pictured with the author at the launch of her Collected Poems in Lusmagh Community Hall, July 2009.

CHAPTER TWENTY-TWO

## *The Bishop's Pastoral Letter: The Homecoming*

Bishop Philbin was clearly becoming more concerned by the day, both from his own observations and from representations which were reaching him about events in Lusmagh, and in the neighbouring parishes of the diocese across the Shannon in east Galway. Typical of the letters received by him at that time was the following one from a clearly concerned parishioner in Lusmagh.

Lusmagh
Banagher
May 17th 1959

Dear Dr. Filban, *(sic)*
I would like to draw your attention to the unfortunate state of affairs in the parish of Lusmagh.

I suggest that you send a priest there to see the parents and the unfortunate youths and have a talk with each of them. The parents are simply distraught at the state the unfortunate parish priest has got their sons into. The youths are disgusted at what they experienced in Mountjoy jail. Obscene language and blasphemy from prisoners there the likes of which they never heard before. They are out on bail now altogether against Fr Fahy's wishes. There are two of them still on the run. They, it appears would have given themselves up but he would not allow them. Nobody knows where he has them. The parents of all, even those who have no child in the trouble, are very upset at the whole state of affairs in the parish. It is a sad state indeed, esp for the future religious outlook.

However, it was a very critical, robust letter from a senior diocesan priest, Fr James Cogavin PP, Eyrecourt, which barely stopped short of outright criticism of Dr Philbin's apparent 'softly, softly' approach to Fr Fahy, that finally spurred him to take immediate action.

He prepared the following pastoral letter – quoted in full in the *Irish Press* on Wednesday 10 June – 'to be read without comment in place of a sermon at all Masses on Sunday June 7th' in those areas which already had or were likely to experience agrarian unrest.

## Bishop's warning against land agitation

A WARNING that "no individual or group has the right to take over land or other property on their own authority, to claim ownership, or to purport to hand over ownership to others in defiance of the law of the land," was contained in a letter from the Bishop of Clonfert, Most Rev. Dr. Philbin, which was read at Masses in a number of parishes of the Diocese last Sunday. 10/6/59.

The Bishop's letter was read at Masses in the parish churches of Lusmagh (Banagher), Portumna, Fahy, Laurencetown, Eyrecourt and Killimor. The letter was addressed, in each case, to the parish priest.

The following is the text of the letter, made available to the Press by Very Rev. M. H. O'Callaghan, Adm., Secretary to His Lordship:

"My dear Father, I feel that events that have occurred in certain parishes, and reports that have reached me make it necessary that I should warn the faithful, through you, their pastor, against activities that are contrary to the Christian obligation of justice and charity towards others, and of obedience to the laws of the State.

"I must ask you, therefore, to remind your people of the following principles: No individual or group of individuals has the right to take over land or other property on their own authority, to claim ownership or to purport to hand over ownership to others in defiance of the law of the land.

"No individual or group of individuals, has the right to interfere with the use of land or other property by its lawful owners or lawful occupiers; thus, it is a sin against the Seventh Commandment to interfere with stock or drive it off land, to till or otherwise change the condition of land which is held lawfully by other people. The fact that a group combine in activities of these kinds does not lessen the guilt of the individuals concerned.

### Condemned

"Secret societies and conspiracies have always been condemned by the Church, and there is a statute of this ecclesiastical province, dealing expressly with them. The offence is greater, not less, when a group are responsible for it, and, in such a case, the danger is also great that injustice will be perpetrated more extensively, and with less realisation of the personal guilt that attaches to each individual involved.

"In this connection, one has to consider not merely injury to property, but also to the character, the freedom of action, the peace of mind and health of those who may be singled out for victimisation. The sin of injustice against the rights of others may be committed in many ways, and sometimes the

harm done may far exceed the intention of those originating it.

"I have, therefore, to ask you to warn the faithful in your pastoral care that anyone who engages, as an individual or as a member of a group, in activities of the kind referred to in this letter, is sinning against both justice and charity.

### Permissible

"To make legitimate political or social demands, to seek by legitimate means changes in the law, or in the administration of the law, are courses which, as everyone knows, are permissible to any individual or group.

"But to conspire to injure the property or the rights of others, or to disobey the laws by which the peace and order of the community are maintained is an offence against the law of God.

"No Catholic may remain a member of any organisation carrying out activities such as are condemned in this instruction. There may be many persons, perhaps even all of those concerned, who without clearly understanding the moral principles governing such matters, have become involved in the activities here referred to. I sincerely hope that they will take this warning to heart and cease forthwith from doing things that are sinful.

"Parents and all those who are responsible for guiding young people are called upon to co-operate in seeing that this instruction is faithfully observed, and that the peaceful and charitable relationships that should exist in every locality are not imperilled by acts of injustice and violence."

Dr Murphy in *Radical Priests* stated that

> Fr Fahy himself read it at Lusmagh, but typically read it with congenial amendments.

Whatever about 'congenial amendments', it is clear from the following letter that while reading the pastoral Fr Fahy's normally vibrant vocal cords experienced a sudden, temporary loss of power.

Lusmagh
6-6-59

Your Lordship,
A letter from you was read at Mass today. It was read in such a way that only those very near the priest could hear what was said in it.

As we and others would like to know what was in this letter so as to obey what was said in it we would like if this letter was read again and explained to us so that we could hear and know what you said as different stories are going around Lusmagh all day.

For great reasons I am afraid to give my name.
*A Worried but Obedient Parishioner*

The bishop's letter was notable for its clarity, lack of ambiguity and repudiation of the philosophy and actions of Fr Fahy and *Lia Fáil*, without specifically mentioning either by name.

Undeterred by this latest episcopal uppercut, Fr John was probably strengthened even further in his determination to accord a heroes' welcome home on 15 June to Dinny Kelly and Ben Killeen after they had completed their twenty-one-day stay in Mountjoy Jail. Still smarting from the appearance of Erskine Childers at the carnival opening just three weeks earlier, he decided that he would 'show the flag' in Banagher first, before heading out to Lusmagh for the official 'welcome home' ceremony on that Monday evening.

Fr John, flanked by Dinny and Ben, led a group of about forty Lusmagh people from the Market Square to the Bridge and back up again before heading out the Lusmagh Road. The procession was headed by well-known Lusmagh musicians, John Coughlan on the concert flute with Johnnie Larkin on the kettledrum and Martin Kelly from Meelick playing an accordion all providing stirring marching airs. At intervals Fr John, wearing his ubiquitous black beret, barked out military commands '*Clé, Dheas, Clé, Dheas*', and occasionally glanced backwards to ensure that his platoon maintained proper marching formation.

Apart from a few provocative comments from one or two bystanders, the event, which had the potential to erupt at short notice, passed off relatively peacefully. Harry Milner, one of Fr John's comrades in the parade, had his car taken to a local sandpit at the back of the convent while he was in Lusmagh at the celebrations which lasted into the night. *The Midland Tribune* on the following weekend (20 June 1959) described the homecoming in the following way:

---

GARDAI KEEP WATCH ON MIDNIGHT MEETING.

# INVASION OF BANAGHER
T, /6/1959 **TOWN BY LUSMAGH**
## LAND AGITATORS

**A** Demonstration took place in the town of Banagher on Monday night on the occasion of the arrival home from Mountjoy Prison of two young Lusmagh men who had served three week's in prison for assaulting, obstructing and resisting the Gardai on May Day—the beginning of the Lusmagh Land Agitation—after they had driven cattle from the lands of Mr. Frank Barry, at Cogran, Lusmagh, that day.

The two young men are Denis Kelly and Brendan Killeen, both of Newtown, who have acknowledged their affiliation to the local agrarian organisation, Lia Fail.

*The demonstrators, numbering forty-three in all, formed up in the Square, Banagher, on Monday night and were headed by six musicians playing two accordeons, flutes and a drum. The procession was led by the Very Rev. John Fahy. P.P.. Lusmagh, who marched between the two returned prisoners while alongside the main body walked Mr. W. H. Milner, of Walsh Island, Portarlington, waving a newspaper in his hand.*

The demonstrators filed out the Lusmagh road and some distance out halted. After a brief few words to those present Rev. Fr. Fahy left the ranks and drove ahead towards Lusmagh in his car. The remainder reformed and marched to Lusmagh Cross where Rev. Father Fahy awaited them at a specially erected platform.

On arrival the numbers had now increased to something over a hundred and these gathered around the platform to hear speeches while two squad cars of Gardai stood by and Det. Garda J. W. Reynolds and Garda Jim Rogers mingled with the crowd around the platform. It was late when the demonstartors arrived at Lusmagh Cross and the speeches went on until around midnight.

The gathering was addressed by Vy Rev. Father Fahy, P.P.; Mr. W. H. Milner, Walsh Island, and Mr. Jack Hynes, London. (Mr. Hynes returned to London next morning).

### Missing Car Found Upturned In Banagher Sandpit

When the demonstration had ended and Mr. W. H. Milner returned to Banagher to drive home his car was missing from where it had been parked in the Square. Next morning workmen going into a sandpit found the Volkswagen car upturned on its side in the pit. It was not thrown down the deep embankment but had been either pushed or driven down the half mile road to the wide pit.

---

The *Irish Times* (17 June 1959) in its account of the occasion, in an article headed 'Band Escort for Two Ex-Prisoners' said that

At Lusmagh, the Very Rev John Fahy PP, welcomed the men home and said they had been through a rough time, but this had failed to break them. He added: 'We know the rights of assembly and the right to hold opinions, and we will see that their homes will not be outraged. Scarcely a home in this parish had not been outraged. We hold the government responsible, and they would see that those thugs responsible would be dealt with. It is horrible to be held in one of those squad cars for hours. This torture will be examined and exposed, and the one or two responsible brought to trial before the Irish nation.'

Mr S. Milner asked the crowd never to do anything that would bring shame. All Ireland was watching them, and their enemies were watching, too. Some recent events had been done by enemies who wanted to bring discredit on *Lia Fáil*. The press in the Twenty-six Counties had not attempted to give the truth to the people of Ireland, yet a Six-County paper, the *Belfast Telegraph*, gave a most impartial write-up.

Civic Guard squad cars attended the meeting.

That June 1959, Lusmagh incursion into Banagher was reminiscent of one nearly a century and a half earlier which concluded with disastrous consequences. It is described graphically by military historian and Irish Army Officer Patrick O'Donnell in *The Irish Faction Fighters of the 19th Century* in a chapter headed *Lusmagh Bid to 'Bate' Banagher Ended in Tragedy*. He outlines in gripping detail how by the time the Act of Union was passed, in 1800, Banagher had become a pocket borough notorious for its parliamentary corruption with Captain St George Armstrong now the dominant political personality. His ancestors had arrived with Cromwell in 1649 and were amply rewarded for services rendered by securing much of the MacCoghlan territory in the Barony of Garrycastle. Lusmagh, for centuries under the jurisdiction of the O'Hoolaghans and the O'Maddens, had seen that ancient rivalry with the MacCoghlans fester and regularly break out in tribal warfare with their Banagher neighbours.

Up to the beginning of the 19th century the Banagher men had been vying with Lusmagh men 'to decide which were the better at the popular sport of stick-fighting'. The champions from each area had regularly met man-to-man. But now the Lusmagh men had resolved, once-and-for-all, to teach their townie neighbours a lesson they wouldn't easily forget.

Once the harvest of 1813 had been gathered:

In different parts of Lusmagh, the Larkins, Carrolls,
O'Maddens and Hoolaghans took out their fighting sticks
and practised. It is recorded that a man who had seen
Brian Carroll wield his stick in practice said 'he'd croosht
a robineen going through a skylight'.

By New Year's Day the Lusmagh men were ready for action.
They posted the following notice prominently in Banagher a
few days before their well-planned assault. They could never
be accused of acting slyly and coming in under the cover of
darkness:

**NOTICE**

We, the parishioners of Lusmagh, give notice to
the town of Banagher that we will go in on Thursday next and give them battle.
Ye may be assured that there is not a man kind
from the age of 12 to 60 that must not turn out.
We are informed of every man that ye are
striking out.
Captain Armstrong says that he will bring his
yeomen on us, but we defy his best, and all the
army in his county. We are able to disarm them if
he attempts it, and take the town ourselves.
Richard Woods had a great deal to say the last
day, but let him, and Boyle and Ramsay and more,
rue the hour that we go in.
No more from Captain Stout.

And so on 6 January 1814 at least 500 men of Lusmagh (pop.
then about 3500) marched on Banagher 'intending to bate them'.

What better way to celebrate the feast of the Epiphany,
Nollaig na mBan, than to have a good physical workout in the
cold dreary days of early January – anything to get the blood circulating, keep the chilblains at bay and banish the post-
Christmas blues!

As the battle was joined: 'Screeches poured out as stick
met flesh and bone and skelps began to fly and a cloud of
dust rose from their feet enveloping the tangled mass like
a fog. Lines wavered and buckled. Witnesses said that
they saw yeomen, but not in uniform, fighting on the
Banagher side.'

The townspeople – many of them in the pocket of the ascendancy – had prepared well for the expected onslaught as

shop windows remained shuttered. Barricades of carts and furniture were built on the Main Street and arrangements made for treatment of casualties.

Fortunes ebbed to and fro until a lull developed during which the Lusmagh men were persuaded to withdraw by Major George Warbuton, at that time in charge of the Yeomanry in Offaly. But as the withdrawal got under way the soldiers responding to a command from Armstrong, who as local magistrate had been observing the scene, shot dead three Lusmagh leaders Joseph Larkin, John Buckley and John Butler 'in the spine, rear of thigh and rear of shoulder respectively, according to the medical report of the military surgeon'. Dozens of others were wounded.

Unsurprisingly in a subsequent official inquiry, both Armstrong and the soldiers were exonerated. O'Donnell concludes the chapter by stating that

Never again did the men of Lusmagh march *en masse* into Banagher to do battle.

It may be noted in passing that Michael Larkin (1837-1867), a native of Lusmagh and a tailor by trade, was one of three men who became known as *The Manchester Martyrs*. His family moved to Birr from where Michael went to England.

After the unsuccessful Fenian rising in 1867, two prominent members of the organisation, Thomas Kelly – 'a Galwegian by birth, a printer by trade and a colonel by courtesy' – and Timothy Deasy were arrested in Manchester and charged with arms offences and involvement in the insurrection. While they were being transported to Salford Jail on 18 September they were rescued from the police van by a large group of supporters, among them Michael Larkin. In the course of the ambush a shot was fired into the lock which accidentally killed Sergeant Charles Brett. Larkin and two others were found guilty in the trial which followed and were sentenced to death for their part in the shooting. The trial was described in the English press as unsatisfactory. In his final message Larkin swore that he never fired a shot in all his life, much less the day the attack was made on the van.

According to Peter Kenny in a fine piece in *The Lusmagh Herb*, Larkin was a grandson of James Quirke, a well-to-do farmer, who was flogged publicly in Banagher by the military for his part in the 1798 rebellion and later deported.

A ballad commemorating the Manchester Martyrs was written, the refrain of which is

'God save Ireland' said the heroes
'God save Ireland' said they all
'Whether on the scaffold high
Or on the battlefield we die
Oh what matter when for Erin dear we fall.'

The monument in the Market Square, Birr recalls the tragic events of 1867 when, as outlined by Peter Kenny

On the morning of Saturday, 23 November after attending their last Mass, William Philip Allen, Michael Larkin and Michael O'Brien mounted the scaffold in front of Salford Gaol and dropped together into eternity and Irish history.

Even a quick glance at the history of Lusmagh from the Middle Ages onwards, when it was part of Co Galway, reinforces the conviction that the people of that parish have long possessed a remarkable spirit of independence and defiance.

Fr Fahy, in leading his followers through Banagher, was consciously or unconsciously re-enacting the events of 1814. Thankfully, on this occasion however there was nothing more sinister or malevolent on the minds of the Lusmagh people than the wish to make a symbolic gesture of defiance at those in Banagher who brought the Minister for Lands to the town to launch the recent carnival.

Harry Milner was clearly convinced that his own life was in danger if he ignored the warnings to keep out of Banagher which he claimed to have received prior to the homecoming parade in June. He took the warnings extremely seriously as the following extracts from an article in the 9th issue of *Lia Fáil* illustrate. His comments were made after a successful *Lia Fáil* Ceilí – under the auspices of the Emigration Action Movement – held in Quigley's Hall, Banagher.

Some months ago Mr Milner's car was thrown into a sandpit belonging to Bantile Ltd, Banagher. There were threats of assassinations etc and warnings to keep out of Banagher.

It was the evening of the home-coming from dark and dreary dungeons of the first *Lia Fáil* patriots. Prior to his visit to Banagher on that evening, Mr Milner had acquired a plot in the local cemetery at Walsh Island – just in case! But the hooligans who are opposed to *Lia Fáil* – and incidentally attached to a particular political party – did not have the courage of their convictions, instead they tried a sneaking attack on a defenceless car. A further proof of the calibre of these people is the fact that when Mr Milner appeared unescorted in Banagher on Sunday 7 January they disappeared into thin air.

Mr Milner very much regretted that to publicly name the people who threw his car into the sandpit might have marred the gaiety on Sunday, but there will be an opportunity of doing so before long. It should be noted that the battalion of police who were in Banagher at the time could not find them. What a contrast with what happened at the hands of the same police to anyone who was suspected of wanting land.

It is rumoured in Banagher that the English-bred Masonic Minister for Lands Mr Childers stated that he would walk through blood and fire to crush this thing – This thing being *Lia Fáil*. He underestimated us. We drove Childers out of the Department of Lands. *Lia Fáil* is stronger than ever. He walked through our blood as far as he could; he may yet walk through fire which the Shannon won't quench.

On 17 June Éamon de Valera won the Presidential election and Séan Lemass belatedly became leader of Fianna Fáil and Taoiseach. Lemass appointed Micheál Ó Moráin – a shrewd Mayo solicitor – as Minister for Lands. Mr Childers was moved to the newly created Department of Transport and Power. It is likely that events in Lusmagh and across the Shannon, combined with the depressed state of rural Ireland, were contributory factors in the Taoiseach's reallocation of portfolios.

# CHAPTER TWENTY-THREE

## *Farewell to Lusmagh*

Bishop Philbin received a steady stream of correspondence and representations throughout that month of June about *Lia Fáil* and Fr Fahy. Almost all of these communications, from a broad spectrum of people including government emissaries, some diocesan clergy and people directly affected in different ways by recent events, were uniformly critical of the manner in which the situation was being handled.

It was now abundantly clear to the bishop that Fr Fahy was blithely ignoring solemn promises he had made. Just over a month earlier Fr O'Callaghan had returned to Loughrea with what could only be interpreted as a clear unambiguous letter from Fr Fahy that whatever involvement he may have had with *Lia Fáil* in the past was now at an end.

The bishop's patience had clearly run out and the 'softly, softly' policy of appeasement and conciliation was now finally to be discarded as the following letter clearly illustrates:

St. Brendan's,
Loughrea.

29 June 1959

The Reverend John Fahy, P.P.,
Lusmagh.

Dear Fr. Fahy,
You are hereby summoned to the above residence for a canonical process on Thursday 2 July at 11 a.m. You will understand the significance of this formal function.

+ William
Bishop of Clonfert.

Given the brevity, tone and content of the letter, a PS along the following lines would not have occasioned too much surprise:

May the angels lead you into paradise;
May the martyrs come to welcome you and
Take you to the holy city, the new and Eternal Jerusalem.

Dr Murphy, quoting a confidential source, states that when Bishop Philbin confronted Fr Fahy he demanded that

he must either publicly apologise to the parish or go …

Murphy further states that

Fr Fahy was broken-hearted to leave but leave he did rather than recant his most cherished beliefs.

Another confidential source has stated that at that fateful meeting on 2 July Bishop Philbin presented Fr Fahy with the following choices:

1. That at Masses in Lusmagh, Bishop Philbin would read a statement in the presence of Fr Fahy, in which among other points, Fr Fahy would admit and confess that he had encouraged actions which were contrary to Catholic teaching. Or:
2. That Fr Fahy would read the statement himself in the presence of Bishop Philbin.
3. A refusal to agree to either option 1 or 2 would result in his immediate transfer and demotion.

The *Irish Times* 6 July opened an article headed 'Parish Priest Resigns' with the following paragraph:

The Very Rev John Fahy, parish priest of Lusmagh, Banagher, Co Offaly, has resigned. He made his announcement at Mass yesterday in St Cronan's Church, Lusmagh, saying: 'My dear brethren, I have resigned my office as parish priest of Lusmagh. I have done so of my own free will. My bishop, who has always been very good and kind to me, has neither asked nor forced me to do this.' Father Fahy then wished God's blessing on every person in the parish of Lusmagh.

Bishop Philbin lost no time in giving immediate effect to the transfer as he conveyed in this letter delivered by hand to Fr Fahy on the following Friday:

Teileafón 15

Coláiste Seoraim,
Gearrbaile,
Béal Áta na Slua.
10 July 1959

My dear Fr. Fahy,

I am hereby appointing you to be Curate at Abbey, Duniry. As you have announced your resignation to the people, I feel that it would be better if you could officiate in Abbey on next Sunday, rather than in Lusmagh, leaving the transfer of your furniture over for another week. I am sure this could be arranged with Fr. Heenan.

On the occasion of your taking up this pastoral office I am bound to give formal instructions that in future you are not to take part in social or agrarian movements that have not ecclesiastical approval, and that you are to dissociate yourself from the persons connected with the Lia Fáil movement, both in Lusmagh and from outside that parish.

I remain,
Yours very sincerely,
+W. Philbin

CHAPTER TWENTY-FOUR

# *Postscript to Lusmagh*

Fr Fahy regularly claimed that there was a conspiracy between organisations such as The Representative Church Body, The Freemasons and some leading politicians to dispossess 'the mere Irish' of their rightful ownership of the land of Ireland. Despite writing many colourful and often vitriolic articles about the alleged conspiracy, he was unable to produce conclusive proof which could bear out his contention.

In *Radical Irish Priests*, Dr Murphy makes an amazing revelation which lends credence to Fr Fahy's allegations when he states

> For the Church of Ireland had in fact secretly set up an Irish Land Finance Company, incorporated in 1913 to act as a lending agency to church members to buy farms and with its working capital supplied by the Representative Church Body, that was active in the land market until it was wound up in 1973, a period when church numbers nevertheless fell 40 per cent between 1926 and 1971; the result of a zealous county Kildare rector's efforts in the 1940s and 1950s to establish 'Protestant blocs' in his parish ('notching up these victories', 'out thrusting the opposition') through the Land Company was that 'blackguards' damaged his parish church in 1959 – *Lia Fáil*'s heyday.

This startling information emerged from a doctoral thesis by Kathleen Annie Garvin in 1977 titled 'The Church of Ireland as a Church in Ireland: a Study of the Anglican Church in the Irish Free State, 1922-1935' (pp. 187-251). This Irish Land Finance Company had its spiritual and geographical centre in Co Laois, 'radiating out to King's, Kildare, Dublin, Wicklow, Carlow, Kilkenny and Tipperary'.

Perhaps in hindsight it was fortunate that Fr John did not know of the existence of that Land Finance Company and its activities at various stages during his many campaigns. Murphy's final comment on the matter was that

If amid the crisis of the fifties news of the Church of Ireland's secret activity in the land market had leaked, then the consequences for church and society alike of land hunger and sectarianism fusing were potentially devastating, turning the ugly Fethard-on-Sea boycott into a trifle by comparison.

The boycott on the Hook Peninsula in Co. Wexford during the summer of 1957 was directed by some local Catholics against Protestant shopkeepers and farmers in the area. That deeply divisive affair was fuelled by among other factors, a long-standing bitterness over land ownership and the *Ne Temere* decree of the Catholic Church concerning what was then called a 'mixed marriage'. A major full-length film, *A Love Divided*, was subsequently made based on those events in Wexford over half a century ago.

The boycott generated deep bitterness and adverse international publicity. It was the following strong condemnation by An Taoiseach Éamon de Valera, quoted in Keogh, *20th Century Ireland*, that brought it to an end:

> I can only say, from what has appeared in public, that I regard this boycott as ill-conceived, ill-considered and futile for the achievement of the purpose for which it seems to have been intended.

In Lusmagh there were divisions and recriminations between some individuals and families in the aftermath of Fr Fahy's departure to Abbey. There were also some financial consequences for the ratepayers of Banagher and Lusmagh arising from the *Lia Fáil* campaign as the following decrees reveal.

*The Midland Tribune* 24 July 1959 outlined in a full page article headed 'Land Agitation Incidents will cost Banagher-Lusmagh Ratepayers £898 … plus.'

In summary, Judge M. J. Binchy at Birr Circuit Court decreed that the ratepayers of the District Electoral Divisions of Lusmagh and Banagher would have to pay, additional to their ordinary rates for public services carried out by Offaly Co Council, a total of £898 5s. 9d. by way of compensation to the owners of the properties concerned.

In addition, the Judge allowed full costs and expenses in each application, the total of those amounts when compiled to be added to the full amount of the orders made by the court.

The several applicants, the amounts for which they were given decrees and the causes in respect of which they claimed, were:

- Mrs Melosine Daly, Cloghan Castle £500; damage to Cloghan Castle building.
- John Francis Barry, Shannon Lodge, Banagher £246; burning of a hay-shed store.
- Albert A. Barry, Invernisk, Banagher £82 10s; burning of hay in above.
- Irish Land Commission, Dublin £35; burning of a dwelling house.
- Wm Henry Milner, Patrick St, Portarlington £24 14s 3d; damage to a motor car.

Respondents in each were Offaly County Council; malice in the alleged damage was not contested in any case; agreements on the amounts for which decrees should be given were reached in the claims by The Land Commission and Francis Barry, and the council contested the amounts in the other cases.

Mrs Daly's original claim was for £900; Albert Barry's for £121 and W. H. Milner's was for £51 10s.

# CHAPTER TWENTY-FIVE

## *Abbey: The Final Years 1959-1969*

Fr John and his housekeeper Catherine (he always referred to her as 'Sister Catherine'), who by now was in failing health, took up residence immediately in the presbytery at Abbey. Despite all the trauma occasioned by his departure from Lusmagh, Fr John retained close links with his former parishioners in *Lia Fáil* and followed closely the legal proceedings which gradually brought an end to a most tempestuous campaign.

The final two issues of the *Lia Fáil* newspaper were published in 1960 with Harry Milner assuming a more prominent role than heretofore. Relations between Father Fahy and Milner clearly deteriorated in the months following Fr John's transfer to Abbey. Letters between the two men during the early months of 1960 reveal an increasing level of bitterness which assumes a more personalised tone of enmity and recrimination between the former colleagues.

A letter from Fr John (30 June 1960) begins with

Dear Milner,
I received your lying and insulting letter today …

In trenchant language Milner is left in no doubt that

*Lia Fáil* is the one and only organisation in the country not infiltrated by a government agent. My guidance of the members secured that.

He is also told bluntly that

The movement was going before you joined it … and that it will keep going after you leave it …

Unfavourable comments by Milner on some Lusmagh men in an earlier note are according to Fr John

not worth commenting on
and the one big idea in your letter is Milner, not *Lia Fáil*.

The letter concludes with Milner being told that

You have yet to learn the ABC of revolutionary leadership ...
You have asked for it.
Fahy

The publication of the final issue (No. 10) of the *Lia Fáil* news-paper in September 1960 brought to an end Fr Fahy's active involvement in national political and agrarian campaigns. He settled down from then on to a low-key participation in local republican affairs.

Fr John's loyal and devoted housekeeper Catherine Fitzgerald died in March 1960 aged eighty-two, and gradually her duties were assumed by Mrs Annie Larkin, the Abbey church sac-ristan, who cared for him with great concern up to his final ill-ness in 1969.

Fr John was prominent among a group who campaigned for years to have a monument erected in Seefin, outside Craughwell, to the memory of Anthony Daly (34) who was hanged there on Good Friday, 8 April, 1820. The agrarian secret society, the Ribbonmen, so called because they wore white rib-bons in their caps, was very active in south-east Galway at that time. Daly was prominent in that secret society which waged a guerrilla war against the landlords through shootings, the mutil-ation of livestock and carrying out robberies in search of arms.

In late February 1820 during a night-time raid by the Ribbonmen on the home of Patrick Cullen, a revenue officer who lived at Coorheen outside Loughrea, Daly was recognised by Andrew O'Geoghegan a servant in the house, a fact which some weeks later led to his arrest. Around the same time an un-successful attempt was made to murder James Hardiman Burke, owner of St Cleran's estate, and his gamekeeper. Daly, a carpenter by trade and originally from Kilrickle, was arrested during the investigation into that failed attack. He was tried at Galway Assizes on 31 March, found guilty of the raid on Cullen's house and ordered to be executed. The prosecution be-lieved that Daly was implicated in the attempt on Burke's life and the crown forces were determined to make an example of him in their determination to defeat Ribbonism. To the end Daly denied any involvement in the St Cleran's incident and stated in court that even though he had only one eye if I had looked along a gun barrel at Burke he wouldn't be here today to swear against me.

Daly also invited the Judge to erect a target to assess his marksmanship, a request which was refused. Local lore relates that another man on his deathbed confessed to having shot at the landlord and his agent.

On the day appointed for the execution, Daly was taken from Galway Jail under armed escort. He was reputedly brought to Seefin Hill, about a mile from St Cleran's, on a cart and sitting on his own coffin. He scorned the opportunity to escape as the Galway militia handed him over to local police near Craughwell for the last bit of the journey.

One version of the execution which survives states that Daly was hanged from the shafts of the upturned cart and that the grass never grows where the wheels rested. The other version indicates that Daly was hanged from a scaffold and that the marks indicating the position of the tripod used for the hanging have remained bare to this day. The *Freeman's Journal* recorded that Daly went to his death 'with the greatest fortitude and res- ignation' and the hanging was witnessed by 'a vast concourse of the peasantry'.

According to Lady Gregory, the renowned poet Antoine Ó Raiftearaí was among the peasantry on that occasion and he later composed a poem – *Antoine Ó Dálaigh* – in praise of Daly. In the course of the poem Ó Raiftearaí uses all his powers of in- vective against James Hardiman Burke, James Daly of Dunsandle, Cullen and his wife, and their servant O'Geoghegan, all of whom gave evidence against Daly. Daly's wife cut her hus- band's wrist after the hanging and smeared the blood on the gatepost of St Cleran's, proclaiming (in Irish) that

no Burke will ever die peaceably in his bed and no rooks will ever again nest at St Cleran's.

Local legend states that those curses remained effective and that Daly's blood was still to be seen on the back gates of St Cleran's before they were demolished. Prolonged illnesses, vio- lent deaths and in the case of O'Geoghegan, a lynching by the Ribbonmen at Cregg Castle near Ballymana, awaited those responsible for Anthony Daly's death. The ladies living in St

Cleran's were prevented from attending the hanging but were able to witness the event through two south-facing windows in the mansion. Burke subsequently had the windows blocked up, which was interpreted locally as a sign of the landlord's guilty conscience. Those windows remained blocked until the estate was acquired by the film-maker John Huston in 1951. The American novelist John Steinbeck, who visited Huston at Christmas 1964, was fascinated by the lore and legends surrounding the death of Anthony Daly.

The interest shown by these two famous men in the story of Anthony Daly did not however result in any creative endeavour on their parts. No book or film about the tragic events ensued.

Sadly, during 'The Troubles' many of the finest 'Big Houses' around the country were burned to the ground. St Cleran's escaped that fate because the owner at the time, a lady called Mrs Studd, who was a Catholic, made a contribution to the local Sinn Féin fund. Volunteer Pat Connaughton who had collected the subscription refused to allow his comrades to set fire to the building.

It is easy to see how Daly's story of betrayal and execution, landlords and their agents, agrarian secret societies and acute poverty in pre-famine Ireland would be of great interest to Fr Fahy. Furthermore, the links between James Daly, the powerful landowner of Dunsandle Castle near Killtullagh, Athenry around 1820 and his mid-20th century descendant, Major Denis Bowes-Daly, the last of that family to own the estate, were not lost on Fr John. In 1959 the Major sold Dunsandle and bought Cloghan Castle, Lusmagh, Banagher, the very building used for a short time by the Lusmagh men while 'on the run' after their rescue from Banagher Garda Barracks.

The efforts of the local committee to keep the story of Anthony Daly fresh in the minds of the people were amply rewarded as the following extracts from an article in the *Connacht Tribune*, 19 August 1961, clearly illustrate:

*Unveiling Of Memorial To Anthony Daly on 15th August*
On Tuesday afternoon last, in brilliant sunshine, a very large attendance saw Rev Fr John Fahy CC, Abbey, Co Galway, unveil a memorial to the memory of Anthony

Daly who was executed on Seefin Hill, Craughwell, on Good Friday, April 8th, 1820.

Last year a small local committee decided to erect a memorial to Daly's memory. There, on Seefin Hill, beside the gallows hole, a platform was erected and on it was placed a nine-foot high Celtic cross, the work of Mr Pádraig Ó Fathaigh of Woodquay, Galway.

The local committee consisted of Mr James Raftery who, as chairman, presided over last Tuesday's ceremonies, together with Mr John Holland, treasurer; Mr Patrick Connolly, secretary; and an executive party of Messrs Martin McHugh, Patrick Geoghegan, Thomas Fahy, Patrick Shiels, Thomas Cannon and Thomas Keighrey. Also present on the platform were Very Rev W. Cummins PP, Closetoken, Rev K. Burke CC, Craughwell, Mr Thomas Doyle, Kiltulla, Mr John Moloney, Craughwell, together with officers and members of the committee.

Speaking in Irish and English, Rev Fr Fahy said that for sheer ruthless tyranny the regime of the English landlords in Ireland has never been surpassed in history.

'How,' asked Rev Fr Fahy, 'did our forefathers survive that tyrannic regime? They survived it because there were men amongst them, men who never surrendered to the robber- invader, men who organised and fought against him until at last he was beaten.'

'Anthony Daly,' he said, 'was a true man, a fearless man, and a loyal man. When offered his life if he would betray his comrades he scorned the offer. His brave mother and courageous wife, who were present at his execution, scorned that offer also. True to his country, faithful to his principles, and loyal to his comrades he chose death rather than be a traitor. Of Anthony Daly it can well be said: "A hero he lived and a hero he died".'

'Today as we look out from this hill-top, on which Daly was hanged, we behold a strange reverse of history. The British landlord garrison has disappeared; its castles are in ruins; and, except for a strip by the Shannon in East Galway, the vast ranches are broken up and the good land of Galway is studded with the homesteads of the native Irish people restored to their heritage. If a similar claim could be made for the provinces of Leinster, Munster and Ulster then Ireland would be a peaceful and prosperous country of ten to fifteen million people.'

Rev Fr Fahy said that our native governments, both Fine Gael and Fianna Fáil, had failed signally to restore the land to the people since they had taken over in 1922.

'We are,' he said, 'as a result, in the sorry plight today that most of Ulster, Leinster and Munster is in the hands of the descendants of Normans, Cromwellians and Williamites and that aliens, Germans, Swedes, Danes, English and Americans are buying up our best land while young Irish men and women have to fly the country at the rate of 60,000 a year.'

He asked the young men of Ireland to work together to restore the lands once robbed from us back to the people of Ireland.

In conclusion, Rev Fr Fahy thanked the large crowd, drawn from all over Co Galway, for attending the ceremony; the Craughwell Band; Mr Paddy Farrell, who had given the site free for the memorial; and all who had given the use of their cars for collecting subscriptions, and all who had subscribed. He paid especial tribute to Mr James Raftery, Chairman of the Committee, to Mr John Holland, Mr Patrick Connolly and the others who had given so unselfishly of their time and labour.

He recalled that thirty years ago he had led a procession to Seefin Hill to honour Daly's memory and had expressed the wish that there would one day be a memorial erected in his honour. James Raftery had been present on that day and had taken his words to heart and had worked down the years to make them come true.

Mr Martin Dolan said that Anthony Daly had died, not because he hated individual landlords, but because he loved his people and wanted to see them happy and prosperous on their own farms. The fact that his memory had been kept green for 140 years showed that the people of Galway recognised the fact that he had laid down his life for them.

A headstone erected by their father in Kilrickle churchyard marks the burial place of both Anthony Daly and his brother Hugh (27) who was mortally wounded in Dunsandle Estate on 9 September 1819, either by a blow during a hurling match or possibly by being beaten to death by a group of the landlord's workmen.

For the most part, Fr John spent his final years in peaceful contentment, reading a lot, reminiscing with old friends, and visiting his extended family and republican colleagues like Barney Kelly and Peadar O'Donnell. But he also enjoyed travelling abroad. He made an indelible impression on a pilgrimage of Cumann na Sagart (a group of Irish-speaking priests) to the shrines of Irish saints in Germany in 1960. The group also visited Munich on that occasion because The Eucharistic Congress was held there at that time. Fr John also travelled to Rome, The Holy Land and The World Fair in New York in 1963.

Sometime in 1962 Fr John drove in his trusty Volkswagen Beetle to Wicklow where he bought an Irish Wolfhound pup which was soon answering to the name 'Bran'. While never becoming quite as famous as his master, it didn't take Bran long to become a familiar sight around the village. It wasn't unknown for him to enter Abbey Church, saunter up the centre aisle, then Arkle-like clear the altar-rail and snuggle down on the sanctuary floor to await the end of Mass or Benediction.

Fr John's lifelong concern for and generosity towards the travelling community was never more in evidence than during his time in Abbey. He regularly arranged for travellers to purchase food and other basic necessities in Holohan's shop and then he paid their bills.

In 1963 Bishop Thomas Ryan, a native of Tipperary, succeeded Bishop Philbin who transferred to the diocese of Down and Connor. Fr Fahy and Bishop Ryan established a most cordial relationship from the outset. It was widely accepted that the bishop was well disposed towards reinstating Fr John as a parish priest but the counsel of some senior clerics opposed to the move prevailed.

Fr John, like older priests all over the world, had to come to terms with new liturgical forms arising from the Second Vatican Ecumenical Council 1962-1965. He was always warmly welcomed at gatherings of the diocesan clergy and brother-priests like Fr O'Reilly, Mons Page, Fr Flannery, Fr Solon and Fr Murray were particularly supportive of him in his final years.

By 1969, as the Six-Counties once more erupted in communal strife, Fr John's health had greatly deteriorated. The volatile volcano of east Galway was about to yield up its final rumble. Down its craggy slopes the molten lava no more would flow.

Fr John was admitted for the final time to Galway Regional Hospital in June where his condition gradually worsened. His cousin, Mother Teresa Fahy from the Presentation Convent, Galway, was with him when he died on 19 July, two months short of the Golden Jubilee of his ordination.

The circumstances surrounding the digging of Fr Fahy's grave in Abbey churchyard are remarkable considering aspects of the story of his life. The local men who undertook the task encountered solid rock about three feet down. The expertise of Denis Sullivan, an agricultural contractor from Woodford, was sought. He found it necessary to conduct a number of controlled explosions with gelignite to reach the required depth. This development caused consternation to the parish priest Fr O'Reilly who was on tenterhooks during the entire blasting operation.

The village of Abbey came to a standstill on the day of the funeral, which by common consent was the largest ever witnessed in the parish.

The *Connacht Tribune* (25 July 1969) carried the following details of the requiem Mass as part of its obituary on Fr John, which was compiled by Bertie Donohue, Loughrea.

> His Lordship the Bishop of Clonfert, Most Rev Dr Ryan, presided at the Solemn Requiem Mass and Office for the Dead, celebrated in Abbey Church, and there were seventy-five priests from the dioceses of Clonfert and Galway; Carmelite Fathers and Redemptorist Fathers.
>
> Amongst those were Rt Rev Dr Winters, Galway; Rt Rev Mons T. Glennon PP, VG, Kilconnell; Rt Rev Mons T. Fahy, Galway; Rt Rev Mons P. E. Mac Fhinn, Galway; Rt Rev Mons P. J. Temple, New York, and V Rev P. McGahey PP, Castletowngeoghegan, Meath, who was closely associated with Fr Fahy in the Land for the People Movement, in the Diocese of Meath.

V Rev M. O'Reilly PP, Abbey, celebrated the Mass; V
Rev T. L. Murphy PP, Ballinakill, was deacon; V Rev J.
Shiel PP, Woodford, sub-deacon, and V Rev M. H.
O'Callaghan Adm, Loughrea, and Rev P. Abberton, CC,
Kilrickle, were chanters.

Amongst the huge attendance at the ceremonies were
groups representing each parish in which Fr Fahy had
served. Mr Oliver J. Flanagan TD was amongst the general
attendance.

Members of the Mid Galway Command IRA wearing
black berets and black armlets provided a guard of honour
at the graveside and an officer laid a wreath on the grave.

The IRA guard of honour had been requested by the Fahy
family to refrain from any armed display at the funeral.

Leaving the churchyard after the burial, Fr Tom Keyes,
Garbally College, turned to his friend John Holohan and said
'Damn it, the man deserved at least a few shots.' Fr John
Flannery and Fr Louis Page were joint executors of Fr Fahy's affairs. A clearance auction of his meagre possessions was
arranged within weeks of the funeral. It was a very local, low-
key affair. The only items of any real value or interest were Fr
John's documents and surviving correspondence, which thankfully were secured for the diocesan archives.

One item which John Holohan, the auctioneer, did not offer
for sale was a very large box of bullets which he found in the
presbytery when preparing the auction catalogue. He took the
ammunition to the bridge over the Shannon in Portumna and
consigned it to a watery grave where, presumably, it rusts to
this day.

In 1970, Fr John's friends in the Republican movement erected
a headstone over his grave with the following inscription on the
base:

On that occasion before a large and representative gathering of friends and former parishioners an oration was delivered by Ruairí Ó Brádaigh at the invitation of Barney Kelly, Mount Temple, Moate, an old friend of Fr John and veteran of the War of Independence. Ó Brádaigh, a Roscommon-based teacher was a Sinn Féin TD for Longford-Westmeath, a former Chief-of-Staff of the IRA and President of the all-Ireland political party, Republican Sinn Féin.

Fr Fahy had visited Ó Brádaigh's mother in Longford in 1958 while her son was interned in the Curragh Military Prison during the Border Campaign in the 1950s. He had led an IRA attack on Derrylin RUC barracks in Co. Fermanagh on 30 December 1956. He was arrested shortly after the attack in Co. Cavan. With his comrades he was sentenced to six months in Mountjoy prison. After completing that sentence he was immediately interned in the Curragh.

Fr Fahy's memory is also publicly perpetuated in Lusmagh. Paddy Byrne, Mick Henchy, Pat Glynn, Francie Kelly and Pat Lantry arranged that a plaque be erected in St Cronan's Church in his honour. It was unveiled by Peadar O'Donnell in 1973. The inscription is as follows:

*Of your charity pray for the repose*
*of the soul of*
*Very Rev John Fahy*
*Parish Priest of Lusmagh*
*1945-1959*
*Erected by his relatives and friends.*

# CHAPTER TWENTY-SIX

# Fr John Fahy: An Assessment

*Never fall out with the extreme men.*
*They are extreme because they are extremely in the right.*
Dr Patrick Duggan, Bishop of Clonfert 1872-1896

Fr Fahy was both radical and conservative. In his introduction to *Radical Irish Priests 1660-1970* (1998), Fr Donal Kerr, former Professor of Ecclesiastical History at Maynooth, states that

> a possible definition of a radical could be one who challenges the established order, political, social or cultural.

Certainly Fr John can be called a radical as he spent at least four decades challenging the political and social order which prevailed in Ireland from the 1920s onwards. Significantly he was the only priest from the 20th century to figure in that fascinating publication. He stood out among the clergy of his day because as Fr Kerr stated

> he took on the forces of an independent Ireland, both Cumann na nGaedheal and Fianna Fáil coming under the lash of his criticism.

From a theological and doctrinal perspective Fr Fahy was very conservative and orthodox. His priesthood was the bedrock of his very being. On a number of occasions, particularly during Bishop Dignan's episcopacy, he risked having his priestly faculties withdrawn because of his political and agrarian activities. However at the last moment he gave, on oath, whatever assurances were required to avoid having that ultimate sanction imposed.

From the 1880s through to the middle of the 20th century, a majority of the Catholic bishops of Ireland were determined in their drive to influence the people in political matters as well as in areas of faith and morals. The hierarchy in general adopted a strong anti-republican stance from the time the Treaty was signed, which coincided with Fr John's return to Ireland from

Scotland. Patrick Murray described how in October 1922 Bishop O'Doherty of Clonfert stated at the Catholic Truth Society conference held in the Mansion House that they (the bishops)

> could not but regard their present (provisional government) rulers as lawful.

Earlier, in August, Bishop Hackett of Waterford

> asserted that he himself held in his own diocese that power which the Pope has for the whole world.

He granted people 'liberty of discussion' but once the bishops had spoken

> all room for doubt is hereby removed.

The bishop rounded off his comments by hoping that he would not have to use

> every weapon that my position as a bishop gives me.

So even on political matters over which it should have been possible for people, legitimately, to hold differing views it was a case of

> *Roma locuta est. Causa finita est.*

That was the backdrop against which Fr Fahy and those sharing his political outlook operated.

In launching *Lia Fáil* in 1957 Fr John was hoping in the words of Brian Murphy that

> the smallholders would yet find their destiny in a Gaelic pastoral society of rural, Catholic, arcadian values cut off from the insidious modern world.

But unfortunately for Fr John and the smallholders of Ireland, government strategy by then was already shifting from the earlier policy of protectionism to one of free trade. Industrialisation, the influx of foreign capital and the fact that henceforth Ireland's economic well-being would increasingly be dependent on forging closer ties with our European neighbours would accelerate the drift from the land and render impossible the realisation of his dreams.

Fr John was reluctant to accept the fact that, however much he despised them, we had our own democratically elected politicians and governments since 1922. By choosing to confront the civil authorities he was backing himself and his supporters into a corner from which it would be difficult to emerge unscathed.

He was less politically sophisticated than priests like Mgr James Horan of Knock or 'the co-operative priest' Fr James McDyer of Glencolumbkille, both of whom quickly realised that political power lay in Leinster House. They worked assiduously with the decision-makers to improve the lot of the communities they championed so effectively.

By contrast, Fr John's fiercely independent spirit and uncompromising nature were in some respects more suited to life and ministry in the final decades of the 19th century. It could be argued that he would have been more at home linking up with the great Patrick Duggan, then Bishop of Clonfert and known as the Bishop of the Land War, in spreading Michael Davitt's Land League message in 1879. Or perhaps in the 1880s when East Galway erupted in what developed into the final phase of the Land War, Fr John would have fitted comfortably during the Plan of Campaign among priests like Patrick Coen, Patrick Egan, Patrick Costelloe and William Roche who gave wonderful support to the Woodford tenants against Clanricarde's agents. Neither is it difficult to picture Fr John as a staunch defender at the siege of Saunders' Fort or giving his last drop of blood in resisting the eviction of 'Doc' Tully at Looscaun on 1 September 1888, events graphically described in *A Forgotten Campaign*.

Fr John had some very important points to make at the height of the *Lia Fáil* campaign. One of his greatest concerns related to the purchase of large tracts of Irish land by aliens.

Unfortunately his message was often lost in the ferocity of his language and in his personalised attacks on famous serving politicians. It was not uncommon for his detractors at that time to accuse him of xenophobia. But in truth he was one of the first people to highlight the acquisition of large farms by non-nationals. Over four years after his departure from Lusmagh, the following article appeared in *The Irish Times* 3 December 1963 under the heading

*Growing concern over foreigners buying land here*

'The new invaders' is the name being mentioned more and more to describe those aliens who have come here since the war to buy tracts of Irish land.

In the past few weeks deputies of the various political parties have been voicing concern in the Dáil at the extent of purchases by these people and for a long time now many organisations have been protesting, mostly by means of resolution, but sometimes by more forceful methods. At least two members of the Catholic hierarchy have raised their voices in condemnation of large-scale foreign purchases of agricultural land and the National Farmers' Association has already carried out a survey to find out the extent of the 'invasion'.

Last March the Minister for Finance, Dr [James] Ryan, said that in the previous 12 months the sum involved in land purchases by foreigners was £1 million. Some time later the Minister for Lands, [Michael] Moran, told the Dáil that from August 1961 up to May of this year a total of 142 properties had been sold or leased to non-nationals.

This involved 11,200 acres and, in addition to these, 2242 acres were purchased for purposes other than agriculture. An additional 4566 acres were acquired for other purposes, and these were exempted from the 25 per cent stamp duty which had been paid on the 11,200 acres.

Recently he had said that before 1961 land sales to foreigners ran, as far as could be gathered, at between 5000 and 6000 acres annually. The picture was still somewhat similar.

Last week it was said in the Dáil that 200,000 acres were bought by non-nationals since the last war. The national councils of Macra na Feirme and the NFA, which examined the position, have asked the government to control all land purchases. The Irish Creamery Milk Suppliers' Association have complained that people with no roots in the country are taking over farms here, and fears of the undesirability of small numbers of foreigners controlling large tracts of land have been voiced even in the Dublin Junior Chamber of Commerce.

Then, in many parts of the country, there have been protests from various organisations, not all of them concerned with the land as much as with the restrictions the new purchasers sometimes put on customs of usage, principally through passage obstruction to seashore or scenic areas.

Very often the foreigners are oblivious to the fact that they are not welcome in a given area and it has been said that they have often made a purchase without being fully informed of this difficulty.

When asked, one such purchaser from Germany said that he thought the only difficulty in the way for anyone buying land here lay in the addition of the purchase price of 25 per cent. He said that he had never been made aware during his negotiations to buy that any unpleasantness might arise.

One person concerned with protests in the past said yesterday that too often the sale of a farm to a non-national has been signed before those living near it realised there was a possibility of it coming on the market.

The NFA believes that well over 12,000 – or double the average the Minister for Lands thinks – go into the hands of the stranger yearly.

Through the 1960s the control and ownership of the land of Ireland continued to be most contentious. In 1970 the National Land League (NLL) was set up by Mullingar man Dan McCarthy. This initiative is brilliantly described by Rosita Sweetman in a chapter of her book *On Our Knees* devoted to McCarthy and the NLL (see Appendix III).

Through his earlier efforts with Peadar O'Donnell to have the Land Annuities issue resolved and later through his constant pressure at local and national level to have the pace increased at which the Land Commission carried out its function, Fr John played an important part in that great social revolution which in the course of a century saw most of the land of Ireland transferred from landlords to tenants. This revolution was not finally completed until 1984 when the Land Commission ceased operations, a landmark event that was formally acknowledged with the passing into law in 1992 of the Land Commission Dissolution Act, 111 years after its inception.

Fr Fahy wrote political pamphlets, a propagandist play, a story (unfinished) relating to the Civil War period, short sketches with strong political messages, and of course most of the *Lia Fáil* newspaper. He drafted political manifestos, wrote a utopian novel and a number of religious publications.

His best known devotional work was *The Sacrifice of the Mass, The Greatest Thing on Earth*, which was published in 1957 by Browne and Nolan. Fr John had been encouraged by the bishop's response after reading the seventy-five-page text as the following indicates:

Quotation from Bishop's letter :—

My Dear Father Fahy,

I think you have done a very useful piece of work and I should like to see it in print. It will convey valuable information as well as edification . . .

✠ W. J. PHILBIN.

# THE SACRIFICE OF THE MASS

*The greatest thing on earth*

*by*

JOHN FAHY

BROWNE AND NOLAN LIMITED
THE RICHVIEW PRESS DUBLIN

In a letter to Fr Fahy (23 March 1957) the publishers indicated that they would 'treat the book as one of their own publications deducting 12.5 per cent for expenses and overheads'. Fr Fahy paid for the printing.

The book was devotional in nature and from a theological perspective it was orthodox in the extreme. In fact what is most striking about it, is that its author could switch so effortlessly

The reproduced title-page images read:

NIHIL OBSTAT:
R. A. CALLANAN, V.G., P.P.,
CENSOR.
CLONFERTENSIS, DIE 3° OCTOBRIS, 1955.

IMPRIMI POTEST:
✠ GUILIELMUS,
EPIS. CLONFERTENSIS.

First Published, January, 1957

PRINTED IN THE REPUBLIC OF IRELAND AT THE PRESS
OF THE PUBLISHERS, CLONSKEAGH, CO. DUBLIN

The Sacrifice of the Mass

INTRODUCTION

IN the rite of the Mass, the Eucharistic Sacrifice is accomplished by the Consecration. The Consecration is the core and centre around which the whole rite of the Mass is built. All the ritual prayers and actions of the liturgy of the Mass are inspired, directed, and dominated by the great Action-Prayer which takes place at that dramatic moment.

From the beginning of the Mass to the Consecration, everything that is done—all the prayers said, all the actions performed—is done in preparation for the Consecration. The preparation is twofold : (1) of the priest offering the Sacrifice, and of the people offering it with him ; and (2) of the things offered, namely, the bread and wine called the " oblata."

Up to the very moment of the Consecration the mind of the liturgy is, first, to prepare the priest and the people offering the Sacrifice with him for the moment of Consecration when the All-Holy One comes to renew for them the Sacrifice of their redemption ; and, secondly, to bless and sanctify and dedicate the material elements of bread and wine whose substances are to be changed into the Holiest Thing in all creation—the Body and Blood of Jesus Christ. As in its first half, even more so in the second half : from the Consecration to the end of the Mass, the great event which takes place in the Consecration—the Real Presence of Jesus Christ on the altar—inspires, directs, and dominates each and every prayer and action of the liturgy that follows.

5

from writing such a conventional, traditional Catholic tract to publishing the often outrageous and possibly libellous articles which appeared in the *Lia Fáil* newspaper.

He also wrote *The Framework of What We Believe* (1953) which he failed to get published either in Ireland, England or the US. The American printing house which specialised in producing Catholic literature of a devotional nature responded negatively to a request from a friend of Fr John seeking information as to why the manuscript was rejected.

October 5, 1953
SS. Placid and Companions

Miss Mary McDonald
6439 98th Street
Rego Park, Long Island

Dear Miss McDonald:

We regret that we do not give out detailed criticisms of manuscripts. However, the decision in this case, (WHAT I BELIEVE, by Reverend John Fahy) was made on the basis of the interest in such a book in the American market. We were not encouraged to think that it would be successful over here.

With good wishes,

Cordially,

THOMAS B. KENEDY

TBK/bs
enc: cc-Rev. J. Fahy

A short letter dated 27 August 1955 from Fr H. Batters SDB (Salesian Press, Surrey Lane, Battersea, London SW 11) to Fr Fahy, returning the 'Framework' manuscript shed interesting light on that episode. Having mentioned the disappointment at being unable to proceed to publication, the letter continues

> I am forwarding with this letter your bishop's letter and that of the censor's too, together with objections sent me by the censor here. The expense for make ready, imposition and proofing is £80-12-0.

The manuscript of Fr John's utopian novel *Urbs Orbis* (it translates from Latin as 'City of The Heavens') was submitted to the Talbot Press in mid-May 1956 with a view to publication. He was evidently very keen to see the novel in print as he wrote the following explanatory letter within a week to Talbot Press:

> St Cronan's
> Lusmagh
> Banagher
> 21/5/56
>
> A Chara,
> A week ago I submitted a MS entitled 'Urbs Orbis' to your firm for your decision re publication. My motivation in outlining such a modern Utopia is the propagation of Christian social ideas so strongly appealed for by our present Holy Father.
> With a world government existing in embryo in the UNO, 'Urbs Orbis' is topical and could be, in the eventuality of a world war, practical politics. It throws out ideas of how the main social problems of the world could be solved. The primary social problem of the world today is food.
> Recently the Holy Father told the U.N. Food Commission that the governments of the world will have to feed the two-thirds of the human race who are underfed. That can be done. 'Urbs Orbis' suggests one way how. Touching on the main social problems affecting humanity today, it should arouse much discussion and criticism.
> If you publish it immediately and if the first edition is not sold out before three months, I hereby guarantee to pay the full cost of printing it.

Hoping to hear from you at your earliest convenience.

I am
Yours sincerely
John Fahy PP

PS: 'Urbs Orbis' has never been submitted to any other publisher – J.F.

On 6 June Talbot Press replied to Father John:

regret inability to undertake publication of 'Urbs Orbis.

These are two excerpts from 'Urbs Orbis':

There was no British and only a very sparse representation from Northern Europe. The Russians had begun the war by hurling a fusillade of atomic and hydrogen bombs on Britain completely obliterating the British people and destroying all life on that island. In the subsequent nuclear hurricane America and Russia practically annihilated each other. Thus, the nuclear war rid humanity of the most warlike section of the human race.

It was in the year 2000 AD amidst the chaos and lawlessness following the collapse of civilisation at the end of what historians now call 'The Lunatic Era' that the foundation stone of the Christian State was laid. A world war fought with atomic and hydrogen bombs, backed by every weapon of destruction that the ingenuity of scientists and nuclear physicists could devise, wrought world desolation. Victims of the radio-active atmosphere, two-thirds of the rural population of the earth withered and died … When the cataclysmic hurricane had passed and the atmosphere had again cleared, one, and only one organisation remained intact on this earth – The Church of Jesus Christ.

After the Talbot Press rejection, Fr John submitted his manuscript to Browne and Nolan for their consideration. They gave the matter some thought because by March 1957 a letter from them indicated that

figures have not yet come to hand concerning the possibility of reducing the cost of Urbs Orbis.

However the book was never published.

Fr Fahy had a deep interest in striving to create a rural Utopia – an imagined perfect place or state of things. Many individuals, religions, political and economic systems and organisations have, through the centuries, sought to bring about what they perceived as a flawless society. Communism, Socialism, other 'isms', The League of Nations, The United Nations and The Welfare State are all attempts in that direction.

An independent 32-county Ireland governed by Brehon Laws administered by *Lia Fáil* was, in microcosm, Fr John's expression of that pipe dream.

Eric Cross in his review of *Utopias and Utopian Thought* in *The Irish Press* (2 August 1969) makes the following perceptive remarks which can be applied to Fr Fahy's unpublished novel

The origin of all aspects of Utopianism is discontent with present circumstances allied with hope. Discontent is the goad and a hopeful faith that man is perfectable is the carrot. But what the Utopian pipe dreamers seem always to have forgotten is that it is just hope and discontent which make man what he is. Remove the discontent – which has sometimes been described as divine – and remove also the hope and you have perhaps an angel or certainly something which is no longer man. Utopia achieved means both the end of discontent and at the same time the end of hope. Furthermore, while man is a member of the race and anonymous, he is also an individual with the individual quirks which make him an individual. When Utopia comes to be achieved the wisdom of the adage – one man's meat is another man's poison – remains and becomes 'one man's Utopia is another man's Dystopia'.

It looks as though Utopia as a form of heaven on earth is, and must always be, a misnomer. Heaven is heaven and earth is earth and never the twain shall meet. Man must always, as man, lie between the angel and the devil. We can never, even by act of parliament, be made perfect. We must, at best, be for ever, not perfect, but pilgrims of perfection. The carrot must for ever dangle and the goad for ever prod.

The following are three examples from Fr Fahy's voluminous correspondence over the years where prudence and tact were discarded and where a flexible or conciliatory approach might have yielded a more favourable outcome.

Coming up to Christmas 1933, diplomatic relations between the principalities of Bullaun (Fr P.J. Dunning) and Ballinakill (Fr Fahy) were strained. At issue according to Fr Dunning were 'these (Fr John's) underhand, persistent attempts you are making to deprive me of my housekeeper.' Fr Dunning went on to say that Miss McGuire (the lady at the centre of this contretemps)

> has shown me all your letters and furthermore she has undertaken to show me all other letters you may send and inform me of any other attempts you may make.

Ballinakill was now on a war footing! On Christmas Day Fr John wrote to Fr Dunning and began by extending 'Greetings and blessings of Christmas,' seasonal sentiments which were immediately negated by the next sentence which read

> I received your insulting and abusive letter today. As to the insults I ignore them on the 'principle of the kid glove.'

After a couple of paragraphs detailing the minutiae of the case, the letter continues

> Remember dear Rev Father that the days of personal chatteldom are over. Your implication that I dare not write to a person in your employment without your permission and knowledge savours of Baghdad.

Two paragraphs further on Fr John throws all caution to the wind and in a stunning flight of fancy delivers the following *coup de grace*:

> With regard to your farcical threat to use my letters to Miss McGuire which you say you have collected, you may use them for all you and they are worth and when you have broadcast them in this island, you may frame them and hang them on Nelson's Pillar, and if that does not suffice you may proceed to adorn the Eiffel Tower with them – not forgetting the Round Towers and the Pyramids of Egypt.

Two further short paragraphs follow before he concludes this yuletide salvo to his diocesan colleague in these self-deprecating tones:

> With every best wish and blessing,
> I am,
> Your humble servant in Christ,
> *Seaghán Ó Fathaigh.*

In one parish Fr John became aware through a contact that a young man with strong links to that parish was wandering aimlessly around Dublin and seriously at risk. He wrote to the young man's older brother who was also in the city and presumably expressed his grave concern at the turn of events.

The following letter duly arrived at Fr John's presbytery (names and addresses have been omitted to preserve anonymity):

> Dublin
>
> Dear Fr Fahy,
> This in reply to your recent letter which I was very surprised to receive. I would now like to assure you that my responsibilities towards my brother are well known to me and I have no intention of listening to any nonsense from you on that score. I don't know who your Dublin informants are, no doubt some busybody with very little to do, and I think you will agree with me when I suggest you would be better occupied yourself tending the needs of your own parish.
> Sincerely Yours,

A few days later Fr John replied in the following manner:

> Sir,
> In reply to your ignorant, cheeky and insulting letter of the 15th inst.
> Your brother's relations here asked me to write to you re _____; also to speak to _____. Also they showed me a letter from there stating that he was roaming round the city as an abandoned dead-end kid.
> Your father and your mother, God rest them, were born and reared in the parish. I am very glad that you were

neither born nor reared in it, and I hope I will be spared
the pain of seeing you live in it.

From what I now know of you I would expect that you
would consider advice from any priest 'nonsense' as you
call it.

Notwithstanding the fact that we priests occasionally
meet ignorant insulting types like you, we still go on with
our charitable work at all times and whenever called
upon.

Yours etc.

In June 1959 at the height of the Lusmagh agitation Fr Fahy
circulated a document (later extended and published in *Lia Fáil*)
outlining the background to the acquisition by Bertie and
Frankie Barry of the land they owned which was at the centre of
the controversy. In the course of that article, Fr John takes a
well-aimed swipe at his neighbour, the parish priest of Meelick/
Eyrecourt/Clonfert, Fr Cogavin who was a personal friend of
Bertie Barry.

Fr Cogavin was very different to Fr Fahy in temperament
and disposition. Prior to his appointment to Eyrecourt in 1945
he had been, for twenty years, an outstanding president of St
Joseph's College, Ballinasloe. Fr Declan Kelly in *People of
Ballinasloe* said that Fr Cogavin was

> very much associated with what may be called the
> Golden Age of Garbally

and that he was

> possessed of a distinguished bearing and cultivated
> clerical gravitas ...

The relevant paragraphs in Fr John's document stated that

> It is sad to relate that when this land-shark Barry, who by
> the way is an RIC man's son, was gobbling up those fami-
> ly farms in Lusmagh, his PP Fr James Cogavin came to
> Lusmagh to assist the land-shark in the work of depopu-
> lating rural Ireland. 'Land should go to the highest bid-
> der' is Fr Cogavin's principle.

According to that principle a multi-millionaire Jew or a Freemason syndicate could lawfully and morally become the owner or owners of all Ireland and constitute themselves The Sovereign Irish Nation.

May we remind the esteemed PP of Eyrecourt that it is the people of rural Ireland, not Barry's type or class, who have always fought and suffered for Faith and Fatherland. Today instead of campaigning against those who are fighting in defence of rural Ireland, as we hear he is, may we remind him that he would be doing better work if he employed his energy to have the vast ranches and estates in his parish divided amongst the young men who are forced to emigrate in hundreds.

Clearly Fr John wasn't a graduate of the Dale Carnegie School of Charm, which among other things claimed to help people to win friends and influence people. He regularly found it difficult to deal with those he perceived as hostile to him. He found it difficult to express his disagreement with those people in a moderate way. If a person, for whatever reason, got on the wrong side of him, in hurling parlance, he wasn't one to spare the timber!

At a personal level Fr Fahy was a complex man. In many ways he was a bundle of contradictions. He was a very humble man who embraced a simple lifestyle. Yet he expected, indeed demanded, that those at the highest levels of government would implement a range of policies proposed by him.

He wrote articles in which he advocated the acquisition and division by the Land Commission of large farms and estates owned by members of the Church of Ireland. Yet for many years he was an active and enthusiastic member of the East Galway Hunt at a time when its members were drawn almost entirely from the remnants of the Anglo-Irish aristocracy and the Protestant land-owning class. In fact he numbered some of the latter group among his closest friends.

Fr John was hot-tempered, impetuous, occasionally provocative and often less than diplomatic. He could be withering or outrageous in his comments and denunciations even from the altar. He inspired fierce loyalty among sections of the laity and from some of his brother priests, but he also provoked opposition and antipathy. He was droll and had a wicked sense of humour.

Stories abound about Fr John. He is reputed to have threatened to withhold Holy Communion from women in Lusmagh who continued to apply a dab of lipstick before heading out to first Mass on Sundays. Maybe he felt they were getting notions from going too often to the pictures in Banagher!

At baptisms Fr John often intervened in steering parents towards selecting a name chosen by him. Paddy and Annie Kelly presented their fifth child – a boy – for baptism on Sunday 5 December 1955.

The following conversation or something resembling it ensued between the proud mother and Fr John:

| | |
|---|---|
| Fr John: | Well Annie, what are ye thinking of calling him? |
| Annie: | Gerard, Father. |
| Fr John: | Now Annie you'll do no such thing. That fellow only became a saint by the skin of his teeth. |
| Annie: | Oh, God, well, what'll we call him so, Father? |
| Fr John: | I'll tell you what we'll call him, we'll call him Joachim, a right good biblical name. |
| Annie: | Joachim, who is he Father? |
| Fr John: | Joachim with his wife Anne were the parents of the Blessed Virgin. If he was good enough to be the grandfather of Jesus, he's good enough for your lad to be called after him. And mark my words, he's going to be either a famous politician or a great sportsman. |
| Annie: | Right so, Father; whatever you say yourself. |

It appears that Paddy (always known to his friends as PK) was content to leave matters theological in the capable hands of 'herself' and Fr. John. In an interesting coincidence Joachim sub-sequently married Anne Larkin, also from Lusmagh whose father Frank was the first treasurer of Lia Fáil. So a modern-day Joachim and Anne couple came into being. What the Irish body-politic missed by Joachim's absence will never be known but what a sportsman he turned out to be.

Joachim helped Lusmagh to an Offaly Junior Hurling title in 1973 and to their only County Senior Hurling success in 1989. He was one of the greatest midfielders of the modern era and contributed hugely to the Offaly Senior All-Ireland hurling suc-cesses of 1981 and 1985. His numerous awards include selection on the All-Stars team. Since his retirement from club hurling in 2000, when he was almost 45, he has been very involved in the emergence of Offaly Camogie teams to the top ranks. Joachim managed the Offaly Juniors to All-Ireland success in 2009 and to the Intermediate crown in 2010, an achievement for which he was selected as 'All-Ireland Camogie Manager of the Year.' A source of particular happiness to Joachim is that one of his daughters, Aoife, a PE teacher, has been a very skilful member of those All-Ireland winning teams.

Fr John's generosity to struggling families and those in need is constantly recalled. In 1968, less than a year before his death he gave his entire savings of £200 to a local collection organised in Abbey for the relief of famine in Biafra, Nigeria. Nobody was turned away from his door. His prayers and intercessions for those with serious health, personal or family difficulties were constantly requested. He was renowned for his matchmaking skills and he rejoiced in the many fruitful and enduring mar-riages he arranged.

Fr John remained true all his life to his deeply held Republican beliefs often at considerable cost to himself and his closest associates. He chose 'the road less travelled'. Personal fame or wealth were anathema to him. He spent his talents and considerable energy in trying to improve the quality of life of the rural dwellers and smallholders of Ireland. He selflessly de-voted himself in a particular way to the well-being of the parishes he served so faithfully. His memory will endure.

Fr Denis Meehan in his book *Window on Maynooth* (1949) de-scribed Maynooth men as 'uncompromising and independent'.

He quoted the 19th century novelist-priest Canon Sheehan 'in words that deserve to stand as their permanent apologia':

> 'Maynooth,' Canon Sheehan said, 'poured forth from its gates the strongest, fiercest, most fearless army of priests that ever fought for the spiritual and temporal interests of the people – men of large physique and iron constitutions … who loved their people and chastised them like fathers, but were prepared to defend them with their lives and the outpouring of their blood against their hereditary enemies. Intense in their faith, of stainless lives and spotless reputations, their words cut like razors; but they had the hearts of mothers for the little ones of their flock.'

Surely no more apt words could be found as an epitaph for Fr John Fahy. May the stony soil of Abbey Churchyard rest lightly on his mortal remains agus *go dtuga Dia a luach dhó i bhfochair naomh na hÉireann.*

# CHAPTER TWENTY-SEVEN

## *Obituaries*

These are some of the tributes to Fr John which appeared in newspapers and periodicals after his death. Some sentences and paragraphs containing for example, biographical detail already covered, have been omitted to avoid unnecessary repetition.

In translating the Irish language obituaries, every effort has been made to remain close to the original meaning. Literal translations were not attempted.

*Ar Aghaidh*
September 1969
*The magazine was published bimonthly by An tAth Eric Mac Fhinn for many years.*

AR AŞAIÐ : Meán Fómhair 1969

## An tАt. Seán Ó Fatais R.I.P.

An 19 iúl v'éag an tАt. Seán Ó Fatais, go nodana Dia gnásta air, san Osburdéal Réigiúin i nGaillim. Di a col ceatar, an Mátair Treasa Ní Fatais, as Clocar na Toirbirte i nGaillim, i n-áinois leis agus é a' págail báis. Tugad an corp go Maimscin Címéil feicín an lá i n-a diaid sin, áit a raib an táigreann ann an tАlao lá agus cuiread é sa Roilig le n-ais na sean-Mhaimscineac. An tАt. Míceál Ó Ragallaig S.P. a can tАfo-Aipreann. Di Tigearna Easburg Cluain Fearca i gceannuis, an tEasbog Sar-Oirrh. Pádraig Mac Giolla Seirhaid i sluag air, roih clér agus tuat, i látair.

As Cill Insín Dioma an tАtain Seán. hOinongead i n-a sagart ó Meádon Fosmair 1919, go luat tar éis don Dr. Tomás Ó Docartaig a beit togta i n-a Easbog ar Cluain Fearca. An Dliadain seo mar sin an a caogad bliadain dó i n-a sagart. Da uncal don tАt. Seán an tАt. Seosam Ó Fatais, a di i n-a sagart pairísce an Ceapac a' tSeagsail vireac roih an tАt. Seán Ó Néill. Go nodana Dia gnásta ar na mairb ar fad.

Ar na h-áiceadai an táit sé tamall ionntu di Dún an Octa, Clocá Stúicín (áit a raib sé i n-a séipliread don tАt. Pádraic Ó Feargail), An Dullán, Daile na Cille (áit an cuir sé páirte roih Cumann na Sagart nGaedealac i an cuir sé féasta ar págail bóid tráctnóra), Lusmag agus, ag deire a saogail, Maimscir Címéil feicín. Cuile áit da oá cráocta an cineacas i an plaicidiacт i biod cuma i n-a diaid nuair v'imtig sé.

Ni raib an tАt. Seán cuеал pаoi cáis an bit da geal leis a plé. (Ceo agat a ráo, má's breág leat, nac bé sáread cúcаl sgaitil). Ni raib sé, pé sgéal é, cúcal pаoi cáis an tSlánuigteóra a plé. Is cuimneac liom sean-Gaedeal—cmeál "sean-Mhaicais," ac nac raib an oiread eolais ag an bpob-

Di an tАt. Seán comaois, mórán, leis an tАt. Míceál Ó Griobta. Nuair vúnhandunsead an tАt. Míceál táinig an tАt. Seán an ais láitreac as Albain. Ofan sé an oi sin a' pairte agus a' guide le h-ais na comrann. Is cinnte go nveаса foodaire an tАt. Míceál i sgionn go mór ar a veancao agus ar a saogal.

Mar camnceoir is mó a mbéid cuimne ar an tАt. Seán. Ní caint poibli atá i sgeise agam, cé go mbiod corr-sеаnamóin uaid a mbiod clú air, agus go noeanna sé corr-píosa camnce i n-áiteacai agus ar ócáidí eile. Cuirhe air mar comráidеi atá i sgeise agam. Nuair veirim comráidúci, b'aige féin a biod an cuir da mó ven caint. Ní h-amlaid go veirim go mbiod sé ag iarraid go bord vaoine eile a scopad ó beit a' caint. Duine lágaс, séim é i measg a cáirde. Ас ni béad roih ort cur isteаd air—cé is moice ve focal anois is anist le cuirle ven caint a mеаllad uaid. Deired pаoi onaorbeact ag an sgaint néir, ceolman, lioñcá, frleаca—long Gaeóilge na sean-vaoine i Cill Insín Dioma an an gcanamainc a bi ar a cuir béarla. Labuirgead sé pаoi na fir boig—ní mó an meas a bi aige ortu ná mar bi ag Seacmán Céirinn. Tagan sé anuas uaid sin go Cat Eаconoma agus na Tринsig. Ас an oiread leis an Reаcтabrac níor misde leis "an Trínseac a' crit i n-a léime".

Seаd, va sagart cartannac, viaganta é. Sgríob sé leabar beag áluinn pаoi'n Aipreann. Is iomdа vuine a bi vuróeac vó agus atа néid roihe, le congnam Dé, "go nglaca siao sin iscеаc ins na h-áiceno síonai ё"—cárla an Soisgéal sin vá léigead an Doimnac a raib sé os cionn clár.

An leaba a bás di sé poigоeас, básca, vuróeac von luct freasтalа agus vo cuaimceoiri. Go séim, sumhneac, fios aige ó cosаd go raib sé go vona ó саoid sláince. Déаo cuma ort eisean feicеал gan ar a cumas ас focal nó vó a ráo. Lá nó vó roih a bás, nuair ceappá nár aicin sé éinne agus nuair

nac raib an oireab eulaip ag an ópon
al paoi—a bí ionraic ionraic agus omó-
sac, ac, an aobar eicint, a bí éirí ab
na Sacraiminti a cleactab. Bí go leon
a' guibe ar a son, go h-áiriu na mná
a mbíob aicne acu air agus iab i gCum-
ann na mban. Bí baoine ag iarraib é
a comairliub. An tác. Seán, nuair a clua
ar go leon eile, a labaim leis agus a
réibcig an sgeal.

cuigeas nac raib sé i nbon caba peic-
eál, cuala sé gut sagaine a táimig is-
teac. "Cé caoi a bpuil tú?" abeir an
tác. Seán—i ngaeoilge—i leac-cogar
íseal agus annsin ainm an csagaint.

Go bcuga Dia luac a saocain bó,
agus luac an csaocain a béanpab sé bá
mbíob an cumact agus an beis aige—
luac na beag-colac a poiceann an Slán-
uigceoir.

p. e. maep.

*Ar Aghaidh*, September 1969

Fr John Fahy RIP

Fr John Fahy died on the 19th July, Lord have mercy on him, in The Regional Hospital, Galway. His cousin Mother Teresa Fahy, Presentation Convent, Galway, was with him at the time. His remains were removed to Abbey the following day where Requiem Mass was celebrated on 21st and burial took place in the adjoining churchyard. The High Mass was sung by Fr Michael O'Reilly PP with the Bishop of Clonfert presiding. Also in attendance were Bishop Winters and a huge congregation of clergy and laity.

Fr John was a native of Killnadeema. He was ordained in September 1919 shortly after Dr Thomas O'Doherty was appointed Bishop of Clonfert. So this year is the Golden Jubilee of his ordination. Fr Joseph Fahy parish priest of Cappatagle immediately prior to Fr John O'Neill was an uncle of Fr John. The light of heaven to them all.

Fr John served in Eyrecourt, Clostoken – where he was curate to Fr Patrick Farrell – Bullaun, Ballinakill – where he welcomed members of the organisation representing Irish speaking priests and entertained them most hospitably – Lusmagh and finally in Abbey (Kilnalehan). His kindness and generosity were always in evidence and his passing was widely mourned.

Fr John wasn't reluctant to discuss any topic of interest to him. (You could say, if you wished, that at times he could have been a bit more reticent.) However he was never slow to engage in matters relating to our Redeemer. I remember an old man upright and honourable similar to, though less well-known than old Matthias in Padraig Pearse's *Iosagán*, who for whatever reason had ceased practising his religion. He had lots of people praying for

him, especially members of Cumann na mBan who had known him. He wasn't short of
advice. When all the rest had failed, it was Fr John who spoke to him and resolved the matter.

Fr John was a contemporary of An tAth Micheál Ó Gríobhtha. When he was murdered Fr John returned immediately from Scotland. He spent that night in vigil praying beside the remains. Without doubt the ultimate price paid by An tAth Micheál greatly influenced Fr John's outlook and indeed his life from that moment on.

Fr John will be widely remembered as a great conversationalist rather than as a public speaker even though the occasional sermon or speech from him will go down in the annals. When I think of conversations with him I recall that he usually monopolised the exchanges though not in any unpleasant manner attempting to silence the others in the group. In the company of his friends he was sociable and gentle. You would rarely interrupt him except to throw in the odd verbal prompt to draw a further torrent of conversation from him. You would be mesmerised by his smooth musical, fluent lyrical expression in English which he acquired from the spoken Irish of the old people of Kilnadeema. He used to speak about the Fir Bolg with the same contempt that Seathrún Ceitinn had for them. He would then move on to the Battle of Aughrim and the Trenches, the landlords. Like Raftery, he'd like to give them a good shaking.

Fr John was a kind and holy priest. He wrote an excellent little book on the Mass. There was many a person greatly indebted to him who has since gone to his eternal reward and who will now, please God, welcome him into the heavenly realms. Coincidentally the gospel read on the Sunday that he was laid out referred to the possibility of our being welcomed into heaven by those who have gone before us.

As the end drew near, he was patient and contented and grateful to his carers and to his visitors. From the outset he was placid and calm and he was fully aware of his rapidly deteriorating condition.

You would be touched to see him barely able to utter a word. A day or two before his death when you would think that he wouldn't recognise anyone and with his sight gone, he heard the voice of a priest who had dropped in. 'How are you?' says Fr John in Irish in a low whisper and then addressed the priest by name.

May God reward him for his life's work and for all he would have accomplished if he had been given the power and the opportunity to do so.

*This is the text of a short homily delivered by Fr Kevin Egan PP Lusmagh on the Sunday following the death of Fr John Fahy.*

Is it not a coincidence that the scripture reading today should be about the Blessed Eucharist when we are re-membering your late parish priest, Father Fahy. I will not presume to talk to you about his many good qualities – his humanity, his concern for those in need – you knew him better than I during his fourteen years living among you. But I would like to draw your attention to his living faith, particularly in the Mass. I am sure some of you have read the book he wrote and published on The Mass. He wanted to pass on to others what he thought and felt about the Holy Sacrifice. He was in the habit of referring to others as 'real brother Christians'. That expression had a deeper meaning for him than many people realised. You proba-bly do not know that he was engaged while in Lusmagh on another work which was not published and which he may not have finished. He was to call it *The Framework of What We Believe* and it was to tell about God's dealing with mankind from the Creation to the Redemption and to show the glory of God in the world around us.

Father John was truly a man of great faith. Nowhere is this better brought out than in the prayer to the Creator which he composed and to which he added the praises of the prophet Daniel.

The following appreciation by Oliver J. Flanagan, Fine Gael TD for Laois-Offaly, was published in the *Irish Independent* on 30 July and in the *Irish Times* on 1 August 1969:

## Late Very Rev. John Fahey, P.P.

### AN APPRECIATION

Father John Fahey, P.P., Abbey, Co. Galway is dead. His loss is felt, not alone throughout his native Diocese of Clonfert, but by his numerous friends in every part of Ireland.

"Father John," as he was affectionately known, was a singularly powerful and attractive personality. Of a remarkably modest and sincere disposition, he was sympathetic, outspoken, patient and understanding of the problems of the poor, the needy, aged and sick.

He championed the cause of the Irish small landowner. From the land he came, and he never lost sight of those who struggled on it for a better standard of living.

He had great gifts of mind and heart and in him shone Christian Simplicity. He was a good and holy priest of God, a skilful counsellor.

All admired his love for his native land; his ambition to see his country free and united; his love for the Irish language and culture.

Those of us whose privilege it was to observe his heroic dedication to his priestly calling can appreciate, at its proper worth, that radiant faith which inspired his work for the people in the parishes of Galway and Offaly whose welfare was always his chief concern.

His charity was boundless and this was exemplified in his generous contributions for the relief of famine in Biafra.

It is told that on his way home with his purchase of meat for a week-end, he got into conversation with an itinerant family —and handed over the parcel of meat so that a good meal could be provided for the children of this family of roadside dwellers.

I have happy memories of his great faith and of his ardent desire to do good for others. Father John was an inspiration to all of us.

All who knew him will miss him but will cherish happy memories of a truly great priest.

O. J. F.

## Laoch ar lár

D'éag an tAth. Seán Ó Fathaigh as deoise Chluain Fearta ar an 21 Iúil. Sagart tíriúil grámhar den seandéanamh a bhí ann, fear a bhí lán de thírghrá agus de dhúthracht ar son a phobail. Chaith sé na blianta tosaigh dá shagartacht in Albain le linn an ama sin toghadh é mar ionadaí na hAlban ar Ard-Chomhairle Bhráithreacht na Poblachta, an t-aon sagart amháin, go bhfios dúinn, a bhain áit cheannais amach san I.R.B. riamh. Ar a philleadh go hÉirinn dó chaith sé é féin isteach go dícheallach sa troid a bhí Peadar Ó Dónaill, An Coirnéal Muiris Ó Mórdha agus cuid den Arm Poblachtánach a chur suas in aghaidh "Blianachtaí na Talún" sna fichidí.

Rinn sé iarracht an troid ar son na talún a athbhunú sna caogaidí lena ghluaiseacht Lia Fáil agus rug na Gárdaí air athuair. Nuair a bhí oilithrigh Chumann na Sagart ag Aerphort Átha Cliath i 1960 ar a mbealach go Muenchen agus chuig Gaelscrínte na Gearmáine, cé tchímid ag an eitleán rómhainn ach an tAth. Seán, gan áit a bheith in áirithe roimhe ré, gan suíochán ar na busanna dó, gan leaba sna tithe ósta. "Tá mé ag teacht libh," ar seisean, "má gheibhim bás ar an bhealach. Murab bhfuil spás san eitleán seo, glacfaidh mé an chéad cheann eile go Francfort.

Murab bhfuil spás sa bhus, glacfaidh mé taxi in
bhur ndiaidh." Cad elle d'fhéadfaí a dhéanamh
le fear a raibh an sracadh sin ann ach fáilte a
chur roimhe agus cúpla duine den mhuintir óg
a chur ar mhullach a chéile. Fuair sé taom croí
an chéad mhaidin i bhFrancfort agus bhí eagla
orainn gur sa Ghearmáin a bhéarfadh an bás
air, ach i gcionn seachtaine nuair a bhí an t-aos
óg claoite leis an teas agus leis an taisteal, bhí
an tAth. Seán ar thús cadhanaíochta ag déan-
amh a shlí trí bhallógaí na mainistreach Gaelaí
i Regensburg a scriosadh in aer-ruathar. "Fia-
fraigh díobh arbh iad na Sasanaigh a rinne é", a
deireadh sé i meascán de Ghaeilge agus de
Bhéarla, mar níor mheas sé go raibh a chuid
Gearmáinise "láidir" go leor lena shoiscéal a
chraobhscaoileadh ansiúd, "agus inis dóibh faoin
chrot a d'fhág Cromail ar mhainistreacha na
hÉireann". Trodaí a bhí ann go deireadh an
chúrsa i ngach rud a bhain lena thír agus lena
phobal féin, agus dalta an trodaí i litir Náomh
Pól guímid go mbronna an Tiarna, an breith-
eamh cóir, coróin na glóire air.

*Death of a Warrior/Hero*
in
*An Sagart*
by
An tAthair (later An Cairdinéal) Tomás Ó Fiaich
*(Winter 1969)*

Fr John Fahy (Clonfert) died on 19th July. He was an ami-able, homely, old style priest, very patriotic and totally devoted to his parishioners. He spent his early years as a priest in Scotland during which time he was selected as Scottish representative on the Supreme Council of the Irish Republican Brotherhood, the only priest ever, as far as can be ascertained, to have been elected to the Executive of that organisation. On his return to Ireland he threw himself wholeheartedly into the struggle being waged by Peadar O'Donnell, Colonel Maurice Moore and sections of the Irish Republican Army against the Land Annuities in the 1920s.

In the 1950s, through his organisation Lia Fáil, he made another attempt to settle the land question but was arrested by the Guards a second time.

In 1960 when the members of Cumann na Sagart (The organisation of Irish speaking priests) were about to depart on pilgrimage from Dublin Airport on their way to Munich to visit Irish shrines in Germany, who did we see at the plane ahead of us but Fr. John who had made no advance bookings of any kind.

'I'm coming with ye,' says he, 'even if it kills me. If they can't fix me up on this plane, I'll chance the next one to Frankfurt. If there's no room on the bus I'll follow ye in a taxi.'

What else could you do with a man like that with such determination but welcome him and let a couple of the younger members of the party double up and make room for him.

He got a heart attack the first morning in Frankfurt and we were in dread that he'd die in Germany. But within a week, with the heat and travel taking its toll on the younger pilgrims, Fr. John was leading the way through the ruins of the Irish Abbey in Regensburg which had been destroyed in an air-raid. 'Ask them,' said he, 'was it the English that had done it' in a mixture of Irish and English as he felt he wasn't sufficiently fluent in German to get his message across. 'Tell them about what Cromwell did to the Irish monasteries.'

He was a great warrior to the end of his days for his country and his community and like the warrior in St Paul's letter we pray that the Lord, the compassionate judge will grant him heavenly glory.

*Midland Tribune*
*Sat. July 26, 1969.*

## Late Rev. John Fahy, Abbey (Loughrea)

The death of the Rev. John Fahy, C.C., Abbey, Loughrea, at the age of seventy-four caused widespread regret for although he was a most controversial figure he was a priest who was sincerely loved by his flock and was himself a man of sincerely held republican principles.

Born in Kilnadeema, Loughrea, he was educated at the Pines, Ballinasloe, and studied for the priesthood at Maynooth. He was ordained in St. Brendan's Cathedral, Loughrea, in 1919, and served for a time in Dundee, Scotland, and also in the Clonfert Diocese in the parishes of Clontoken, Ballaun and Ballinakill before being appointed Parish Priest of Lusmagh, Banagher.

When the land agitation incidents attributed to the local agrarian group called Lia Fáil reached a peak he resigned his position as Parish Priest and retired to Abbey (Loughrea) where he served as a curate. He was in failing health for some years past.

Throughout his life he was a dedicated nationalist and in Dundee he became President of the Scottish Division of the Irish Republican Movement.

Coming back to Ireland he was a familiar figure in South West Offaly and took part in the annual Manchester Martyrs commemoration ceremonies in Birr.

As a pastor he was deeply conscious of the spiritual and temporal needs of his flock and his concern for their welfare was that of a kind and good priest.

He will ever be remembered by those he served and all join in extending to his brothers Peter (Craughwell), and Thomas (Kilnadeema), deepest sympathy in their loss.

## REV. FR. JOHN FAHY, C.C., ABBEY

*Connacht Tribune Friday, July 25, 1969.*

# PRIEST-CHAMPION OF

# THE FARMERS

It was with a very deep sense of regret that the people of Clonfert learned of the death of Rev. Fr John Fahy, C.C., Abbey, Loughrea.

The end came to him peacefully as the climax to a life of extraordinary—indeed one might say unparalleled — energy and zeal.

Of Fr. Fahy it can be truly chronicled, that throughout his lifetime he worked every waking hour of every day towards a goal in which he believed passionately—the welfare of his fellow man both spiritually and temporally.

By his death, the Church in Ireland loses one of its most colourful and controversial characters. The Fr. Fahy who was in his 76th year, was born in the Parish of Kilnadeema, near Loughrea—an area pregnant with historical, ecclesiastical and agrarian associations. From his boyhood, he took a deep and abiding interest in all three and the hardships endured by his neighbours in their battle to survive on uneconomic holdings beneath the shadow of the Slieve Aughties, enkindled in him a burning desire to help them to help themselves.

His education began in the local National School and later he studies in The Pious, Ballinasloe, before entering Maynooth where he read a brilliant course. He was ordained in St. Brendan's Cathedral, Loughrea, in 1919 and would have celebrated the Golden Jubilee of his ordination a few weeks hence.

Fr. Fahy's first appointment as Curate was in Dundee, Scotland, and it was to make an indelible impression on his young mind. There he saw hardships amongst the people akin to those of his native place and he threw himself wholeheartedly into the Scottish Nationalist Movement to break its ties with the British Empire. He was later to get the signal honour of being elected President of Scottish Nationalists. When this conferred, the late Rev. Fr. Michael Griffin, was murdered by Crown Forces, Fr. Fahy returned home to attend his obsequies in Galway and funeral to the grounds of the Cathedral in Loughrea.

Afterwards, Fr. Fahy ministered in the parishes of Kilconieran, Bullaun, Ballinakill and was appointed Parish Priest of Lusmagh, Banagher, Clonfert's only parish across the Shannon, by Most Rev Dr. Philbin.

In each of these parishes he became a legend in his own time. His selfless devotion to his work, his great charity and his saintly life, won him veneration at home and far beyond the boundaries of his native diocese.

His passionate desire to see justice done for the poor, the downtrodden and the oppressed so suffered his life that even when it brought him into conflict of the law of the land, he refused to deviate one iota from the course in which he believed with every fibre of his being As a result he was imprisoned for a period after taking steps to prevent the seizure of a widow's cow, during his curacy in Bullaun.

Later his leadership in the Land for the People movement was to make his name a household word throughout the whole country. His precept and example were an inspiration to others in the struggle to retain the land of Ireland for the Irish

His dynamic leadership, his genial personality and his gifted eloquence, endeared him to one and all and made him welcome everywhere. He wanted nothing for himself personally and the donation by him last year of all the money which he possessed, £200, to the Biafra Famine Fund was typical of this great-hearted man.

After serving in Lusmagh for a number of years, Fr. Fahy resigned and took up an appointment in his final curacy at Abbey. There he continued to work with the same dedication and indefatigable perseverance that had ever marked his career.

Despite failing health he laboured unceasingly for every section of the community. Not least of those were the itinerants questionably—God's people. He helped and sheltered countless numbers of the poor and downtrodden. By his passing they have lost a real friend and the people of the parish will tastly miss the guidance, direction and experience, which he brought to their deliberations and the sense of fair play which he ever displayed.

Fr Fahy's great interest in the farming community was well known and he never ceased advocating their claims to more liberal Government consideration. Like the late Most Rev. Dr. Duggan, who admitted to being an 'extremist' in that he was 'extremely right' in his belief that the farmers were the hardest worked and worst paid section of the community when they should be regarded as the backbone and mainstay of the nation.

Fr Fahy persevered as their fearless and outspoken champion. He moved amongst his people with Saint-like simplicity and is deeply mourned by them.

His Lordship the Bishop of Clonfert, Most Rev. Dr. Ryan, presided at the Solemn Requiem Mass and Office for the Dead, celebrated in Abbey Church, and there were seventy-five priests from the dioceses of Clonfert and Galway; Carmelite Fathers and Redemptorist Fathers.

Amongst those were Rt. Rev. Dr. Winters, Galway; Rt. Rev. Mons. T. Gleeson, P.P., V.G. Kilconnell; Rt. Rev. Mons. P. Fahy, Galway; Rt. Rev. Mons. P. E. Mac Fhinn, Galway; Rt. Rev. Mons. P. J. Temple, New York, and V. Rev. P. McCabey, P.P., Castletowngeoghegan, Meath, who was closely associated with Fr. Fahy in the Land for the People Movement, in the Diocese of Meath.

V. Rv. M. O'Reilly, P.P., Abbey, celebrated the Mass; V. Rev. T. L. Murphy, P.P., Ballinakill, was deacon; V. Rev. J. Shiel, P.P., Woodford, sub-deacon, and V. Rev. M. H. O'Callaghan, Adm., Loughrea, and Rev. P. Abberton, C.C., Kilrickle, were chanters.

Amongst the huge attendance at the ceremonies were groups representing each parish in which Fr. Fahy had served. Mr. Oliver J. Flanagan, T.D., was amongst the general attendance.

Members of the Mid Galway Command I.R.A. wearing black berets and black armlets provided a guard of honour at the graveside and an officer laid a wreath on the grave.

Fr. Fahy was brother of the late V. Rev. Martin Fahy who died two years ago, and his survived by his brothers, Mr. Peter Fahy, Roo, Craughwell, and Mr. Tommy Fahy, Kilnadeema, Loughrea; by his nephews, Rev. Fr. Fiacra Fahy, White Fathers, Zambia, and Mr. Tom Fahy, Roo; his niece, Sister M. Declan, Mercy Sisters, India, and by a wide circle of cousins, relatives and friends.

---

## Hospital Downgrading

AT Monday's meeting of Roscommon Co. Council, Mr. P. Concannon asked was there any word from the Department about the down-grading or otherwise of the Co. Hospital.

Mr. Concannon said a question was asked in Dail Eireann last week but the answer given was not satisfactory.

Mr. S. Scott said Mr. Childers was now Minister for Health and a deputation should be sent to him.

Mr. E. Miley said the former Minister for Education had announced publicly that the hospital would be upgraded. The Council should ask the Taoiseach to confirm that statement.

Mr. J. Smith said that when Mr. Childers was a Parliamentary he got £3,000 for roads in the Tauchmacconnell area. He felt that if a deputation went to Mr. Childers about the hospital they would get a sympathetic hearing

These comments formed part of the tribute to Fr John by *The Scottish Catholic Observer* 8 August 1969:

> An Irish priest who became a legend in his life-time has died at Clonfert, Galway. He was Fr Jn Fahy CC (75) of Abbey, Loughrea, whose first appointment was at St Joseph's, Dundee. Fr Fahy demonstrated throughout his 50 years in the priesthood a deep commitment to the temporal as well as the spiritual welfare of the people. In Dundee he never ceased to protest against the hardships of the workers and he was prominent in the ranks of the Scottish Nationalists.
>
> When he returned to Ireland to take up an appointment in the diocese of Clonfert Fr Fahy led the 'Land for the People' movement. His name became known far beyond the West of Ireland. His qualities of leadership were outstanding, his gifted leadership made him welcome at campaign meetings and he was at all times a pious and humble priest. He wanted nothing for himself and it was typical of this priest – champion of the farming community last year, he gave all he possessed – £200 – to the Biafra Famine Fund.

*In 'The Fountain' (1970)*

*Garbally College Annual*

## BROTHER JOHN
### – an appreciation

I have been asked by the Editor of *The Fountain* to send him a brief account of Father John Fahy's life and career. It is a labour of love. My only regret is my inability to do justice to any portrait of that noble, self-sacrificing soul. A "brief account" of Father John is very apposite. A record of details would be only a repetition of the pattern. Never was the aphorism more true, "the child is father of the man".

John Fahy was a native of Kilnadeema, belonging to a family that gave distinguished service to Church and State. Along with a younger brother, to whom he always affectionately referred as Máirtín, he entered the old college at the Pines in the latter years of the first decade of the twentieth century. Only such stout landmarks are worthy signposts in the careers of these two strapping boys. Boys they were in every sense of that pregnant term, full of the zest for life, full of fun and "divilment", revelling in the exchanges of the football field. A stranger who saw the brothers on opposite sides would never suspect the deep bond of affection that bound them to the last, notwithstanding the staid elder's periodic fraternal corrections.

Those sturdy, handsome, country boys were, by no means, dull intellects. Without much effort and with a healthy contempt for academic distinctions they held their place in the class and were happy at that. In those far off days the evangelical counsel— "spare the rod, and spoil the child"—was a dictum much in vogue with pedagogic pundits. The young Fahys were stout-fisted lads and shrugged off the ministrations of the rod. Those boys were never spoiled and no rod would bar their headway once their compass was set in any direction.

In due course both matriculated and embarked in different courses, on the study of philosophy and the sacred sciences in preparation for the priesthood. In due course, also, after eventful and occasionally stormy voyages, both became devoted priests, throwing themselves heart and soul into their work, and leaving fragrant memories of their services in their field of activity. Father Martin, after a fruitful career in pastoral work in the U.S.A., retired in ill health and predeceased Father John by a few years.

John Fahy entered Maynooth in the year 1912. From the beginning John was a "character", probably the best known student in his division, not merely in his class. He was friendly, good-natured, communicative, quick-witted, quick-tempered and tenacious of his "bone", whether on the hurling field, the formal debate or mere casual encounter. In the occasional *contretemps* the fun was never far beneath the surface. The ready smile was always round the corner, and the warm handshake. John could "give it", but he could "take it" without resentment. He was a popular figure among his companions in Maynooth.

John Fahy's ecclesiastical academic career was cast in one of the most eventful periods of Ireland's chequered history, the years immediately preceding and following 1916, a wonderful time for any Irishman to be alive, but very heaven to be young for an ardently patriotic soul such as he was. The Maynooth students are always, in the main, a fine lot of boys, generous, open-hearted, intelligent, witty and humorous, and intensely patriotic. Their formal debates, especially where the subject of discussion touches them closely, are always worth witnessing. As a rule there is/in every class some outstanding character whose contribution is always in demand. This was John Fahy's milieu. During the critical days of the Rising in Dublin it is recorded that John was one of the forthright enthusiasts who counselled active participation in the fighting, following the Maynooth tradition of 1798. Wiser counsels prevailed. They were all aware that survival in the battle would be no guarantee for survival in Maynooth and nobody wanted to part with a devoted comrade.

Father John Fahy was ordained priest in the year 1919 in the Cathedral, Loughrea. His first appointment was in Dundee, Scotland. He threw himself with ardour into the busy pastoral duties assigned to him. He was always a deeply spiritual man, no fringes or tassels, solid piety "rooted in charity", as St Paul has it. No labours on his part were too much for the souls entrusted to him, and it was so during his whole priestly career.

After a brief span in Dundee Father John was called home to work in Clonfert, and henceforward his lot was cast amongst us. The call came, it is said, not a moment too soon. The Irish com-

munity was everywhere in ferment during those troubled years and where trouble was brewing Father Fahy never made himself scarce. Involvement was the watchword in every sphere of his career as student and priest. Feelings ran high and the lot of Irish exiles in foreign lands was often embittered by national and religious prejudice. Father Fahy's ardent political and patriotic convictions marked him out for the special attention of the minions of the law.

Before being fully launched on my theme I seem to hear the Editor's warning, "cut it short". Father Fahy's pastoral work in the various parishes of Clonfert was marked by the same spirit of zeal for the welfare of his flock. Any movement for the people's economic or cultural development had his wholehearted support, and no effort was too much where the people's welfare was at stake. On political and civil affairs his opinions were often outsized and in the eyes of some perhaps *outré*. But the man was transparently honest and self-consideration never entered in. Father Fahy was trusting to a fault, and sometimes as a result he became the unsuspecting victim of designing people whose ends were at variance with the noble ideals that inspired the priest's activities. Personally he was a most kind-hearted man and would share his last shilling with the man in need. Father Fahy's devotion to duty was duly rewarded by the gratitude and affection of a people who understood him and appreciated him. During the funeral services the "good word" was to be heard on every side.

Among the priests in Clonfert Father Fahy was welcome at every gathering. He had an intimate knowledge of local history and folk-lore and where evidence was wanting, Father John's vivid imagination supplied the deficit. He had a command of parabolical language that invariably created hilarious amusement.

In his latter years Father Fahy's health was failing. He resigned from the parish of Lusmagh and accepted a less arduous appointment in Abbey. In those years Dr Ryan had become Bishop of Clonfert and from the first the bishop recognised the sterling qualities of Father John and with a father's solicitude did everything in his power to make these latter years happy. Father Michael O'Reilly, his senior colleague in the pastoral care of Duniry and Abbey, proved himself with characteristic loyalty a genuine "brother", as Father John liked to call his fellow-priests. The memory of Father John Fahy will long remain fresh and green in his native Clonfert. Ar dheis Dé a anam uasal.

The following is the entry in *The Lusmagh Herb* (1982), written by Fr Tom Kennedy about his predecessor:

Father John Fahy (1945-1959) put Lusmagh on the map as author of the book *The Sacrifice of the Mass* and his active involvement in all the problems of his parishioners. He continued the rural electrification scheme in the parish and maintained that every young farmer should have a wife and forty acres, no more no less. He campaigned actively for these objectives. He had a commanding manner and like Father James Madden before him he did not fight shy of championing the cause of his parishioners. 'The land for the people and the bullock (rancher) for the road.'

He bestrode the parish like a colossus and had a horse to match, Simon by name. He rivalled Fr Callanan for growing flowers especially on the occasion of confirmation. He is dearly remembered for his great sympathy for the poor and his loving kindness and attention to the sick. He died in Abbey, Co Galway on 19th July 1969 and there he awaits the resurrection. There is a plaque to his memory in Lusmagh church.

# APPENDIX I

## *The Fahys – Clanricarde's Opponents*

*The following article first appeared in* Clanricarde Country, *published by the Woodford Heritage Group (1987) and is reproduced here with the permission of the author, Jim Fahy, Western Editor with RTÉ News.*

The Fahys are an old Gaelic clan, or group of clans, whose history in Co Galway can be traced with some degree of success through 1500 years. Their story is inextricably linked with 'Clanricarde Country' and family tradition has always maintained that they were the very last of all the native clans to yield up their lands to Clanricarde hands.

For most of the 1500 years they appear to have been a relatively minor clan, never achieving the power or importance of their Gaelic neighbours and overlords such as the O'Kellys, the O'Maddens, the O'Flaherties, or the great Anglo-Norman de Burgos. Yet there are today few family names which are as unmistakeably linked to a particular county as are the Fahys to Co Galway.

The Fahys are not, however, an exclusively Galway family, because numerous Fahys are also to be found in counties Tipperary and Waterford. Whether there is a direct link between these families, or whether they may have sprung from different roots and ancestors, hasn't so far been established. There are some grounds for believing that they may have entirely different roots and emerged at entirely different times in history.

The Galway Fahys have a tenuous claim to a 1500-year-old pedigree going back to about the year AD 500. In Munster we know that the year AD 891 was a significant date in the story of the Tipperary/Waterford Fahys.

Clan and tribal names existed for a considerable time before hereditary surnames came into being and the present day Fahys first crop up as members of tribal groupings like the Muintir Fathaigh, the Cinél Fathaidh and the Uí Fothaidh.

In Co. Galway the sites of most interest to those probing O'Fathaigh or Fahy beginnings are:

- Finnure in the Parish of Mullagh where lived a 6th century Úi Máine chieftain, Aengus Loman, whose son Fathadh may have been the progenitor of all the Fahys.
- Claregalway, which has been identified as the location of the '14 townlands of Muintir Fahy' referred to in an old Gaelic poem dating from about 1089 ... and again in the annals for the year 1247.
- Athenry, where there is a strong tradition that '700 Fahys fell' at the decisive battle of 1316 and where the townland name of 'Fahysvillage' still survives.
- Kilthomas Parish, which in 1585 was known as 'Pubbelmoynterfahie', where the Fahy Clan according to the Composition Book of Connaught owned seven quarters of land (probably about 1000 acres).
- Dunally, near Peterswell, where according to a 1574 survey, an O'Fahy castle existed. This is the only known reference to a Fahy castle. Its owner is listed as 'Shane O'Fae'.
- Woodford/Ballinakill, which by the middle of the last century (1856) had one of the single greatest concentrations of Fahy families in Co. Galway, after they had been driven from their ancestral lands and forced to eke out an existence on small mountainy holdings.

The distinguished historian John O'Donovan discusses the beginnings of the clan and the Fahy name, in both his notes on the *Annals of the Kingdom* (otherwise the *Annals of the Four Masters*) and in his *The Tribes and Customs of Hy-Many*. He says 'it is possible though not certain' that the 'Cinél Fathaid' were the ancestors of the present day Fahy and O'Fahy families.

The 'Cinél Fathaidh' were an Uí Máine tribe who occupied an unspecified part of the territory we now call east Galway between AD 500 and AD 800 ... and the Fahys strongest claim to a 1500 year old pedigree lies in trying to establish a link with the Shadowy 'Fathadh' who gave the tribe its name. He is listed in Uí Máine pedigrees as the great great grandson of Máine Mór, the warrior chieftain, who carved out the Uí Máine kingdom in present day South Roscommon and East Galway in the fifth century.

Fathadh was one of five sons of Aengus Loman, who is described as being from Finnure – located in the present day parish of Mullagh – and if we accept even the possibility that his descendants, the Cinél Fathaidh, were the people who afterwards assumed O'Fathaigh as a surname, we can then begin to look at Finnure as the possible starting point for a 1500-year exploration of Fahy roots.

In the *Book of Lecan*, Fathadh is listed with Eochaidh, Eochaidh, Ainmire and Carrthach 'a race of brothers' who were the sons of Aengus Loman. O'Donovan traces the 'Cinél Fathaidh' pedigree through thirteen generations down to about the year AD 800. After this they fade from the pages of recorded history. Other Fahy families subsequently crop up in several other parts of the country ... but there are no links with the Finnure area in medieval records. However, a most interesting geographical clue turns up in the 1683 *Petty's Atlas* of Co. Galway, which lists a townland of 'Gortnurfahy' right beside Finnure ... greatly strengthening the area's claim to having been Fahy patrimony and a likely starting point for the Fahy story in Co. Galway.

Another possibility is that one or other of the present day Fahy families may have been descended from either Fergus, son of Fothadh, King of Connacht, who died in the year AD 843, or from Fothadh, son of Conall, who lived three centuries earlier and died in the year AD 552. Of these two men we know virtually nothing, except that their deaths are recorded in the annals. Shortly after the death of Fergus son of Fothadh, the 'Uí Fothaith' and 'Uí Fathaidh' tribes appear in the same annals (AFM).

The same annals refer to the Tipperary Uí Fothaith in the year 891, when they went on a plundering raid on Loc Dacaech (present day Waterford Harbour). In his commentary on the *Annals of the Four Masters*, John O'Donovan says the 'Uí Fothaith' were a tribe situated in the Barony of Iffa and Offa in Tipperary – a territory which stretches the entire length of the Tipperary–Waterford boundary. He then links the Tipperary 'Uí Fothaith' and the Galway 'Cinél Fathaidh' and 'Cinél Fothaidh' as possible Fahy and O'Fahy antecedents.

So we have to consider that there may have been two or three separate Fahy or Ó Fathaigh families in the Middle Ages in Connacht and Munster. There is an even remoter possibility that the Fahy's may have a lineage going right back to the dawn of recorded history to the era of the Fir Bolg, when 'Fathach' was the poet of the Fir Bolg at the time of the Battle of Moytura ... which was fought in either Sligo or North Galway in mythological times.

In dealing with the meaning of the Fahy name, Professor Edward MacLysaght raises another possibility. In his *Irish Families*, he says the most obvious derivation of the name Fahy would appear to be from the Irish word 'fathach', a giant, the genitive being 'fathaigh'; but he claims that this is not what he describes as 'an acceptable assumption' and suggests that the name is derived from another Irish word 'fothadh', meaning a 'foundation'.

The present day Fahys may therefore be descended from either a historical or semi-historical personage such as:

- Fathach, the Fir Bolg poet
- Fathadh, the 6th century Uí Máine tribal chief
- Fothadh, son of Conal, who died in AD 552 or
- Fergus, son of Fothadh, King of Connacht, who died in AD 843

Or from tribal groupings such as:

- The Cinél Fathaid who lived in Uí Máine from AD 500 to AD 800
- The 'Uí Fothaid' who plundered Waterford in AD 891 or
- The Muintir Uí Fathaigh who lived around Claregalway in AD 1089

Or from a clan or group of people who took their name from a place such as:

- The 'Uí Fothaith' or 'Uí Fothaidh' who may have been so named because they lived in the vicinity of some kind of 'fothadh' or 'foundation' of which no trace or no folk memory now remains.

Chronologically then we can trace our Fahy references from the 'Cinél Fathaidh' who existed in East Galway from AD 500 to AD 800 ... to Fergus Mac Fathadh, King of Connacht, who died in AD 843 ... to the '14 townlands of Muintir Fahy' (in the Claregalway area) referred to in an old Irish poem dating from about AD 1089 recorded in O'Flaherty's *Iar Chonnacht*.

After this, history remains silent for another 150 years until the *Annals of the Four Masters* confirm that the Fahys were still in possession of their lands in the Claregalway area – but in the year 1247 that land was being laid waste by Turlough O'Connor on his way to 'burn Galway', then an Anglo-Norman strong-hold. The annals describe how Muintir Fathaigh were overrun by Turlough O'Connor.

A half a century later in 1316, there was a bloody and deci-sive battle between the Anglo-Normans and some new found Irish allies on the one side and the old Gaelic chieftains and their Scottish supporters on the other at the gates of Athenry. It was a disaster for the Irish and the flower of Connaught's manhood, as almost every prince and chieftain on the field perished. There is no historical record of the Fahys being involved – but there has always been a tradition in the family that 700 Fahys fell on the day – almost wiping out the entire clan in one fell swoop.

For the next 200 years we hear nothing more about the family ... until they crop up in various Elizabethan records in the year 1585. This time we find them back again in East Galway. One lot of seven O'Fahys are being given 'pardons' for various offences. Among them is a 'Cornelius O'Fahy – a priest.' Most of the seven are located in O'Madden territory. In 1585 we also find in the *Compositon Book of Connaught* that 'Pubbelmoynterfahie' – in other words the Fahy clan – owning seven quarters of land (prob-ably 1000 acres) in Loughrea Barony. No exact location is given but Pubbelmoynterfahie has been identified by many historians as being Kilthomas Parish near Peterswell/Gort. The *Composition* also records a 'Conor Oge O'Fahy' in Longford Barony.

From now on there are increasing references to the Fahys in connection with East Galway – the old 'Cinél Fathaidh' territory – in the documents of the English administration. In 1641 the *Book of Survey and Distribution* lists 25 Fahys in Poblemunterfahy (Kilthomas Parish) owning 700 of the 1700 acres in the parish. But by 1663 every single one of them had been dispossessed and it is only in nearby Kiltartan that any of the O'Fahys were able to hold on to their land. There is a strong tradition referred to by

John O'Donovan in his *Tribes and Customs of Hy-Many* that the Fahys were in fact the last Gaelic clan to surrender their ancestral lands to the de Burgo Clanrickards.

South Galway historian Pádraic O'Fathaigh in his unpublished manuscripts held in the National Library (Ms 21288) gives a most colourful description of the O'Fahy/Clanricarde confrontation.

## PARÓISTE CILL TOMÁIS

The Parish of Kilthomas otherwise Peterswell, was also known at one time as Pobal Muinntir Uí Fhathaigh.

The O'Fahy Clan had their headquarters at Dunally, where their castle stood until it was pulled down some time ago in order to get material for the building of a big house nearby, which was never finished. It was mysteriously falling down.

The Ó Fathaighs had free land long after the other clans had been subdued, but the De Burgoes did not interfere, until a famous dueller named Uilic de Burgo (or Burke) vowed he would make them pay rents and rates like everyone else.

Taidhg Ó Fathaigh, ie Taidhg an tSléibhe, was then chief of his clan, and one Sunday when he and most of his clan were hearing Mass at Kilthomas, De Burgo had the chapel surrounded with his soldiers. Hearing of what was on foot, the clansmen came running with their weapons to augment those that were at Mass. Seeing this de Burgo challenged Taidhg an tSléibhe to a single handed contest, to decide the issue and save the lives of the clansmen and soldiers.

De Burgo was seldom if ever beaten in a duel, and he was confident of victory. Taidhg however was trained at fencing in France and knew every thrust and turn of the sword as good as Ulick and perhaps better. The contest was not long in progress when de Burgo discovered that he had bitten off more than he could chew. It was a long and bloody struggle, and although Ó Fathaigh was severely wounded he had the strength left to overcome the representative of the English government, whom he left dead outside Kilthomas Chapel.

Clanricarde's soldiers took their dead chief, threw him into a cart and left the Ó Fathaigh triumphant. The Ó Fathaigh clan had free lands then until a Scot named Mac Giolla Breith

(Galbraith) made them yield. He took their lands and pushed them into the Sliabh Aughty Mountains.

They were great workers and managed to eke out a simple existence from their poor farms and the paltry pay received from the Landlord. Eventually the people were able to crawl back again and purchase or retrieve their farms which their ancestors owned, while the Landlords were gradually swept into oblivion.

The story of the Galbraiths is told in *The Irish Genealogist* (1968 iv) and it confirms that 'Major Hugh Galbraith' was the first of the family to settle in Ireland, having as family records put it 'appropriated' the Cappard districts ... hitherto O'Fahy property. The family continued to occupy Cappard, according to the article from 'the close of the 17th century to the late 19th century'. The family was descended from the Galbraiths of Balgair Castle, Stirlingshire.

The story of the Galbraiths of Cappard is traced from the marriage of Major Hugh Galbraith to Jane Dudley Persse of Roxboro in 1729, to the death of the last of the direct line, Richard Hugh Balgair Galbraith in 1908.

Whether there is a solid historical basis for the story of the Ulic de Burgo/Taidhg (an tSléibhe) duel has yet to be established, but two interesting facts have come to light.

1. The Patent Rolls of James I, list Taidhg Antlevy (an tSléibhe) Fahy as a South Galway landholder in the year 1620 (p. 440).
2. The Bibliotheque Nationale in Paris has a record of the granting of a coat of arms to a 'Jean Fahy', an architect and burger of the city of Lyon, in the year 1696.

Could it possibly be that this French branch of the Fahy family provides us with evidence to support Pádraic O'Fathaigh's claim that 'Taidhg an tSléibhe was trained in fencing in France'?

The 1700s saw Co. Galway being carved up between the great Anglo-Irish landowning families ... those whose activities would impinge most on them by then well scattered and dispossessed Fahys, would be the de Burgo/Clanricardes; the Dillon/Clonbrocks, the Trench/Clancartys and a host of minor Burke families, i.e. of Marble Hill, Ballyduggan, etc., it was in this period that the remnants of the Peterswell Fahys in particular waged an 'agrarian war' on those who had grabbed their lands and Pádraic O'Fathaigh, again in his unpublished manuscripts, describes in considerable detail the activities of the 'Terry Alts' and some of the Fahy leaders, including one of the best known 'Ned Rua'.

By 1856 Griffiths Valuation plots the rise and fall of the Fahys ... listing almost 600 'land occupying' – not landowning – Fahys in Co. Galway, the largest concentrations being in the south and east of the county.

The returns for Ballynakill parish show that the village of Dooras was Fahy heartland in 1856. Situated in present-day Woodford parish on the shores of the River Shannon at the centre of Lough Derg, Dooras had at one time fifteen different Fahy families.

There were 48 Fahy families in Woodford/Ballinakill according to Griffiths Valuation in 1856, even though 34 Fahys emigrated to Australia between 1830 and 1850. In modern times, therefore, Woodford has been the principal home of the Fahy clan and may well have been their original birthplace too.

On the international scene the story of the West Indian Fahies has also to be explored. Probably the most prominent member of the family was Rear Admiral Sir William Charles Fahie, President of His Majestie's Council of the Island of Tortola, who was granted the coat of arms – which most Fahys now use – in the year 1825. Smith's *The General Armory* describes him as of 'an old Connaught family'. So the family has two distinctive and different coats of arms – the French one granted to Jean Fahy of Lyon in 1696 and the English one granted to Sir William in 1825. Father Fahy of Argentina is probably the best known Fahy émigré, and though born in Loughrea, his family originally came from Derryoober, Woodford.

## APPENDIX II

# *Fr Fahy and other radical priests*

Fr Fahy was one of the most outspoken anti-Treaty priests with strong Republican sympathies to have been involved either in the War of Independence, The Civil War or in the years and decades following the establishment of the Free State. But he was not the only one to defy the authority of church and state in nailing his convictions firmly to the Republican mast.

A brief account follows of three such priests, each with his own distinctive personality, attributes and political vision.

## *Fr Thomas Burbage 1880-1966*

Fr Burbage, a priest of the diocese of Kildare and Leighlin was a curate from 1916 to 1924 in Geashill, a village a few miles from Tullamore. He was interned in Ballykinlar camp during the War of Independence and had been vice-chairman of the County Offaly Executive of Sinn Féin in 1917. He was as implacably opposed to the Treaty and to those who supported it as he was to the British forces in the years from 1916 onwards.

Like Fr Fahy he used the pulpit during Masses to attack the Free State government over its execution of Republican prisoners. So scathing and inflammatory were some of his sermons that the Commander-in-Chief of the Free State Army, General Richard Mulcahy, felt compelled to protest to Bishop Foley about the conduct of Fr Burbage. General Mulcahy had been informed by an officer of the Free State Army who attended Mass in Geashill. Mulcahy's accusation against Fr Burbage was that he incited

> certain people to take part in or aid and abet an attack on the National Forces in that he at the Roman Catholic Church, Ballinagar, Offaly on the 25th Day of February 1923 encouraged the congregation there assembled to rise against the National Forces.

Fr Burbage, though forbidden to appear at an anti-Treaty meeting in Tullamore in April 1922 before the outbreak of Civil

War, insisted on accompanying de Valera and Harry Boland on the platform at a rally in Portlaoise where he renounced the Treaty in the most forthright terms.

During the War of Independence he had been a Republican Court judge. On the occasion of his release from internment in Ballykinlar, Co. Down, he was joyously received back into the fold by his bishop and fellow-priests and presented with an address praising, according to Patrick Murray,

> his character and judgement ... and celebrating his work for the Irish language, the revival of Irish industries and a rebirth of a spirit of self-reliance in the people.

Supporters and people in his parish presented him with a

> beautiful two-seater Morris Cowley motor car as a token of their esteem.

In October 1925 Fr Burbage was secretary to the committee which welcomed back to Ireland for a speaking tour Archbishop Mannix, former Professor of Theology in Maynooth and now presiding over the diocese of Melbourne, Australia. Mannix was highly critical of the pro-Treaty stance taken by the overwhelming majority of the Irish clergy and used a number of speaking engagements to point out that the Irish hierarchy had erred in making claim to 'infallible sanction in political matters'.

Over thirty years later Fr Burbage as PP of Mountmellick gave practical and moral support to Fr Fahy when he founded *Lia Fáil*. He regularly attended at Tullamore and other locations during the court appearances of *Lia Fáil* members in 1959/1960.

There is a fine monument to the memory of Fr Burbage facing the village green in Geashill. It bears the following inscription:

*Fr Thomas Burbage, Priest and Patriot*
*Curate in Geashill 1916/1924*
*in recognition of his active participation in the fight for freedom*

## Fr Michael O'Flanagan 1876-1942

Fr O'Flanagan, a priest of the diocese of Elphin, is another man who fits easily in the group of clerics who advocated a strong republican line in the national independence movement and a radical approach to the question of land redistribution. Inevitably he too fell foul of both the civil authorities and his church leaders. Like Fr Fahy in the following decades, he gave open and vocal support to young men who received prison sentences as a result of their actions in trying to improve the lot of subsistence farmers and landless people.

In 1917 Fr O'Flanagan was vice-president of Sinn Féin and by the following year his bishop, Dr Coyne, had suspended him from public ministry because of his refusal to cease political campaigning. He was most vehement in his opposition to the Treaty and during Peadar O'Donnell's editorship of *An Phoblacht* he was a regular contributor.

At the outbreak of the Spanish Civil War in 1936, he organised support for the Republican anti-Franco side with Frank Ryan, George Gilmore and O'Donnell.

One of Fr O'Flanagan's ongoing crusades was directed at the Irish hierarchy, who in his opinion was totally inconsistent by ordering priests to desist from political involvement while simultaneously turning a blind eye to clerics who became involved on the pro-Treaty Free State side.

He set out clearly for lay Catholics how they could act independently of their priests in political affairs. This matter is covered extensively in Denis Carroll's biography of Fr O'Flanagan (1993)

> It is your duty to make up your own mind, and pay no more attention to the views of your pastor than you would to any man of equal political intelligence.

For priests who, he contended, had 'the right and duty to speak out as citizens where justice and freedom are threatened in a situation of conflict' he had somewhat similar advice:

> You are not bound to follow the leadership of your bishop in political affairs ... it is your duty to form your own mind and pay no more attention to the views of your bishop than to the views of any other man of equal political acumen or the reverse!

In 1925 he formulated the principle 'that the good of the people was the supreme law (*salus populi, suprema lex*) and this to him seemed more fundamental than the commands of an individual bishop.

Fr O'Flanagan also believed that

by making religious authority the basis of political decisions we broke the very bedrock of democracy.

With equal vigour he rejected interference of civil authority in matters properly religious.

Fr O'Flanagan invoked no less a figure than St Augustine to drive home his point:

In all things necessary, unity;
In all things doubtful, liberty;
In all things, charity.

In 1939, largely through the intercession of the Papal Nuncio at the time, Dr Paschal Robinson, Fr O'Flanagan was permitted to say Mass in public again on his appointment as chaplain to the Carmelite nuns in Roebuck and Kilmacud, Dublin.

The Catholic newspaper *The Standard* (14 August 1942) wrote as follows about Fr O'Flanagan after his death:

Like Pearse he was a student and teacher with thought and sympathy for youth; like Thomas Clarke he seemed in his person to typify the spirit of resistance to oppression; like James Connolly he loved the people who work in poverty.

## Fr Patrick Browne 1889-1960

Patrick Browne was a native of Grangemockler, Co. Tipperary. After studying at Rockwell College, Clonliffe seminary and in Paris at the Sorbonne, he was ordained in 1913 for the Archdiocese of Dublin but was immediately appointed Professor of Mathematics and Natural Philosophy in Maynooth in succession to Éamon de Valera. He was also a brilliant linguist and translated classic works from Greek, French and Italian into Irish.

Fr Patrick, or An tAth Pádraig de Brún as he was also widely known, held strong republican views. He regularly encouraged his students to express in word and action their own nationalistic fervour.

At the Maynooth prize-giving ceremony in June 1916, the college president Fr John Hogan used the occasion to address the students on the need to show proper respect for authority, an approach which drew a very noisy response from the student body. Fr Corish in his *History of Maynooth* is in no doubt that it was An tAth Pádraig who orchestrated the protests against the president.

He was heavily involved in the Cavan by-election of May 1918 on behalf of Sinn Féin candidate Arthur Griffith, then a prisoner in Gloucester and whose victory on that occasion was probably the final nail in the coffin of John Redmond's Parliamentary Party.

Within a month of that election and largely because of de Brún's involvement in it, the Trustees of Maynooth (The Bishops) issued a directive to the staff of the college to the effect that any future political activity by them would first have to be sanctioned by the president and the local bishop. De Brún was severely reprimanded. He said in his defence that he had obtained permission from local parish priests to attend and speak at a number of meetings but that in future he would desist from all such activity. This promise was very similar to assurances given by Fr Fahy a decade later – promises neither man took too seriously.

In July 1922 during the Civil War, William T. Cosgrave wrote to Archbishop Byrne of Dublin complaining that de Brún had, according to Patrick Murray 'visited the Irregulars in the Swan Public House, York Street for the purpose of hearing their confessions' and that 'this action could not fail to be interpreted by them as implying complete approval of their unlawful activities.'

At the end of October 1922 Pádraig de Brún was one of a small group of academics which included Seán T. O'Kelly's wife Cáit, lecturer in French at University College Dublin, who were selected to draft a comprehensive letter in French to the Pope. The letter would present a coherent and detailed summary of the republican position as a response to the pro-Treaty pastoral issued by the hierarchy on 12 October which imposed heavy episcopal sanctions on those choosing to disobey its contents. The letter was prepared over a number of weeks and ran to almost ninety pages. It was presented at the Vatican by Professor Arthur Clery, Dept of Law at University College Dublin and Dr Conn Murphy a civil servant who had been staunchly anti-Treaty. Dr Murray points out that Murphy was 'dismissed from the Civil Service that year for political reasons and rein- stated in 1928.'

An tAth de Brún continued his active political involvement on the republican side much to the dismay of both the Cosgrave government and the Maynooth authorities.

In the following February a Free State Army operation involv- ing de Brún is graphically recorded by Dr Murray as follows:

In February 1923, in the course of an army raid on Sinn Féin headquarters in Suffolk Street, he was arrested in the company of Mary MacSwiney, Mrs Tom Clarke and Kathleen Barry. The circumstances of the raid were com- municated by Army Headquarters to Monsignor MacCaffrey, President of Maynooth College, who in turn reported them to Cardinal Logue and the other College Visitors. The arresting party searched Browne, who 'styled himself Father Perry of Maynooth,' and the three women, and claimed to have found an assortment of sub- versive documents, one of these 'inciting to the murder of the Governor-General' in retaliation for having 'con- firmed the sentences of execution' of Republicans. The soldiers also found a copy of a poem by Browne signed Pádraig de Brún 'apparently extolling the action of five deserters from the National Forces who took a machine gun and rifles from Baldonnel Camp.' The army authori- ties also alleged that Browne gave the officers 'a consider- able amount of very unpriestly abuse,' and that it was this fact that led to his being detained. He also embarrassed the authorities even further by refusing to sign the under- taking normally required of all suspected prisoners be- fore being released. In the circumstances, the Maynooth authorities felt obliged to take action against Browne. The College Visitors instructed the President to draw his at- tention to the Statute which forbade any official of the col- lege 'to take public part in politics by presence, word or writing without the approbation of the President.' He was also told to comply strictly with the statutes 'as long as he remained an official' of Maynooth.

Regarding his name being noted as 'Father Perry of Maynooth', it has been suggested by Fr Corish in writing about that same incident that 'one of the women had referred to him as Fr Paddy of Maynooth and that the president of the college was instructed to notify him (de Brún) that

> in view of the impression which prevails among the clergy and people of the country that you have been associated with the activities of the Irregulars, the bishops deem it their duty to direct your attention to the terms of the College Statute II, 16.

The undertaking which An tAth de Brún was unwilling to sign required a suspect

> not to take up arms against the parliament elected by the Irish people or the government responsible to that parliament nor support in any way such action nor interfere with the property or persons of others.

Almost a year and a half after de Valera's command to his supporters to lay down their arms, officially bringing the Civil War to an end, de Brún was still loath to withdraw from the fray.

In September 1924 he maintained an all-night vigil outside Beggars Bush Barracks in Dublin with Mary MacSwiney and Erskine Childers, son of Erskine Childers senior, a close ally of de Valera who had been executed in November 1922. Word had circulated that the Free State authorities were about to exhume the remains of Childers for removal to a secret location. In fact the planned removal was abandoned at short notice.

It is perfectly clear that neither Maynooth College Statutes, presidential directives nor Free State Army surveillance were enough to curb a man so firmly rooted in his political convictions.

Todd Andrews, a founder member of Fianna Fáil, was keenly aware of the importance of being able to count the intellectual de Brún as a high-profile supporter of the Republican cause, especially when the overwhelming majority of the bishops and priests were unrelenting in their criticism of de Valera, his associates and their political stance.

His mere presence as a priestly sympathiser with the Republicans,' Andrews claimed, 'assuaged any feeling of guilt I might have had as a result of abandoning my allegiance to the church, although I would not have imagined myself going to him for confession.'

Patrick Murray's verdict on this was that

the attachment of such notable clerical sympathisers as Browne to their cause inevitably mitigated the republicans' sense of alienation from the church.

It should be noted that Pádraig de Brún and his family made a notable contribution to the church and state during the 20th century. Two of his brothers were also priests, one of them becoming a Cardinal and head of the Dominican Order worldwide. His sister, a lecturer in Irish in UCD, married Seán MacEntee, a formidable minister and one-time ally of Dr John Dignan, Bishop of Clonfert. MacEntee's daughter, Máire Mhac an tSaoi, distinguished Irish poet and Gaelic scholar, is the wife of the late Dr Conor Cruise O'Brien.

An tAth Pádraig was a long-serving chairman of the Dublin Institute for Advanced Studies, a position from which he resigned in 1945 to become president of University College Galway.

## APPENDIX III

# Clann na Talmhan,
# Dan McCarthy and The National Land League

An outline follows of two of the best known organisations, Clann na Talmhan and The National Land League which, like *Lia Fáil*, were set up to improve the lot of the smallholders of Ireland at different times in the 20th century.

### Clann na Talmhan

Clann na Talmhan, which translates as 'Family of the Land' was set up at a meeting in Athenry in June 1939. Michael Donnellan emerged as its leader. He put his considerable energy and political skills at the disposal of this new organisation which hoped to drag Irish farming out of the economic mire into which it had slipped.

Like Fr Fahy, Donnellan had strong republican sympathies having been active in Sinn Féin. He was also a Fianna Fáil county councillor for some time. Both men like so many others had gradually become disillusioned with the way a hard-won freedom was being managed.

A native of Dunmore, Donnellan had been an outstanding club, county and Railway Cup Gaelic footballer in the 1920s and 1930s. His sons John and Pat went on to win All-Ireland senior medals with the great Galway three-in-a-row teams of 1964-1966 and to add further lustre to his rich football legacy, his grandson Michael was one of the stars on the successful Galway All-Ireland winning teams of 1998 and 2001.

Donnellan's analysis of the plight of the country was very similar to the conclusions reached by Fr Fahy. The rise and fall of Clann na Talmhan are comprehensively outlined by Dr Tony Varley (School of Political Science and Sociology, UCG) in *Galway – History and Society.*

Donnellan, like Fr John, had a very acerbic turn-of-phrase. Regarding the political elite of the day he said, according to Varley, that:

You could take all the TDs, all the senators, all the ministers and members of the judiciary and all the other nice
fellows and dump them off Clare Island in the broad
Atlantic. Still Ireland would succeed. But without the
workers and producers the country would starve in
twenty-four hours.

Having severed his links with Fianna Fáil Donnellan did not
spare his former political colleagues. Varley states that

a recurring image in Donnellan's fair-day speeches was to
liken Fianna Fáil to a banana that started life green, then
went yellow before finally going rotten.

A further striking similarity between the Clann na Talmhan
leader's understanding of the reasons for the malaise in Irish
rural life and the views later expressed by Fr Fahy can be detect-
ed in Donnellan's contention that

the rightful position of farmers had been usurped by
politicians, civil servants, monied professionals as well as
by cliques of Jewish and Freemason usurers.

Initially the Clann na Talmhan grouping intended to be non-
political but that policy was eventually discarded. In the 1943
general election, Clann na Talmhan succeeded in having 13 TDs
elected. In subsequent contests through the 1940s and into
the 1950s the party fared less well despite participating in the
two inter-party governments of 1948-51 and 1954-57 in which
administrations Donnellan held the position of Parliamentary
Secretary to the Minister for Finance with responsibility for the
Board of Works. Joseph Blowick, the party leader, became
Minister for Lands. In co-operation with James Dillon, Minister
for Agriculture, he oversaw a large afforestation programme
and a nationwide land reclamation scheme. Donnellan ensured
that the Corrib–Clare drainage project became a reality and
reaped a rich political dividend, particularly in his own constituency, as a result.

The participation of Clann na Talmhan in those inter-party
governments helped to break the sixteen-year stranglehold on
power which Fianna Fáil had held, and according to Varley:

as the movement was to be ultimately absorbed by Fine Gael, Clann na Talmhan became the means of transferring farmer votes in the west from Fianna Fáil to Fine Gael.

However, by the late 1950s the party was in terminal decline. Varley contends that by participating as a political grouping the lasting significance of Clann na Talmhan

> was in demonstrating the ultimate bankruptcy of direct farmer involvement in party politics. Farmers that organised along party lines could only become active accomplices in their own subordination ... and the experience of Clann na Talmhan became an exemplary case of how NOT to organise Irish farmers.

Sadly, Mick Donnellan died suddenly in September 1964 on The Hogan Stand as he watched his son John captain Galway to All-Ireland glory over Kerry on a scoreline of 0-15 to 0-10. John was elected as a Fine Gael TD in the subsequent by-election.

In a political career spanning twenty-five years, John served as Minister of State in a number of departments. He invariably expressed himself in a forthright manner and sometimes found it difficult to adhere to strict party discipline. A good example of this independence of spirit occurred in 1987 when on a particular policy issue, he publicly criticised his leader by declaring that

> if 'twas raining soup [Alan] Dukes would be outside trying to gather it with a fork.

In the process he clearly showed that the talent for coining a colourful phrase was not confined to the Mick Donnellan or John Fahy generation.

## Dan McCarthy and The National Land League

*This account of Dan McCarthy and The National Land League was written by Rosita Sweetman. It is an abridged version of the chapter on Dan McCarthy which first appeared in her book* On Our Knees *(1972) and is included here with the author's permission.*

Dan McCarthy, the man who is the driving force behind the National Land League was born into a small farming family in Mullingar. The second of six children. At thirteen he left school to go to work as a labourer on a neighbouring farm. At eighteen he packed a suitcase and left for England. Forced off the land which couldn't support more than the one family, and that was his elder brother's right; forced from his country which could scarcely provide jobs for industrial workers, let alone 'redundant farmers sons'. But if he left he didn't leave willingly. He vowed he'd come back.

For ten years he worked on different building sites around England. He met hundreds of fellow small farmers' sons also forced from the land. He joined a trade union in the building trade and rose to the rank of shop steward. He worked and saved. Didn't smoke, or drink, and slowly hardened his views. Why were the farmers being driven off the land? Why was he here in England with all these other small farmers' sons? What could he do about it? He saved enough to buy himself a small cottage in Mullingar, his home town, so he'd have something to come back to, and when he had £2,000 in the bank he returned. This time with a wife he bought a small farm, stocked it and considered the situation around him.

An estate belonging to an old family in Westmeath came on the market in 1959. 1,300 acres, bordering a number of small farms. The local farmers tried to get the Land Commission to purchase, but failed. A certain foreigner bought 500 acres of land for £17,000 and three years later sold the same land for £40,000 to the Duke of Mecklenburg. Mecklenburg later enlarged his estate to 2,000 acres. The small farmers met. They wondered, what could they do?

'At first,' says Dan, 'we did all the usual things. Contacted our local TDs, you've got to understand that in the country nobody goes to the toilet without asking their TD. We asked the Land Commission to acquire the land, went on deputations. We got nowhere. Finally we decided to write to the Duke of Mecklenburg ourselves. We told him we wanted the land, that we needed it. We told him that our quarrel was not with him but with the Land Commission and with the government officials who stood by as the land was sold over our heads. We also pointed out politely, but firmly, that he should hand the land back to the Land Commission and receive due compensation – by that we didn't mean speculator's prices, but what he paid for it. We also said that if he made it awkward for us then we'd have to consider our next move and direct our agitation against him. We got no reply.' Whether the Duke ever received the letter or not is unclear. However the land was eventually sold to the Irish Land Commission and is currently being rented out to the local small farmers.

In the beginning the farmers thought of organising a big meeting in the town with big names to come and speak at it. Peadar O'Donnell, a veteran in the struggle for small farmers' rights, advised against it. 'If you have something worthwhile on your minds,' he advised, 'stand up before your neighbours and tell them about it. If it makes sense to them you are on the way to launching a movement. When your movement becomes strong the powers that be will listen to you.' That advice was taken and it laid the basis for the Land League structure. The small farmers are the leaders, the organisers and the initiators of the league.

Their first meeting was such a success that they decided to hold a conference inviting everybody – church, business and social – in the county to send delegates. The purpose of the conference was twofold. Firstly to show that the men behind the League were simply small farmers. This was to forestall slurs of 'outside agitators', a weapon easily used to effect in a hesitant, conservative community. The second purpose was to enlist the help of as broad a section of the population as possible – 'like the Civil Rights Movement in the North' comments McCarthy.

The basis was laid. A committee appointed. A plan of campaign drawn up. Farmers from all over the country began contacting the League. New branches were set up. In July 1970 a National Council of eleven members was appointed with

Dan McCarthy as President, to meet bi-monthly. A National Executive of five members to meet at a moment's notice was also appointed. A membership fee of £1 per annum was fixed. At the last count over 7,000 members were enrolled.

The aims of the League can be broadly divided into three categories:

1. They want the 'unit for land distribution to be the viable family farm'. To achieve this they want 'the break up of all large estates, foreign or Irish owned'. The viability of the family farms to be ensured by abolishing the present annuities (a rent payable to the Land Commission for 'new' land), and a complete overhaul of government subsidies for farmers, of which McCarthy reckons, 80 per cent are going to the big farmers.
2. They want an optimum acreage for the family farm unit to be fixed, depending on the land value in different areas, and that all land above and beyond this re-apportionment to be placed in a Bank of Land to create new holdings where desirable.
3. They want the future large unit farms to be made up of voluntary farming co-operatives between family farms, and the banning of large privately owned estates.

On the face of it their battle would seem hopeless. Nobody will admit quicker to the innate conservatism of the small farmers than Dan McCarthy. Deflected from outright agrarian warfare in the late 19th century by the Land Acts, which made them poor, peasant proprietors, rather than just poor tenants; weakened over the years by the massive emigration of the brightest and ablest young men and women from the land; and 'hypnotised like bloody rabbits' by various politicians, chiefly Fianna Fáil, whom they elected in the hope of a better deal, and who kept them quiet by dividing up a bit more land, coughing up a few more subsidies.

Perhaps a great deal of the League's success to date – the break-up of the Mecklenburg Estate, and its planned division among the small farmers at the moment, the numerous stoppages of private sales, the increasing awareness of the Land Commission that small farmers must be consulted – is attributable to Dan McCarthy's trade union experience.

You'd wonder though how trade union activity could be used in land agitation? ... 'We hear of a piece of land that's to be sold. Before the sale we have a branch meeting in the area. We work out how much we think the land is worth per acre. We contact the Land Commission and tell them. The branch then appoints somebody to organise a picket outside the farm, prior to the sale. We have banners saying 'Grabbers Go Home', 'Scabs Out' – things like that. This is important, because the people coming down to view the land, see the picket and know there's some trouble on. We've even had foreigners taking photos of us! It also makes the sellers aware that we're watching them.'

'Then we appoint another man to attend the auction. Once the deeds and that have been read out our man stands up and asks the people not to bid. He says he's from the National Land League, and that the local farmers have been watching this piece of land. That we don't dispute their right to buy it (it's important that, McCarthy stresses slowly, otherwise we might be accused of intimidation), but if they do buy the land they'll be regarded as scabs and grabbers by all the local people.' McCarthy watches your face to see if the message has sunk in, 'that usually works. The man with the money doesn't want pickets on his house, or trouble on his land.' Who does?

They can be ignored though, threats, or whatever you like to call them. To broaden the scope of the pressure the League can bring to bear Dan McCarthy is having discussions with one of the biggest trade unions in the country. 'If monied interests, the ranchers, come in and buy land over our heads, then we'll ask the local trade unionists to black them. We'll get the trade unionists in the sales yards to black them. We'll get the local shopkeepers and suppliers to black them.' If you can't frighten them out, starve them out? Isn't it all a bit anti-foreigner, petty nationalism for a dying cause? 'No, we're not anti-foreigner at all. We'll welcome them, but they cannot take possession and control of our land. We will oppose all those who use their money to exploit us – native or foreign.'

Is it lack of education that's kept the farmers so beaten down? 'Not at all. We don't need books to see the problem. We look out our windows and we can see it.'

'We see our elected representatives collaborating with our enemies. We can see it clearly because we're the victims of it.' Of well-intentioned people and their well-intentioned reports to improve the lot of the farmers he's equally derisive: 'Let the countryside once get angry and we'll sweep past these well-intentioned people. It's not in them to lead. To lead you must not only see the light – you must feel the heat, feel the anger, the blazing awareness of the injustice we suffer; the national betrayal that bears heaviest on us.'

What do they want so, and where do they want to go?

'We've no ambitions to be millionaires. We want to be able to live with our families on the land. This is being made impossible for us. I came back to the fields and the hills that I grew up in as a boy. To bring up my own children here, and give them a chance to roam the countryside as I did. If they want to go off afterwards that's all right. At least they'll have the choice.'

'The National Land League was literally forced into existence because of the exploitation of the people. What we've to learn is to define our enemies, and we've done that. We'll make it hot for them, and if this government and the institutions of this state won't work for us then we'll use whatever force is necessary to make them.'

'An ordinary man, Dan McCarthy, with an extraordinary task.'

(*Dan McCarthy is now eighty-two and no longer directly involved in farming. He led the National Land League until the Land Commission was dissolved in the 1980s. He was active in the Irish Creamery Milk Suppliers Association and became Chairman of its National Rural Development Committee. Still a man of great energy, he is a member of Westmeath County Council representing the Labour Party. —J.M.*)

# APPENDIX IV

## *Childers' Memorandum to Government*

5 Bealtaine, 1959.

MEMORANDUM FOR THE GOVERNMENT

<u>LAND AGITATION</u>

1. Lia Fáil was founded in 1957 by Father Fahey, P.P., of Lusmagh, Co. Offaly.

   In the first issue of Lia Fáil, the official organ of the organisation, the aims were clearly set out:-

   (a) To seize the lands of ascendancy families still in residence without compensation;

   (b) To seize the lands of aliens who bought land in the 1940-50 period, without compensation.

   An analysis made in 1950 revealed that, exclusive of owners of small properties and Northern Ireland residents, about 200 persons had bought 50,000 acres, mostly in Kildare, Meath and Wicklow. A good many of these were, in fact, Irish in origin and the reports were based on the nomenclature of the owners. Much of this land had been sold since. It represented about .3% of the land area. Most of those left give reasonable employment.

   (c) To take possession without compensation in two years of all land owned by Landowners in excess of 100 acres.

2. Two incidents have been directly connected with the organisation,

   (a) the Barry/Ryan case (See Appendix at Page 6 ), and

   (b) the attempt to disrupt Land Commission migration in Co. Mayo at Hollymount, where local holders, most of whose holdings were over standard, tried to prevent the occupation of Land Commission lands by migrants from the Mayo area.

   Further information will be available from the Department of Justice.

3. The organisation is believed to be small. No report was available on the proceedings of a convention in Portarlington. The

   /circulation

circulation of Lia Fáil is some 2000 - 3000 copies.

(a) The following is a brief analysis of acquisition cases, occurring since 1957, where incidents took place but where all is now quiet and all action has ceased.

| | |
|---|---|
| Westmeath | 1 |
| Limerick | 1 |
| Tipperary | 1 (Trivial) |
| Total | 3 |

(b) Ditto cases where the original agitation is of pre 1957 standing but where incidents occurred since 1957.

| | |
|---|---|
| Kerry | 1 |
| Mayo | 1 |
| Leitrim | 1 |
| Total | 3 |

(c) Ditto cases where some agitation continues

| | |
|---|---|
| Carlow | 1 |
| Westmeath | 1 |
| Offaly | 1 (present case - Barry) |

(d) There were one or two cases where newspapers gave exaggerated reports of agitation but where in fact nothing objectionable occurred.

(e) There were twelve cases of agitation over land distribution since April 1957.

The total number of cases in the year is not regarded as seriously abnormal, the participants in most cases being persons not likely to be awarded land (with exceptions).

4. No reports of large-scale acquisition by aliens have been received and it is not believed that they are likely to occur. Stud farms and demesnes not suitable for land division exchange ownership in certain Eastern areas without agitation taking place.

In the Minister's view, the left wing extreme nationalist element represented by Sinn Féin and Lia Fáil exists in many areas but to what extent he is uncertain. The only partial antidotes are those offered by Macra na Feirme, Muinntir na Tíre and by the acceptance of the Programme for Economic Expansion.

6. The usual crop of agitations occur every year and it may be noted that most of them are ephemeral – they die down without gaining any objective.

7. During 1958/59, the Land Commission acquired or resumed 18,165 acres and, in addition took over 15,196 acres through exchanges giving a total intake of 33,361 acres. The total area allotted, including re-arrangements, was 57,000 approx. representing about twice the normal distribution programme. This entailed a special drive to dispose of arable lands on hands for two years and upwards. 10 year records, or near records, were established in all aspects of field work.

8. The government examined at very great length Land Commission policy in all its aspects, including possible changes in acquisition methods. Briefly –

   (a) It was decided not to acquire land of under £30 Valuation;

   (b) To ensure that big estates were given priority. They always were but the Inspectors have been reminded of their duties.

   (c) To facilitate long-term lettings.

9. (a) The Government was unanimous in deciding not to acquire well-worked estates.

   (b) An examination was made into the proposal that no individual should own land above a certain acreage.

   It was pointed out that –

   (i) The arable and pasture land in estates of over 500 acres amounted to only 260,000 acres. The employment lost by acquisition would far outweigh the social advantages of acquisition.

   (ii) The Bureau of Statistics revealed that only medium size farms were increasing in numbers the upper size limit being 200 acres.

   (iii) To limit the size of farms would result in division among relatives in most instances and would require a tremendous organisation to deal with private sales in the country, and quite impracticable. Other political and economic objections could be mentioned.

                                                                                /10.

10. ~~At the time the Bill was started and subsequently it was decided~~
to ignore the propaganda and the Minister for Lands in consequence
took no special action.

11. Lia Fáil differs only in intensity of belief from the nebulous
attitude held by a small number of persons who see land within
their grasp, and demonstrated by agitation from time to time from
1923 onwards and which has been resisted by successive governments
using the same arguments.   Namely,

(a) that the congestion problem is insoluble;

(b) that a great effort is being made to provide holdings for those
living in western agricultural slums and for as many others as
circumstances permit.

(c) that the right to private ownership of property is guaranteed
by the Constitution subject to possible delimitation by law
"with a view to reconciling .... with the exigencies of the common
good";   well worked land cannot, save in the most exceptional
circumstances, be acquired:

(d) that even in the case of badly worked land, humanitarian
considerations must operate and as a result appeals are granted
in the Land Court;

(e) that some 1,198,000 acres have in fact been allocated under
Land Acts 1923-54.   It should be noted that in a high percentage
of agitation incidents, the persons agitating are not qualified
to be allotted land.

12. Ministers for Lands do not make speeches about the steady work
of the Land Commission nor do they make any pronouncement on
cases of agitation unless compelled by particular circumstances
to do so, for obvious reasons.   To speak of the Land Commission's
limitations involves more agitation;   to speak of its limited
success invites envy among the 165,000 uneconomic landholders.
On the occasion of the Estimate Deputies, with the exception of
a very few, do not comment on the work of the Land Commission in
a way that necessitates arguments to refute Lia Fáil propaganda.

/The

The present Minister has maintained this tradition.   Apart from
the Estimate speech in relation to acquisition, framed on
conventional lines, he has made only two general pronouncements
since April 1957 of a purely conventional type.   He has been
compelled to deal with two cases of agitation in local areas
but, apart from parliamentary questions, any statements were
largely confined to the area in which the agitation took place.

13. The Minister for Lands seeks the advice of the Government on
    steps, if any, required to deal with Lia Fáil,

         (a) at present,

         (b) on the Estimate coming shortly before the House,

         (c) on other future occasions,

    And how far he should participate if at all.

    The Minister for Justice will no doubt have observations to
    make on the law and order aspect of this agitation.

Estate Barry, Co Offaly, S 20597:

Area 94.5 acres, Cogran, R.V. £60.

Land Commission instituted proceedings for this Estate in 1953 and the
owner's objection was heard and allowed on 21/1/54.

There was some local congestion but the lands, mostly craggy or subject
to flooding, were not considered very suitable as they contained only
about 26 acres arable. As well, the owner, who was a retired London Co
Council official, with a small pension resident in Banagher was dependent on the lettings for his living and represented that it would be a
hardship on him and his two dependent sisters if his land was acquired
unless he get about £4,500. He had bought the lands in 1937 in a very
neglected state and spent £1,500 in draining and reclamation but then
had not enough capital to stock them and was forced to let. The Land
Commission had offered him £2,500 which they considered the Market
Value of the farm.

After full hearing the objection was allowed.

No representations have since been made to the Land. Commission
about the place.

His brother Albert Barry who holds 140 acres in Co Galway nearby also
has 107 acres in Incherky Island, Co Offaly, in the river Shannon. All
but a few acres of the Island is subject to flooding so that the land
is summer grazing only. All Albert Barry's lands were well farmed
according to Inspector's report in 1953.

Albert Barry is a rate-collector.
Estate: Ryan,
Co Offaly, S 20364.

Patrick O'Leary of Ballynasragh was approved for migration to the above Estate, 12 miles away. He was to surrender 31 acres and 1/2 share of 14 acres (R.V. £18.1. in all) in Ballynasragh. The exchange was carried out on 17/4/1959 but it was necessary to let the surrendered holding (which he had manured and partly cultivated) back to the migrant until the end of the year. Proposals for the disposal of the O'Leary holding have not been settled yet but it is almost certain that it will be disposed of to local smallholders.

# APPENDIX V

## *Pages from* Lia Fáil

This appendix includes some pages from different issues of the *Lia Fáil* newspaper to give a sample of the articles published.

"There is no reason why we should not have a population of from fifteen to twenty million people living on the land of Ireland. That is the vision of Lia-Fail."

# LIA·FÁIL

**ORGAN OF THE LAND AND INDUSTRIAL ARMY OF IRELAND**
(Under the Patronage of Our Lady of Victories)

| NO. 1. | AUGUST 1958. | PRICE THREEPENCE |

## Birth of Lia-Fail

On November 1st, 1957, the people of Lusmagh, Banagher, Offaly, held a meeting to discuss the problems of emigration. The Parish Priest, Father John Fahy, presided at the meeting, and Francis Kelly, Lusmagh, was appointed secretary. From that meeting Lia-Fail was born.

... the unanimous ... the meeting that ... matter of vital and ... necessity for the sur... the Irish people in ... the problem of ... Land of Ireland be tack... led and solved immediately.

When we got our own Government in 1921 this was the first problem that our rulers should have tackled and solved.

Through ignorance, incapacity, treachery and insincerity, our politicians not only neglected their duty to the Irish people in this matter, but allowed are still allowing foreigners — English, Dutch, Germans, etc.—to come in and purchase the best land of our country. Ireland is being conquered through the Bank of England!

A new plantation is taking place! Irish boys and girls are being shipped out of Ireland in greater numbers than when under Cromwell, whilst Englishmen and other aliens are being 'planted' on the best land of Ireland!

To counteract and undo this horrible treachery of our politicians the meeting at Lusmagh launched a movement called "Ireland for the Irish." The Secretary had the following leaflet printed containing the aims of the Association:—

### RELAND FOR THE IRISH

"The Ireland for the Irish Association was launched in Lusmagh, Offaly, on 1st November, 1957, when the following provisional committee was appointed:

President: Fr. John Fahy, C.P., Lusmagh; Secretary: Francis J. Kelly, Newtown; Treasurer: Frank Larkin, Bream. Committee Members: Patrick Kelly, Tim Bennett, Denis Kelly, Martin Sullivan, Paddy Greeanes, Jeem Donegan, etc.

**Purpose of the Association**

"1. To secure that all the sources of wealth in Ireland are preserved for the Irish people.

"2. To make it illegal for any alien to purchase land, property or any source of wealth in Ireland.

"3. To have annulled forthwith all sales of land, property and sources of wealth to aliens, contracted since the establishment of the Irish ...

was ordered by Lord Midleton to secure the British Garrison in the lands they had plundered from the Irish people.

"5. To divide the land of Ireland among the young men of Ireland.

"6. To limit private ownership of land to one hundred acres so long as young men have to emigrate from the countryside.

"7. To re-instate the dispossessed Irish people on the good soil of Ireland from which their forefathers were driven by the robber-invaders, who are in possession still of the good land of Ireland,"

### CREATED A SENSATION

As soon as the above leaflet stating the aims of "Ireland for the Irish" got around, our correspondents from all parts of Ireland poured into Lusmagh. Political and social organisations, societies, clubs and individuals wrote approving of the Association and requesting membership of it.

For years isolated groups in various counties had been agitating to have estates and ranches divided by the Irish Land Commission.

There was "The Kildare Land Division League"; "The National Land Division League" functioning in Limerick, Clare, Tipperary, and the Roads, and in Mayo the the "Bonaparte Land Division Club" in Carlow; the "Land for the People League" in Westmeath; and many other similar groups.

### HOW IT ALL BEGAN

Under the leadership of "Ireland for the Irish" all these Land Associations came together, agreed to a common policy, formed a Provisional National Executive, and called the new movement "Lia-Fáil."

Lia-Fáil's first objective is to put the young men of Ireland on the good land of Ireland. It will concentrate all its energies on that problem until it is solved.

Today Lia-Fáil is launching its paper, Now that it has its own paper, all the Irish people will soon be told what its policy is and how it means to carry it out.

May this generation not pass away before Lia-Fáil's vision comes true—the laughter of Irish children filling the countryside and that baby stretches from Cavan to the ...

### The Pope on Landless Men

Men without land have the right to cultivate land laid down in a letter of the Vatican Secretary of State sent by His Holiness the Pope to the 16th Annual Social Week, being held in Vigo, Spain.

If we bore in Ireland made a similar statement, we would be attacked as extreme revolutionaries or even communists.

## Little Accomplished After 36 Years of Freedom

After thirty-four years of native Government, it is a lamentable fact that an organisation has to be formed to solve the problem, which was the very first problem that our own Government should have tackled and solved. When we won our freedom in 1921, the British Garrison was in possession of most of the good land of our country. Their only claim to it was the title of the robber-invader. Having defeated the robber-invader, our first duty to the Irish people was to deprive that robber-invader of his loot and restore to our own people the lands that were robbed from their forefathers.

The British Garrison staked their claim on the success of British arms. When the British arms failed, most of them packed up and were ready to leave if ordered. Unfortunately our leaders failed us. Either they knew nothing about what freedom really meant or they were too busy murdering each other for jobs. Through ignorance, incapacity, selfishness or what ever the reason was, the Sinn Féin leaders allowed the British Garrison to retain the good land and wealth of Ireland, and left the dispossessed Irish people where they were—on the bad lands and bogs and mountains.

Similarly with trade and commerce. For over thirty years our people have waited in hope on the bad lands and bogs and mountains. At last, realising that they were let down, that our own native Government had not the slightest intention of restoring them to their patrimony, and that they and their children after them were doomed to a life of poverty and misery, whilst the robber-invader lived in luxury on the fat of the land, they decided for their children's sake to clear out and seek a living in foreign lands. After holding on doggedly for centuries to be let down by your own flesh and blood! What poignancy! "The bodac" is bloated luxury in the garden of Ireland, "the Gael" on the emigrant ship! Wealthy professional parasites of all classes talk, and lecture on "the flight from the land." There is no "flight" from the good land! They don't lecture on the flight of aliens into the good land. Oh no! That might not please the dastardly traitor politicians! It would expose their treason! The only flight of the Irish people is from the mountains and bogs and bad lands.

With God's help and the help of His Blessed Mother Mary, Lia-Fáil will organise a flight of the Irish people from home and abroad into all the good land of Ireland.

● Ireland is being planted with aliens. The Government has no mandate from the people to allow foreigners to buy up the land that belongs to the people. The Dáil could solve the problem with

## ONE HOUR'S WORK

The Dáil could in one hour solve the whole problem that Lia-Fáil has been established to solve. They have all the means at their disposal to do so. One comprehensive Land Bill would solve it all. Fianna Fáil with a majority over all the combined parties in the House could solve it themselves. What is more they have the power and the legislative authority to do so. They have an obligation to the Irish people to do it.

In one hour in the Dáil they could solve this problem once and for all. There is nothing ... or anything, except their own unwillingness. That is the simple naked truth that nobody can deny. Why then don't they do it?

Do they think they were elected to banish the Irish people from Ireland and plant Ireland with aliens?

Do they think that they have a mandate from the Irish people in whom English ... when they allowed a syndicate of British - Orange - American Freemasons to purchase Kilbr...

Do they really think that the chief purpose for which the Irish people elected them were to banish the Irish from Ireland, to organise a new English invasion of Ireland, to put in concentration camps the Irish... who are striving to undo the partition of our country, and use Ireland's Army and police force to preserve inviolable the boundary that ...

... all, secure and safeguard the vested interests of the British Garrison in our country?

We ask the Taoiseach, the master of duplicity and evasion to give a straight answer, if it is possible for him to do so, to a couple of straight-forward questions:

(1) Does he think that he has a mandate from the Irish people for the above policy?

(2) If he does not believe that he has that mandate why is he carrying it out?

### LIA-FÁIL

Editorial Offices at Newtown, Lusmagh, Banagher, Offaly, to which all communications should be sent.

Approved advertise...

# Cancer on the Body Politic

THE accursed Civil War which split open our nation thirty-six years ago, and produced the cancerous growth of putrid party politics as we know them today, has left our people disillusioned and disgusted.

Our Irish martyrs died that Ireland might be free and Gaelic. We are neither free nor Gaelic. Our economy has collapsed. Our main exports are our people and our money—our money to the tune of hundreds of millions sterling invested in Britain and elsewhere; our people to the tune of fifty to sixty thousand per annum. Our six northern counties are held at bayonet point for Britain. Our land in the Twenty-six, is quietly passing over to British hands. Our resources and industries are being offered freely for exploitation by the foreigner.

YET OUR SMUG POLITICIANS WHO DURING THAT PERIOD HAVE VAPOURISED AD NAUSEAM, CONTINUE IN THE SAME STRAIN, OBLIVIOUS TO, AND CARELESS OF THE NATIONAL ROT WHICH HAS SET IN. THEY THINK THEY CAN INDEFINITELY CONTINUE TO BEFUDDLE THE PEOPLE. WE WONDER.

Just now three widely read Sunday newspapers are devoting pages to a re-hash of Civil War details. Why? The older generation knows too much of that tragic chapter in our history. The less the younger generation knows of it the better for them and for Ireland. Is there a conspiracy on their part to divert the eyes of Irish youth from the present and future to that time of hate and shame, at this critical epoch, when young Ireland is becoming conscious of its bondage, resenting and resisting it in no unmistakable manner?

Recently that sanctimonious humbug who guides the destinies of the Fianna Fáil party, was much on the air through the taxpayer's Radio Éireann, and in the columns of the daily papers.

Had he discovered the solution of the Border problem? Had he to announce the exclusion of foreigners from ownership of Irish land, or the expulsion of the foreign land-owners already here? Had he a solution to the unemployment and emigration problems? NO! to all these questions.

He had however a proposition for what he considers a Comprehensive Insurance for his Fianna Fáil party—the abolition of Proportional Representation.

At his party Ard Fheis too he advocated the teaching of patriotism, through the medium of schools and suitable school books. This seems interesting! DOES HE ENVISAGE THE ERECTION AND MAINTENANCE OF FURTHER CONCENTRATION CAMPS TO HOUSE THE PATRIOTS, AND ANOTHER NATIONAL INDUSTRY TO ADD TO LEMASS'S LIST OF INDUSTRIAL TRIUMPHS?

## Patriotism 'à la Fianna Fáil'

Or what peculiar brand of patriotism does this party 'Mortho' hope to inculcate? Presumably patriotism 'à la Fianna Fáil.' If so the Irish children must be able to answer such questions as:

Who may save Ireland—God or Dev?

How can you become a good Fianna Fáiler?

What is meant by 'pull'?

How would you work a 'pull' for, say, Rate Collector, Home Assistance Officer, etc.?

Have foreigners a prefect right to Irish land?

Is Mr. Childers really fond of fish?

What indulgence may Fianna Fáil grant to one who shields 'Up Dev'?

Before leaving "Dadh" and "Mama" what should Fianna Fáil parents teach their children to say?

Why is an overall majority for Fianna Fáil a more precious ideal than national freedom?

A fair imagination can formulate many other questions. Any old F.F. lackly knows all the answers. But Dev would be able to know them too.

*"... that sanctimonious humbug ..."*

LITTLE PATRIOTISM LEFT IN YOU, YOU CAN BEST SHOW IT BY GETTING OUT AT ONCE TO LIVE ON YOUR SPOILS OF OFFICE, AND HAND OVER TO IRISH YOUTH TO WHOM THE FUTURE BELONGS.

YOU AND YOUR RIVAL PARTIES HAVE BROUGHT THINGS TO A SORRY PASS IN IRELAND. UNSCRUPULOUS SELF-SEEKING SYCOPHANTS, AS YOU ALL ARE, YOU MUST REALISE THE MISFORTUNE YOU HAVE BROUGHT ON OUR COUNTRY. YOU HAVE DONE ENGLAND'S WORK EVEN BETTER THAN SHE COULD HAVE DONE IT. GET OUT, THE LOT OF YOU!

## 'Fishy' Minister for Lands

Resolutions re land division and purchase by aliens brought the usual consolation from the 'fishy' Minister for Lands. He assures all and sundry that the Land Commission knows its job and is doing it, and greater relief will—that no aliens are purchasing Irish land. Musha, Erky Hamilton, a gradh gil, will you forgive us. We thought they were, but, Ah Blimey! it must have been foolish imagination.

Strange how Fianna Fáil delegates from Carlow and elsewhere were so 'unpatriotic' as to formulate and move such blasphemous resolutions. However, now they know the truth and have them home handy.

Oh Irish martyrs, have you died in vain?

Will may Mother Eire

## TO HELL WITH THE IRISH !

THE people of Carlow have been asking the Government for a good while to have the Dunleckney estate, divided among local uneconomic holders and landless men.

A few weeks ago they picketed the auctioneer's office in Dublin (North's) where this estate was put up for sale. While the mere Irish of Carlow were picketing the Fianna Fáil Ard Fheis over another Carlow estate bought by an alien, THE DUNLECKNEY ESTATE WAS PURCHASED PRIVATELY.

"Free sale is sacred and fundamental," says Childers. That means, in practice, that the land of Ireland is for the wealthy class, alien and native.

The firm which bought the Dunleckney estate we are told, has already bought a good slice of Kildare. This firm, Keenan Bros., who are also informed, makes its money selling farm equipment—bysheds, etc.—to farmers.

Using the farmer to spoliate the farmer. What will the farmer spoliate his spoliators?

## Catholic Ireland Insulted

AIKEN, DE VALERA'S MINISTER TO THE UNITED NATIONS, HAS, BY HIS ACTION IN THAT ASSEMBLY, INSULTED THE CATHOLIC PEOPLE OF IRELAND; HE HAS INSULTED THE MAYNOOTH MISSION TO CHINA AND EVERY COLUMBAN FATHER AND MISSIONARY PRIEST WHO WENT TO THAT COUNTRY TO PREACH THE GOSPEL OF JESUS CHRIST TO THE CHINESE PEOPLE.

By upholding the pirate atheistic gangster government who persecuted, tortured, martyred, and expelled Christian missionaries in that country he has implicitly approved of their inhuman and anti-God policy; he has scoffed at the Holy Father and jeered at His Holiness's pronouncements; he has insulted and outraged the feelings of the Irish race and of the Catholic Church in the United States of America; he has created hostility between the people of America and the people of Ireland; he has falsely and treacherously broadcast to the whole world that this Catholic people of Ireland are an ally and friend of Communist China and Soviet Russia; he has outraged Irish hearts by brazenly announcing that Catholic Ireland is on the side of anti-Christ and opposed to the teaching of the Holy Father and the Catholic Church; he has desecrated the millions of Irish martyrs for the faith; he has defamed and fouled Ireland's fair name; he has belied and outraged the deepest sentiments of Irish Catholics; he has diabolically misrepresented the Irish people by sponsoring in their name, atheism and Communist tyranny; he has scandalized and horrified the christian world by marching under Ireland's flag, in the ranks of anti-Christ!!

PEOPLE OF IRELAND!! FOR TRUTH'S SAKE, FOR SAKE OF IRELAND'S HONOUR, AND MEMORY OF IRELAND'S COUNTLESS THOUSANDS OF MARTYRS FOR THE FAITH, DON'T LET THIS SCOUNDREL OF A POLITICIAN OFF WITH SUCH DEFAMATION AND DESECRATION OF YOUR RACE.

RISE UP IN PROTEST, AND LET YOUR HOT "RESIGN YOU SCOUNDREL, YOU DON'T REPRESENT US!" BE HEARD FROM SEA TO SEA.

# IS LEMASS MAD?

## Ireland Has Been Betrayed
## Again—By Her Own

### A TERRIBLE INDICTMENT

AFTER centuries of domination by a foreign power, we native Irish have had for almost forty years control of the greater part of our country. One of the primary obligations of our native government was to secure the integrity of the soil of the nation: to see that the land of Ireland which belongs to the people of Ireland was preserved inviolably for the Irish people.

Every independent government on the earth safeguards for its people the integrity of its country's soil. For the Frenchman the soil of France is a sacred thing to be defended with his life's blood. So for the Belgian, the Spaniard, the Portuguese and all free peoples.

#### Abhorrent Idea

THE IDEA OF ALLOWING FOREIGNERS OR ALIENS TO COME IN AND PURCHASE THE SOIL OF THEIR NATION IS AS ABHORRENT TO FREE PEOPLE AS THE IDEA OF ALLOWING AN INVADER TO COME IN AND ROB HIM OF IT BY FORCE. THAT BASIC NATIONAL PRINCIPLE OF THE INTEGRITY OF THE SOIL OF THE COUNTRY IS WRITTEN DEEP IN THEIR CONSTITUTIONS AND FULLY PROCLAIMED IN THEIR LEGISLATURES.

Having scanned the integrity of the soil of the nation by enshrining it as a basic principle of our Constitution our government's next duty was to see that the land of Ireland, which belongs to the people of Ireland, was equitably distributed among the native Irish people. In 1921 there was nothing to prevent our native government fulfilling these two primary obligations. They had the power, the authority and the means to do so. The hour had struck to right the wrongs of a thousand years.

#### Politicians Failed Us

Alas, the politicians who climbed into power on our backs failed us — the real Irish people — then, and they have failed us ever since. Not only have they not safe-guarded the integrity of our country's soil or made an equitable distribution of it among us, but, horrible to relate they are shipping the remnants of our people from it faster than Cromwell shipped our forefathers, and, treason most heinous, they are establishing "a new Plantation' of English, Dutch, Swedes, Norwegians, Russians, Jews all Freemasons and heretics who hate our race and our religion — upon the best land of our country!

FORTY YEARS OF IGNORANCE, INCOMPETENCY, EGOISM, SELF - AGGRANDISEMENT, GRAFT, JOBBERY, NEPOTISM, SQUANDERMANIA, TREACHERY, TREASON AT THE HANDS OF POLITICAL GANGSTERS!

YOUNG MEN OF IRELAND, AT HOME AND ABROAD, BAND YOURSELVES TOGETHER AND GET RID OF THE DEN OF THIEVES WHO ARE SELLING YOUR BIRTHRIGHT, AND WHO WILL LEAVE YOU WITHOUT A HOME OR A COUNTRY

Mr. Lemass

## Lia-Fail is Catholic and Irish

"LIA-FAIL" is a Catholic Irish paper. It is Catholic first and Irish second, because it puts first things first. The Creator precedes creation, in truth, fact and justice, too, and these things pertaining to God, should have priority over man and the things pertaining to man. Man's first duty as a creature of God is to worship God. Religion is the virtue through which man worships God. Therefore a man's religion or a people's religion should take priority over his or their politics. A man's religion should take precedence over his patriotism. Patriotism is a minor virtue prescribed by religion. The international political gangster would understand the alpha and things of all religion. We in Lia-Fail put first things first as in truth and justice we are bound to do, and we press no apology to an anti-publican or gangster, Englishman or Orangeman, Freemason or heretic. We are Catholics first and Irishmen second, and we are all the better Irishmen for that. A good Catholic will not conscientiously will not be a fonds or publ ful gangster, will not sell his country.

The Catholic Church is the one and only true church in the world and we think that for the infallible privilege of being members of that one and only true church.

#### IMPORTANT

Form a branch of Lia-Fail in your parish. Help in the recomquest of Ireland.

## WANTED--

1,000 young men to implement the first stage of Lia-Fail's "Back to the land" policy. Please write to the Secretary of Lia-

RECENTLY in Dublin the above question was put to a member of our organisation. The man who asked it is manager of one of the largest Irish business firms in the city and takes an active part in every aspect of our national life, cultural, social, industrial. In thanking Lia-Fail for helping to focus public opinion on the treachery and treason of De Valera's government IN SELLING THE LAND AND INDUSTRIES OF OUR COUNTRY TO ENGLISHMEN AND OTHER UNDESIRABLE ALIENS, reference was made to one of the most recent acts of treachery—the purchase that week by an English company of the Gypsum Factory in Cavan. It was that reference that elicited the question: "Is Lemass mad?"

ONLY A MADMAN OR A TRAITOR OF THE DEEPEST DYE WOULD ACT AS HE IS ACTING: HE IS ISSUING LICENSES TO JEWS, ENGLISHMEN, DUTCHMEN AND OTHER UNWANTED ALIENS TO START ALL KINDS OF SO-CALLED INDUSTRIES HERE, AND IS FINANCING AND SUBSIDISING THEM WITH THE MONEY OF THE IRISH PEOPLE.

#### Undisguised Treachery and Treason

The greatest problem many countries have is to get rid of foreign vested interests. LEMASS IS HELPING FOREIGN VESTED INTERESTS TO GET A GRIP OF OUR COUNTRY. That policy is undisguised treachery and treason. He has neither the mandate nor authority of the Irish people to help undesirable aliens to own and control our industries. Does he think he owns Ireland? Only the owner of a thing may dispose of it. Have Irishmen lost the faculty of thought? Do they realise what a menace Lemass is?

- Will they stand idly by while he hands over our country to the English and Dutch — the aliens who for a thousand years murdered, robbed and persecuted our forefathers, desecrated and plundered our churches and and who would do the same to us today is they had us in their power?

- Lemass is doing with our industries what Childers is doing with our land — handing them over to aliens! And over the whole transaction De Valera presides!

- Irishmen, will you allow a hatter's son from Flanders hand the industries of your country over to Jews, Englishmen, Dutchmen and other most undesirable aliens?

- Will you let an Englishman's son hand all the good land of Ireland over to Englishmen, Dutchmen, Danes, Norwegians and Swedes?

- Will you allow the Spanish gardener's son to succeed where Cromwell failed?

J. J.

## Anti-Climax

FROM 12 P.M. TO 9 P.M. ON THURSDAY 18th SEPTEMBER, I WAS AT DUBLIN AIRPORT. ALL THE TIME A BUSY STREAM OF TRAFFIC WAS PASSING THROUGH: PLANES LANDING AND TAKING OFF WITH LOURDES PILGRIMS. IN THIS PROFITABLE STREAM OF TRAFFIC THE LARGER PLANES, FLYING THE LION JACK, CARRIED THE MAJORITY OF THE PILGRIMS — TWO OUT OF EVERY THREE; THOSE BRITISH PLANES DOMINATED THE AIRWAY WHILE THE SMALLER AER LINGUS MACHINES KEPT WELL BACK OUT OF THEIR WAY!

Another shocking act of treachery against our country — to allow our one and only enemy to come in and take most of the air passengers of Ireland! From Dev and his treasonable politicians save Ireland, O Lord!

Dev arrived back from Lourdes accompanied by his publicity agents, photographers and political toadies, all aglow. As he approached the lorries a young Dublin draughtsman, Hugh Sweeney of Britanmas, home from England for his brother's marriage, confronted Dev and asked him: "What about the few who have to emigrate to earn one bread?"

The anti-climax so shocked Dev that he got weak and had to be taken aside to a seat to rest for a while.

IT IS HOPEFUL TO SEE YOUNG MEN ASSERT THEIR RIGHT TO A LIVING IN THEIR OWN LAND.
—EDITOR.

● HELP TO PROMOTE THE

#### De Valera v. Cromwell

Which — Dev or Cromwell — banished the most native Irish.

Which of them planted most aliens in Ireland?

Is Dev and his Freemason a greater menace to the Irish people than Cromwell and his Dragoons were?

Why did the members of the Church-Body subscribe to Dev's party and canvass for them at the last general

#### QUESTION & ANSWER

Q What was the Norman invasion for?
A To get the land of Ireland for Englishmen.

Q What was Cromwell's invasion for?
A To get the land of Ireland for Englishmen.

Q What was William Orange's invasion for?
A To get the land of Ireland for Englishmen.

# BOYD-ROCHFORD HAS NO WINNER THIS TIME!

THOUSANDS of farmers, road workers and others interested attended a tremendously successful meeting held after Mass last Sunday, August 31st, in Castletown-Geoghegan, Co. Westmeath, to consider the latest phase in the unrelenting effort to restore the Boyd-Rochford estate to the people.

The nearby estate was snatched in the past—like so much of the best land of Ireland—from the people by members of the planted ascendancy.

Descendants of scores of the original dispossessed and evicted owners were present to applaud the inspiring words of Eamon Ginnell, Tom Kavanagh and Pat Clarke, who spoke of the work of Lia-Fáil and the renewed efforts to have this fine land speedily and equitably divided.

References were made to the shocking disinterested attitude of the Department of Lands towards the further division of this estate, and to the criminal apathy of the Minister (Childers) whose cynical couldn't-care-less attitude in the matter had roused the anger of the people.

# 400 Families Driven From Their Homes in Westmeath

LESS than a century ago there were 400 Irish Catholic families living on what is now called the Boyd-Rochford estate, which the Protestant-Freemason Englishman, De Valera's Minister for Lands, now claims to own.

# A Family On the Land

# TUSSLE WITH MY P.P.

# FOREIGNER IN LIMERICK GETS 127 ACRES MORE

## OXLEY'S
GENERAL DRAPERY
BANAGHER

## B. Hunt
BANAGHER - OFFALY

## Mrs. Brigid Lyons
Main St. - BANAGHER

## Arthur Bridge Ltd.
Main Ford Dealer - BIRN

Ford Cars, Trucks, Vans
Fordson, Major and Dexta Tractors

● The Only Answer to the Future of Ireland—

# Back to the Brehon Laws

FROM the pre-Christian era to the time of the Norman invasion of Ireland, title to or ownership of Irish land was decided and governed by the Brehon code of law.

The Brehon code of law was the law of the land in Ireland prior to the conquest; it was the legislature or system of laws devised by the wisest men of the race (Brehons) to safeguard the person and property of the citizens and was enforced by the rulers as the law of the State. Under that system of laws our pagan forefathers lived and prospered and attained a high degree of culture.

When in the fifth century St. Patrick had converted them to Christianity, he blessed and consecrated their Brehon code of laws as being in perfect consonance with and conducial to, the Christian way of life.

Let us see how the Brehon Law regulated titles to and ownership of land. In his "History of the Land League" (chapter xxii, p. 190) Michael Davitt lays down the Brehon Law on titles to Irish land. "Under the Brehon Law," he writes, "ownership of land in Ireland rested in the people themselves . . . Under the Brehon Law the land in Ireland was the absolute property of the people. It was held in commonalty, so much being allotted for pasturage, so much for agriculture and tillage. The lots were not owned by their occupants as the title was invested in the people at large. But the occupant of a lot, was the owner, de facto, as long as he had need of it . . .

"Under the Brehon Law the land was leaned by the people to the individual, and when the individual no longer needed it, it was resumed by the people. In no case was the title parted with, and in no case did the title vest in any individual. The Chief Prince or King who was elected by the people, got pasturage as the land under the same law as the people got it . . . On the death of his Prince or King, the land they had the use of lapsed to the owners i.e. the people."

Thus, under the Brehon Law, the land of Ireland belonged to the people of Ireland. Neither individual nor chieftain, nor Prince nor King had a free title to one perch of Irish soil. Every perch of the soil of Ireland was to absolute property of the Irish people, and apportioned by them for the greatest good of the greatest number of Ireland's citizens.

A thousand years before Fintan Lawlor was born the law of the gaelic state was that the land of Ireland was the absolute property of the Irish people and was disposed of by the people as they thought best fit.

It was that land law, St. Patrick blessed and gave the sanction of the Church to, and it was under that land code that our race attained its highest peak culturally, spiritually, materially and nationally. That era of the Brehon code especially from the fifth to the thirteenth century has been called by all historians 'The Golden Age of Irish History,' and truly it was, it was so because no other race of people known to history ever devised for themselves, and lived under, a legislative system so closely in accord with God's Devine and Natural law.

There are many aspects of the Brehon land-law that we would like to bring before our readers, but space and urgency compel us to confine this article to one aspect only of that law, namely disposal, or control. In view of what is taking place in our country today the matter is of vital importance to every member of our race.

How did the Brehon Law divide land, disposal of land and allot land? In the first place, there was no such thing as sale of land under the Brehon code. Neither Prince nor individual nor government dare usurp the people's title. That the land of the people, the very basis and foundation of their terrestrial life, would be gambled at the whim of casinos, or by syndicates, or individuals was a crime inconceivable to our Gaelic sires. Such a crime against the people and all in the year's of citizenship, with racial extermination. The Brehon Law in motion that

reason and the Natural law. To deprive a man or family of his or their only means of existence on this earth is tantamount to depriving him and them of their lives. Grabbing in land pursued to its logical conclusion, means that the most successful gambler, or the ablest financial crook, could become the owner of the earth, and thereby have power of life and death over the entire human family. Our Gaelic fore-fathers realized that and legislated against it.

It is a crime against the Devine Natural Law to have the land of a country gambled by individuals, syndicates, governments or anyone whosoever. When the land that belongs to the people of a country like ours is allowed to be gambled and purchased by aliens, hostile to our religion, our culture and our Christian way of life, there is no word in any language capable of describing the heinousness of that crime against the people and the treachery and treason of the dastard-authority that sanctions and allows it—it is absolutely diabolical, Satanic, devilish—and that is what is happening to most of the good land of Ireland today. It is being bought up and gambled by speculators and gombeen-men at home, and, horrible-dictu, it is being purchased and monopolized by English syndicate and the Protestant Church-body, who, for centuries have tried to exterminate our race and destroy our religion, and would do the same today if they got the chance and De Valera and tresonable government, as we will prove to him and them (for he won't be able to suppress us as easily as he is suppressing the young patriots who are hurling themselves at the Border; are not only allowing and conniving at the sale of the land of our people to our alien enemies, but are helping that treacherous and treasonable and criminal transaction) Gaels! Arise and impeach the traitors!!

JOHN IRELAND.

## "Yes" or "No"

WE ask De Valera to give a straight answer to the following questions. We, the real native Irish, have a right to be answered:

Is his Minister for Lands, Childers, chairman of the Protestant 'Church-Body?'

Is Childers, his Minister for Lands, a Freemason?

IS THERE ONE T.D. CATHOLIC AND IRISH ENOUGH TO RAISE THIS QUESTION IN THE DAIL?

Has Oliver Flanagan lost his moral courage?

Is McQuillan man enough to hold Dev. to an answer?

Hundreds of thousands of Irish people want an answer, as De Valera will soon find out.

When, some time ago, the question of T.D.'s being members of the Knights of Columbanus was raised in the Dail, De Valera, as the Dail records can show, took great pains to inform the country that none of his T.D.'s were members of this Catholic Society. Oh yes. We call on Dev to show equal zeal in telling the Irish people here that none of his Ministers or T.D.'s is a member of a secret anti-Christian, anti-Catholic and anti-Irish Society called Freemasonry which is condemned by the Holy Roman Catholic Church.

We in Lia-Fail, tell De Valera that he has desecrated the millions of martyrs for our faith and fatherland by putting an Englishman, a

If resignation of Irish Catholics and immigration or invasion of English and often heretics continues at their present rate for another few years, the alien-heretics will outnumber the native Irish Catholics here in Ireland. Already those aliens have got control of most of the wealth of Ireland! Every decent Irish Catholic who is not a member of Lia-Fail should join the ranks at once.

## OLD CAMPAIGNER TO THE YOUTH OF IRELAND

I HAVE been in the Land-War and in the fight for freedom from 1916 to the end of the Civil War and I want neither land nor a job, nor a pension, nor to be a T.D. I see no hope for Ireland today unless you, the young men of Ireland, take over your country.

There never was such a 'clearance' in Ireland as now under our own politicians! Since the 'Flight of the Earls' there never was such a 'plantation' of English, Dutch, and other aliens as is taking place NOW! The life-blood of Ireland, physically and financially, was never 'drained' as fiercely as NOW!

Our politicians have sold us, they have built up a parasitical juggernaut of jobbery and graft that is crushing Ireland to death! Worse than Cromwell and the Yeomen, they are wiping out the real Irish people and, in bloated complaisance, they smilingly look on, while aliens rape Mother Eire!

Young men of Ireland don't be handmaidens, legger-men or toadies to those absential politicians!

Band yourselves together and form your own leadership, for your own sake, for Ireland's sake, and for Christ's sake of

## A word to the young men of Ireland

YOURS is the richest and most blessed land in God's good earth. The Danes saw it and tried to rob you of it. You drove them into the sea.

The Normans, by cunning, intrigue and force robbed you of it, and drove you into the bogs, bad-lands and mountains.

Cromwell, by murder and robbery, planted his yeomen on it.

William of Orange completed the confiscation of the land of the Gael and gave it to his soldiers.

Through all those centuries of robbery and plunder, your forefathers kept up resistance and lived in hope.

Today we have our own Government in control of our country.

The first duty of that Government is to restore the dispossed Irish people to the patrimony of their fathers.

What else does Irish Freedom mean? The term "Irish Freedom" is meaningless unless it means that the Irish people own their country—Ireland.

Young men of Ireland, the politicians have failed to do their duty to you and to Ireland.

They have failed to restore to you the patrimony of your fathers. They have done worse! They have secured the land-robbers in the lands that, historically and merally, belong to you.

Only political tradies and degenerate slaves would tolerate such treason!

Have you the courage, the manhood, the patriotism to band yourselves together and tackle this problem which affects so vitally yourselves and your country?

If you have, Lia-Fail will show you how to solve it.

# Offaly Shows the Way

**WE were shocked into a thoughtful silence on Monday at the fair on being introduced for the first time to a young farmer who spoke only of farming matters and the future of Ireland during the pleasant hour or two that we spent in his company and that of his friends.**

He is from Offaly, and he assured us that there is an acute awareness among the people down there—and among the farming community in particular—of a crisis in national policy. He told us sincerely and simply of a new movement that may (and we share his hope) one day solve the affairs and problems of the nation.

The new movement—it is not yet, and we do not know if it ever will be, a "party" in the narrow, accepted political sense of the word—is known by the title "Lia-Fáil"—"The Voice of the Land and Industrial Army of Ireland." It has followers, estimated to number about 11,000 at present, in Carlow, Kerry, Cork, Offaly, Kildare and Westmeath; and, while most of them are young farmers, a few priests, office workers, tradesmen, teachers and shop workers are also taking a leading part in spreading the light and preaching the new gospel.

### DIFFERENT

THE Offaly farmer and his companions shocked us in a pleasant and refreshing way. They didn't ask us the usual questions which we are regularly called on to answer—"Were you at the match yesterday?" "What are you going to back today?" "Were you at the picture in the Odeon?" "Did you hear about the ructions at the carnival in——?"

They are serious but by no means angry young men. We discovered that they like football and hurling and dancing and films but have, even at an average age of 25, learned to put these pastimes and amusements in proper perspective. Football to them will always be a good game—merely. Something to help the young to keep fit and to develop a sense of fair play and a willingness to give and take hard knocks. Nothing more. Football must never be allowed to develop into big business, to be ruled by controlling hierarchy, and followed and cashed-in on by unscrupulous knaves.

### SENSIBLE ATTITUDE

THAT is the sensible attitude of followers of "Lia-Fáil" to all games. They see clearly through the false and stimulated enthusiasm of the big newspapers, Sunday and Provincial, that devote pages to games of little importance and build and blow up obscure young men who, when their hour of glory is over, too often fail to fit easily into their old place on the farm or in the shop, and who turn out to be pathetic and boastful bums weeping into their empty tumblers and relating for the benefit of the loungers at the bar the technical points of the game they did so much to win in the dear, dead days of the forgotten past.

### NOT FANATICS

THESE young men are not, we discovered with joy, too much concerned with abstract ideas of freedom, are not relying on bombs or guns to achieve their aim of making Ireland a fit place for the Irish to live in.

### AIMS AND IDEAS

They are not out to bulldoze their way to popularity, but are quietly convinced that the majority of the people share their views and opinions and need the sort of a lead that "Lia-Fáil" is prepared to give, unselfishly and with the highest motives.

They are, of course, fundamentally concerned with the the land and have plans for getting the best out of the wasted and neglected acres of Ireland.

They refuse to tolerate the idea of allowing the best and biggest farms to go to foreigners who can put up the biggest money, and point out that aliens are not allowed to buy land in most of the progressive countries of the world.

They'd take over badly managed and neglected land, develop it with the most modern machinery, and spare no expense to make such land fully productive. The money for the machines and the development would—or could—come solely from the profits that good productive land could earn.

### PARISH PLAN

THEY spoke enthusiastically of a parish plan for the joint ownership of the best machinery and an organised group of workers in each area to do every farm job. They know only too well of the hit and miss system of working that allies itself to the unpredictable weather to bedevil the efforts of the small, individual farmer. They know that half the farmers of the country are up to their eyes in debt and are working year after year to pay off the money they owe to banks, and to credit companies and to Ford and Ferguson. One good set of first-class machines properly used and maintained could do all the work on a dozen Irish farms, and all the work could be done in a fraction of the time it takes at present with organised and planned methods.

### PRACTICAL IDEAS?

ARE their ideas shared by many? We think so. We have heard many say that the canals and navigable rivers should be used for the transport of such commodities as petrol, oils, coal, timber, turf; that the CIE railway services be exclusively used for the haulage of all heavy freight—particularly cattle—and so save our roads and the millions of pounds spent on the upkeep of the highways.

### REVIVING IRISH

THEIR ideas on education are sensible, almost revolutionery. They'd scrap the present curriculum and go back to the subjects taught so successfully 60 and more years ago—the three R's, botany, practical farm work and gardening, house and homecraft, science, music, languages.

They'd revive Irish by the simply plan of making it a likeable and desirable language to learn. At present all students of Irish are turned against it by stupid rules of grammar and syntax and confused methods of pronunciation and spelling.

They'd instal a film projector in every school and have educational films used regularly. They are fully aware of the tremendous influence films have on the young—so would use the cinema for all educational purposes.

They'd see that TV is established in this country immediately. As with the school films the TV would be fully used to instruct children and grown-ups to get the best out of life by showing them how to do things—cook, sew, plant, hoe . . .

They would not, under any circumstances, allow the TV or radio programmes to be put on by a "sponsor"; or allow any commercial propaganda that would encourage people to smoke more, or eat more rubbishy foods, or drink more doubtful liquids, or gamble, or waste their money on luxuries.

### MANY IDEAS

THEY see Ireland as a geographical island entity democratically and economically governed by honest men with the minimum of pomp and ceremony.

They may not have an immediate plan, but they know that they will not need a second chamber, an army, an air corps, a navy, elaborate institutions at home, ornate embassies abroad, or the help of any outside power in building up the Ireland they visualise.

They see clearly how to settle three times as many on the land, how to end emigration, to establish Irish air and shipping lines, and—among many things—how to encourage the complete manufacture here of all things necessary for the maintenance in comparative comfort of an island race.

### NEW PAPER

ALL the aims and ideas of "Lia-Fáil" are, we now learn, fully outlined in the paper of the same name, the first issue of which is now out and is widely distributed.

"Lia-Fáil" is a stimulating little paper—and will probably be called provocative by many. It is not too literary and has many faults from a technical point of view. But its sincerity cannot be doubted; and it is certain to play an important part in getting all the people who share its views into a compact and orderly mass that may (even sooner than we all realize) play a big and important part in the future history and destiny of Ireland.

—THE LONGFORD NEWS.



# ALIENS

HERE are the names of aliens who have purchased land in just one corner of a county. Names of aliens from other counties will be given in our next addition:

MICHAEL NARISN — 840 acres at Ballytore, Co. Kildare.

GLENMALORE PRODUCTION CO.—400 acres at Ballytore, Co. Kildare.

COLONEL ALLEN—200 acres at Dollardstown, Athy.

COLONEL BUTT—150 acres at Danistown Mer, Co. Kildare.

BURY—500 acres at Charlville Estate, Tullamore.

COLONEL SMALLMAN—100 at Ballytore, Co. Kildare.

AN ENGLISHMAN—500 acres at Kilcullen, Co. Kildare.

PORTLAW TANNING CO. purchased two tanneries at Ballytore, Co. Kildare, and closed them.

MR. WHITEHEAD — Buildings and Sites at Ballytore, Co. Kildare.

MR. HAROLD—2,000 acres at Brown's Hill, Co. Carlow.

MR. HAROLD—2,000 acres at Oak Park, Co. Carlow.

MAJOR BEAUMONT—1,000 acres at Harristown, Brannockstown, Co. Kildare.

# Our Freedom Song

(Tune: Slattery's Mountain Foot.)

Come on me boys the day is here
We must not tarry long
But go to work without delay—
Singing a marching song.
Fall in behind our leader
He's a soldier brave and true
We'll fight the grabbing English
And we'll smash the red and
blue.

We'll plough the plains of
Ireland
And build our homes therein
We'll raise the flag of freedom
And a marching song we'll sing.
Sing a song of marching men
Who hate to use to sword
But be it forced upon them
Shall strike without a word.

Grabber men with robber rights
Must go this very day
And leave the land behind them
And its owners to their way.

We'll plough the plains of
Ireland
And build our homes therein
We'll raise the flag of Mary
And a marching song we'll sing.

"An Irish Boy."

**WARNING TO ALIENS**
**The Irish people object to your buying Irish land.**

# MESSAGE OF HOPE AND ENCOURAGEMENT

FROM Offaly where Lia-Fáil was born and where the Lia-Fáil Minister for Lands and Secretary live, the following message of encouragement and hope has come to us from one of Ireland's noble warriors:

"Dear Mrs. Kelly, your Lia-Fáil programme to settle the maximum number of Irish people on the lands of Ireland has my approval.

"The decline in the agricultural population with our increasing unemployment and emigration, capped by the new form of ranching in foreign combines seizing thousands of our fertile acres in many parts of the country, calls for **immediate and remedial** measures to **stem the national haemorrage.**

"The continued struggle for national freedom from **British domination** and **tyranny** and undoing of partition and **wiping out** of the British Crown colony in our Six Northern Counties must keep abreast with the struggle against the **economic strangulation** of our ancient nation by enemies foreign and domestic.

"Faithfully yours,

Seán McGuinness."

# JEALOUSY

THE world and the devil are jealous of our religion! This is very obvious from the way that, in this stage of the world's history, anti-Christs are being paid—yes paid—to come in here to Ireland and possess it.

Ireland withstood persecution after persecution for the 'Faith of our Fathers' and it surely has God's blessing for that. It is clear from what is going on today that the powers of darkness in human form are making a last and final effort to have Ireland for themselves.

For this reason it is unnaturally contrived to send and banish our innocent youth to foreign cities where every diabolical trap is laid ready to wean them from what they were so carefully taught at their mother's knee. Young men who don't drink are laughed at in clubs.

Young girls who would blush at an innocent joke before leaving Ireland, must now paint, pluck and donn gaudy fashions or they won't be kept in jobs. They must keep up with the times.

It is anti-Christ's work that employment for youth is impossible here: a foreigner from anywhere is more looked-up-to. The daily papers prove this by giving great praise and publicity to the work of foreigners. In every paper you read about Miss So and So (foreign, of course) who loves Ireland. She is now a dress designer in Dublin.

Mr. So and So (foreign again) is now enjoying a holiday with his friends on such an estate, and so on.

I could relate numerous instances of Satan's cunning in human form to banish religion from the only country where heresy was kept out.

His final efforts will be flouted, with God's help and that of His Blessed Mother.

AN EYEWITNESS.

Printed by THE LONGFORD NEWS at 1, Harbour Row, Longford, and published at the office of Lia-Fail, Lusmagh, Banagher Offaly. AUGUST, 1958.

## APPENDIX VI

## TITLE DEED TO LAND

The following is a copy of the 'Title Deed to Land' which Fr Fahy drew up and issued to a number of Lusmagh people in 1959:

## TITLE DEED TO LAND

at

Lia Fail

On behalf of the people of Ireland to whom the land of Ireland belongs

HEREBY GRANTS to citizen

The land in the townland of

in the County of Offaly containing


Dated the 1st Day of May, 1959

Signed on behalf of Lia Fail

Red seal

# Bibliography and Sources

Campbell, Fergus, *Land and Revolution. Nationalist Politics in the West of Ireland 1891-1921*. Oxford University Press, 2005.

Canning, Rev Bernard J., *Irish-Born Secular Priests in Scotland 1829-1979*. Bookmag, Inverness, Scotland, 1979.

Carroll, Aideen., *Seán Moylan Rebel Leader*. Mercier Press, 2010.

Carroll, Denis, *They have fooled you again. Mícheál Ó Flannagáin 1876-1942*, Columba Press, 1993.

Carroll, Joseph, *Ireland in the War Years 1939-1945*. David and Charles, New York, 1975.

Casey, Michael (Fr), 'Easter 1916 Remembered' in *Vexilla Regis*, 1966.

Coogan, Tim Pat, *Ireland in the 20th Century*. Arrow Books, 2004.

Corish, Rev Patrick J., *Maynooth College 1795-1995*. Dublin, 1995.

Corish, Rev Patrick J. (Ed.), *A History of Irish Catholicism Vol V. The Church Since Emancipation*. Gill and Macmillan, Dublin, 1970.

Corkery, Daniel, *The Hidden Ireland*. M.H. Gill, 1956.

Dooley, Terence, *The Land for the People: The Land Question in Independent Ireland*. UCD Press, 2004.

Egan, Rev Patrick K., *The Parish of Ballinasloe*. Kenny Bookshops, Galway, 1994.

English, Richard, *Radicals and The Republic: Socialist Republicanism in the Irish Free State 1925-1937*. Oxford University Press, 1994.

Fahy, Jim, 'The Fahy Clan – Clanricarde's Adversaries', in *Clanricarde Country*. Woodford Heritage Group, 1987.

Fahy, Rev John, *The Sacrifice of the Mass*. Browne and Nolan, 1957.

Fanning, Tim, *The Fethard-on-Sea Boycott*. Collins Press, 2010.

Foster, R. F., *Modern Ireland 1600-1972*. Penguin Books, 1989.

Gilmore, George, *The Irish Republican Congress*. The Cork Workers' Club, 1974.

Guinan, Canon Joseph, *Annamore or The Tenant-at-Will*. Burns and Oates and Washbourne Ltd, London, 1924.

Kavanagh, Patrick, *Collected Poems*. Martin Brian and O'Keefe Ltd., 1972.

Keane, John B., *The Field*. Dublin, 1993 edition.

Kelly, R. J., *A Patriot Prelate: The late Most Rev Dr Duggan, Bishop of Clonfert 1872-1896*. Veritas Reprint, 1987.

Kelly, Rev Declan, *Meadow of the Miracles: A History of the Diocese of Clonfert*. Editions du Signe, 2006.

Kelly, Rev Declan, *Ballinasloe, From Garbally Park to the Fairgreen*. Nonsuch Publishing, 2007.

Kelly, Rev Declan, *Between the Lines of History. Vol. I. People of Ballinasloe*. 2000.

Kelly, Denis (Compiler), *Famine: Gorta i Lusmá*. 1995.

Kennedy, Fr Tom (Ed.), *The Lusmagh Herb, The Annals of a Country Parish*. 1982.

Keogh, Dermot, *The Vatican, The Bishops and Irish Politics 1919-1939*. Cambridge, 1986.

Keogh, Dermot, *20th Century Ireland, Nation and State*. Gill and Macmillan, 1994.

Lee, J. J., *Ireland 1912-1985, Politics and Society*. Cambridge University Press, 1989.

Lyons, F. S. L., *Ireland Since the Famine*. Fontana Press, 1990.

McCarthy, Kevin, *Footsteps in Time*. C. J. Fallon, 1997.

McDonald, Walter (Rev) *Reminiscences of a Maynooth Professor*. Mercier, 1967.

McInerney, Michael, *Peadar O'Donnell: Social Rebel*. O'Brien Press, Dublin, 1974.

McManus, Francis (Ed.), *The Years of the Great Test 1926-1939*. R.T.E. and Mercier, 1967 (Thomas Davis Lecture Series).

Manuel, Frank E. (Ed.), *Utopias and Utopian Thought*. Souvenir Press, 1969.

Masterson, Rory (Ed.), *Offaly Heritage Vol. 5, 2007-8. Journal of the Offaly Historical and Archaeological Society*.

Meehan, Denis (Fr), *Windows on Maynooth*. Clonmore and Reynolds, 1949.

Murphy, Brian S., 'The Stone of Destiny: Fr. John Fahy (1893-1969), *Lia Fáil* and Smallholder Radicalism in Modern Irish Society', in *Radical Irish Priests 1660-1970*, Gerard Moran (Ed.), Four Courts Press, 1998.

Murray, Patrick, *Oracles of God, The Roman Catholic Church and Irish Politics 1922-1937*. UCD Press, 2000.

Neeson, Eoin, *The Civil War in Ireland 1922-1923*. Mercier, 1966.

Newman, Jeremiah (Rev), *Maynooth and Victorian Ireland*. Kenny Bookshops, 1983.

O'Donnell, Peadar, *There Will Be Another Day*. Dolmen Press, 1963.

O'Donnell, Patrick, *The Irish Faction Fighters*. Anvil Press, 1975.

Ó Drisceoil, Donal, *Peadar O'Donnell*. Cork University Press, 2001.

O'Looney, Pat (Ed.), *Killeenadeema Aille, History and Heritage*. 2008.

Ó Tuama, Seán, Kinsella, Thomas, *An Duanaire 1600-1900: Poems of the Dispossessed*. Dolmen Press, 1981.

Ó Tuathaigh, Gearóid, 'The Land Question, Politics and Irish Society 1922-1960', in P. J. Drudy (Ed), *Ireland: Land Politics and Society, Irish Studies 2*. Cambridge, 1982.

Shiel, Michael, Roche, Desmond (Eds), *A Forgotten Campaign and Aspects of Heritage of South-East Galway*. Woodford Heritage Group, 1986.

Smith, Raymond, *The Football Immortals*. Dublin, 1971.

Sweetman, Rosita, *On Our Knees, Ireland 1972*. Pan Books, 1972.

Varley, Tony, 'Farmers Against Nationalists: The Rise and Fall of Clann na Talmhan', in Gerard Moran and Raymond Gillespie (Eds), *Galway History and Society*. Geography Publications, 1996.

White, Lawrence William, 'Fahy John', in James McGuire UCD and James Quinn RIA (Eds), *Dictionary of Irish Biography. 9 Volumes*. Cambridge University Press in collaboration with the Royal Irish Academy, 2009.

White, Robert W., *Ruairí Ó Brádaigh: The Life and Politics of an Irish Revolutionary*. Indiana University Press, 2006.

Whyte, J. H., *Church and State in Modern Ireland 1923-1970*. Dublin, 1971.

# Newspapers and Periodicals

*The Irish Independent*
*The Sunday Independent*
*The Evening Herald*
*The Irish Press*
*The Sunday Press*
*The Evening Press*
*The Midland Tribune*
*The Connacht Tribune*
*The East Galway Democrat*
*The Connacht Telegraph*
*The Tuam Herald*
*Lia Fáil*
*The Farmers' Journal*
*The Bell*, O'Donnell, Peadar and Ó Faoláin, Seán (Eds)
*An Sagart*, Ó Fiannachta, An tAth Padraigh (Ed.)
*Ar Aghaidh*, Mac Fhinn, An tAth Eric (Ed.)
*The Fountain*, Edited and published by the students of
St Joseph's College, Garbally Park, Ballinasloe.
*Vexilla Regis*, Maynooth.
*An Phoblacht*
*Christian Scotsman*
*United Ireland*
*Scottish Catholic Observer*

## Archives Consulted

Ardagh and Clonmacnoise Diocesan Archive, Longford.
All Hallows College Archive, Dublin 7.
Clonfert Diocesan Archive, Loughrea.
Fr K. P. Egan Archive.
St Patrick's College, Maynooth Archives.
The National Archives, Dublin 2.

Dáil Éireann Debates.